Bird Song

IDENTIFICATION MADE EASY

Common Yellowthroat

Bird Song

IDENTIFICATION MADE EASY

ERNIE JARDINE

with illustrations by Don Cavin

NATURAL HERITAGE / NATURAL HISTORY INC.

To the memory of my Father,
For Mum, Lise and Dorothy,
and my own Justin and Ann Marie

Second Printing May 1997

Bird Song: Identification Made Easy
by Ernie Jardine

Published by Natural Heritage / Natural History Inc.
P.O. Box 95, Station "O", Toronto, Ontario M4A 2M8

Design and typesetting: Robin Brass Studio
Printed and bound in Canada by Mothersill Printing

Canadian Cataloguing in Publication Data
Jardine, Ernie
Bird song identification made easy

ISBN 1-896219-11-X

1. Birdsongs – Canada – Identification. 2. Birdsongs – United States – Identification. 3. Birds – Canada – Identification. 4. Birds – United States – Identification. I. Title.

QL698.5.J37 1996 598.259 C96-930476-5

Natural Heritage / Natural History Inc. acknowledges with gratitude the assistance of The Canada Council, The Ontario Arts Council, and The Association for the Export of Canadian Books.

Contents

---

* Denotes a northern breeder which would only be seen on migration in many areas.

DISTINCT SINGLE NOTE REPEATED / Slower delivery (measured notes)

DISTINCT SINGLE NOTE REPEATED / Faster (less deliberate)

TWO NOTES REPEATED / Slower (measured notes)

TWO NOTES REPEATED / Faster (less deliberate)

Preface

Birding (or birdwatching) is a hobby that is enjoyed nowadays by millions of people throughout North America. When I started as a nine-year old in 1954, it seemed that there were very few of us and it was almost mandatory to hide the fact. The image portrayed by "birdwatchers" was something less than flattering. Over the years though, and in tune with the growing emphasis on (and growing awareness of) the environment and ecology, birding has gained a greater degree of respectability. We have all been pulled closer together in our appreciation of the natural world around us and of the need to protect it. Numerous clubs and organizations have grown up and nurtured this new awareness, emphasizing the benefits (if not the necessity) of protecting and preserving wilderness areas and their various forms of wildlife. New books, magazines and television programs, new businesses and even ecology-oriented holidays have carried the message further. We are beginning to realize that nature is not the only beneficiary of this concern. We benefit too – in our new-found joy in observing nature, as well as in preserving our planet for future generations. One of the "spin-offs" of this new awareness and attitude is the tremendous interest generated in birding.

In a sense it is this increased awareness that indirectly stimulated my interest in writing this book. Some sources claim that birding is the fastest-growing hobby/sport in North America, and judging from my own experience, I find this easy to believe. Over and over, friends and acquaintances have asked me about birds they have seen and heard ("What bird makes this sound?"), and their song descriptions have left me wondering. I thought there had to be a way to organise 25-30 of the more common bird songs so that a person, new to birding, could identify them by their songs and, more importantly, identify them right there in the field, while they were listening. The problem is that even the most common bird songs heard by people are "hidden" in bird guides, or in tape recordings, impossible to access without having first physically identified the bird. Often we hear birds quite clearly and easily, but we have great difficulty in actually spotting them. The song haunts us but we have no method for quickly locating and identifying it, using guides or tapes. I decided that there had to be a better way.

I set out, in my own way, to remedy this situation. I compiled a list of 25-30 of the most common birds found in the east. I then organized them into four main song categories which would allow for "easy" identification, based on my system. Within a year, my "game" had become much more serious and my goal had risen to 100 birds. I was beginning to think that this project might have an appeal for people beyond my own friends and acquaintances. In fact it could be used by anyone with more than a passing interest in bird song – even by serious birders looking for an easy-to-use, ready-reference on bird song. As time passed, I elaborated on my original concept, all in an effort to make identification easier or more efficient. I added a section on "Habitat" which limits choices by associating a bird (and its song) with a specific habitat. Then I added a section called "Going for a Walk" which leads the reader through each habitat, emphasizing where to look, what to listen for and what to expect in each case. After adding information for an additional 25 birds near the end of the book, I then created, as a "quick reference," overviews of all 125 bird songs, organized by habitat.

For a beginning birder, or simply for anyone with an interest in the outdoors, it provides the challenge of "playing detective" in the wild, while learning these various bird songs. For the more established birder, who already has a good grasp of many bird songs, this guide should provide a ready-reference to further enhance this valuable skill. As with any field guide, the more one practises the easier it is to use. Mastering these 125 bird songs would just about admit one into the ranks of expert birders, and it should also make it easier to learn the songs of other birds, not covered in this book, if only by the process of elimination.

I wish everyone the best in birding, using this guide and remember that practise makes perfect. I hope that you'll be able to answer your friends when they ask "What bird is it that...?" – or better yet, recommend this book.

ACKNOWLEDGEMENTS

I have been amazed at the number of people that I have come in contact with during the course of this project. I have been even more amazed at the willingness of people at all levels to become involved and offer help. The following people all gave of their time and expertise.

First, I would like to thank Roger Tory Peterson, J. Murray Speirs, and Gord and Dan Gibson for reviewing my manuscript. Clive Goodwin was very helpful and shared his ideas in the early stages of my enterprise. At a later stage, Allison Tilley provided me with help, encouragement and her own special enthusiasm. I would also like to thank Allison's father, Alex Tilley, for his support of my project. Dan Kimball was enthusiastic about my idea from the beginning, and his invention, the Song Wand, has always intrigued me. I would like to thank Harry Foster for his help, encouragement and interest, as well as my own publisher, Barry Penhale and his wife, Jane, for sticking with me and providing me with many good ideas. Thanks too to Robin Brass for his more than strictly professional interest in this project and for his unique ideas.

I would like to thank my field testers, Ian Harnarine and Mike Hong, for their time and their ideas, Bernie Kelly for his early work and for letting me "see the light" concerning computers and word processing, and my friend, fellow birder and artist/illustrator Don Cavin. I was glad he had the time available so that we could work together on this project.

Finally, I would like to thank my father (one of those who originally sparked the idea) for his support along the way (until his passing in1992), my sister Lise Andrews, who has always supported me in this project and in any other, my mother for helping me through the rough spots (and for that first pair of binoculars at 11 years of age – which I still have), Ron Anderson, Bob Thurston and Hugh Calderwood who always give me something to think about. I thank Ron, in particular, for his field testing and for proving to me that the system does work.

Ernie Jardine

Introduction

I ORGANIZATION

This book deals with 125 of the more common birds of eastern Canada and the eastern U.S. The area of focus is roughly the Manitoba/Ontario border (in Canada), south to Texas, and all points east of this (from Florida up to Quebec, Newfoundland and the far north). It should be added however, that many of the birds have ranges that extend further west, and, as a result, the book could prove useful beyond the western limit outlined here. Although most of the birds are quite common, some are more locally common than others, and still others are "northern breeders" that would be seen only in migration in many parts of the east. They all but abandon the eastern U.S. (and southern Ontario) in summer. Many of these "northern breeders" are warblers, a spring favourite for all levels of birders. The songs used in this book are the versions most commonly heard. However, in some cases, one, or even a number of alternate songs are included. It must be admitted that in certain specific cases it is not possible to outline all of the common alternate songs, since these particular songs are so variable. However it is hoped that the examples given, along with habitat information and song characteristics, will provide the necessary information to allow for positive identification with such birds. In the book there are four main song categories and, within each song category, the birds are presented in the same family groupings and order (evolutionary) as would be found in other bird guides.

II SYMBOLS

Various symbols are used throughout this book in order to describe the various songs or their components. These symbols and representations are meant to clarify and amplify my word descriptions. First it must be understood that the word **"note"** in my category breakdowns (song descriptions) is synonymous with **"syllable"**. For example, three notes repeated means three syllables repeated: "WHIP-POOR-WILL", or the Carolina Wren's "TWEEDLE-DEE TWEEDLE-DEE TWEEDLE-DEE" (also described as "TEA-KETTLE TEA-KETTLE TEA-KETTLE"), or the "WITCHITY-WITCHITY-WITCHITY" of the Common Yellowthroat.

The "Song Representations" used in Part I are meant to illustrate in a general way the pitch, speed and quality of each song. THEY ARE NOT SONOGRAMS, nor indeed anything as scientific, simply my personal interpretation of the song in each case. In these song representations each note (or syllable) is represented by a dot or a line. The length of the line signifies the length of the note, and the space between notes, the speed of delivery of the song. Some examples and other notations follow:

Short notes, very close together – a trill.

Longer notes and longer pauses – short, separate notes.

Long notes and similar pauses.

Groups of three notes (first note longer, second and third shorter), repeated after a pause.

A note slurring upward.

A note slurring downward.

A three-syllable song first slurring upwards, with a prolonged middle section, and then slurring downward. When notes or syllables are joined, as in this case, it signifies that they are "slurred" together.

A rough line represents a harsh, buzzy or raspy quality

A block of sharp, jagged notes represents a harsh rattle or chatter, or sharp "twittering".

A wavy line represents a tremolo or wavering quality.

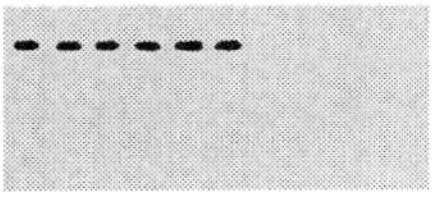
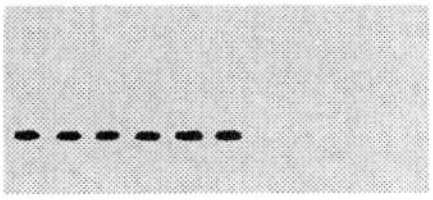
The position of the notes in the box also represents the pitch of the song, whether higher, as illustrated in the first box, or lower, as in the second box.

Similarly, when "word representations" are used in the text, hyphens and spaces are used to signify longer or shorter pauses:

"DEE – DEE – DEE – DEE..." signifies long pauses. (Killdeer)

"KEE-KEE-KEE-KEE..." signifies quicker repetition. (Northern Flicker) (also described as "WICK-WICK-WICK-WICK...")

Sometimes spaces are used to separate phrases in a song and to avoid confusion, by the use of too many hyphens. In this case simply follow the established speed through each phrase: Least Flycatcher – "CHE-BEK CHE-BEK CHE-BEK..." Simply follow through with the rapid repetition of the two-note "CHE-BEK" phrase. As mentioned above, in addition to the word representations, the text and song representation will also help to clarify the speed of delivery in each particular song.

How to Use This Book

PART I: BIRD SONGS

This section has been designed in such a way that it can be a useful tool in identifying common bird songs, right in the field. In order to do this, the bird songs have been organized into four main categories, or types of songs. Further divisions aid in "keying in" closer on the song, and then the detailed descriptions of song and habitat should allow for specific identification. What follows here is an explanation of the four main categories, along with examples, in order to illustrate the system and its basic organization. (Remember that the word "note" also means "syllable". This should help with quick deliveries or slurred notes.)

THE CATEGORIES

I VERY SHORT SONGS

– Single-note song
– Two-note song
– Three-note song

II REPEATED NOTES

– Single note repeated: i) trills, ii) distinct notes
– Two notes repeated
– Three notes repeated

III SHORT SONGS – VARYING NOTES

– Several varying notes
– Containing a distinct repeated note or phrase

IV LONG SONGS – VARYING NOTES

– Many varying notes
– Consisting of short, variable phrases

EXPLANATION

I VERY SHORT SONGS

This category is reserved for birds that have only a one-note, a two-note or a three-note song. It includes songs that might be repeated sometimes, but are also commonly given as a single one-note song (or a two- or three-note song). For instance, the American Crow often repeats its "CAW–CAW–CAW..." call, but may also utter one simple "CAW". Therefore it is included in this category. Also, some birds repeat their songs so slowly on occasion, that the single note (or two notes or three notes) seems to stand alone as a very short song. The Northern Bobwhite, for example, has several seconds between each two-note delivery. [Note also that many birds have a single "call note". These call notes are not included here.]

II REPEATED NOTES

This category includes the birds whose songs consist of

(A) A single repeated note ("CAW–CAW–CAW...")

(B) Two notes repeated ("WEE-SEE WEE-SEE...")

(C) Three notes repeated ("WHIP-POOR-WILL WHIP-POOR-WILL...")

The division for single repeated notes is further split into (i) those songs which are rapidly repeated single notes in the form of a chatter or trill, and (ii) those songs which consist of a distinct and separate single note repeated. For example, the Chimney Swift has a high-pitched, noisy, twittering or chatter. The Black-capped Chickadee, on the other hand, gives a series of distinct and separate "DEE-DEE-DEE-DEE..." notes.

All the songs in this category are characterized by repetition of a specific note or phrase. However the delivery varies from very rapid to quite slow, some with quite obvious pauses between each note or phrase (a few seconds).

III SHORT SONGS – VARYING NOTES

This category includes those birds whose songs are (1) fairly short and (2) consist of a variety of notes. "SHORT SONGS" means that each song contains several notes and is not noticeably prolonged – "VARYING", that there are at least two or more different notes in the song and that any repeated pattern is broken. There are two divisions within this category:

(A) Short songs with several varying notes

These birds have short songs, consisting of several notes, which vary in pitch. The Eastern Meadowlark has a song that consists of five notes, the first three slurred downward, the last two, starting high again, but also slurred downward. They are, thus, several notes that vary in pitch (in a short song).

(B) Short songs containing a distinct repeated note or phrase

These birds have short songs, with two or more varying notes, but each contains a distinct repeated note or phrase within it. It should be noted though, that in each case the repeated pattern is broken. For example, the Magnolia Warbler sings a song that has two-note phrases, repeated three times, and finishes with a different, higher note ("SEEYA-SEEYA-SEEYA-SOON", last note higher). The Cerulean Warbler has several rapid, buzzy notes on one pitch, and finishes with a higher-pitched, buzzy note ("ZREE-ZREE-ZREE-ZREE-ZREEEE").

IV LONG SONGS - VARYING NOTES

This category contains songs which are (1) noticeably longer than the average bird song, and (2) contain a variety of notes or phrases. There are two divisions within this category:

(A) Long songs with many varying notes

These birds, as has been pointed out above, have songs which are noticeably longer than the average bird song and they contain a variety of notes or phrases. For example the Warbling Vireo has a long, warbling song, that wavers up and down, and ends on an upswing. It is composed of a variety of notes and is noticeably longer than the average bird song.

(B) Long songs consisting of short variable phrases

All of the birds in this category are vireos and their long songs consist of variable short phrases delivered over and over with a noticeable pause between each phrase. The Red-eyed Vireo delivers many short sweet variable phrases, with a short pause after each one.

LOCATING A SONG
HOW THE SYSTEM WORKS

In order to categorize a song you simply ask yourself the following:

[ALWAYS IN THIS ORDER]

Is this song

1. a VERY SHORT SONG (one-, two- or three-note song),
   or
2. a series of REPEATED NOTES (trills, one, two, or three notes repeated)?

If not, then it is either

3. a SHORT SONG – VARYING NOTES,
   or
4. a LONG SONG – VARYING NOTES.

This decision should be quite easily made and the "keying-in" process should begin. It is important to eliminate the initial two categories first, when identiifying a song, in order to avoid confusion. If a bird has a "long song" made up of repeated two-note phrases, we look at repeated notes as our priority. "Long songs" applies only when there are "varying notes" or breaks in the repeated pattern – either (a) several different notes or (b) repeated notes or phrases finishing with a higher or lower ending.

As well as dividing the songs into the categories listed above, an attempt has also been made, in most of the categories, to separate the songs into those with a slower delivery (measured notes), and those with a faster delivery (less deliberate). This is done in order to help narrow down the possibilities, and thus, the "search time", when trying to identify a song. It should be noted, however, that, just as there are variations in song, within the same species, speed of delivery can also vary. As a result, although the divisions should prove quite dependable, there may be the odd exception to deal with, in specific cases.

Where a bird has a variety of different songs, I have included each song in its proper category and then indicated by a number in brackets after the bird's name that this is the second song [2] given for this bird, or the third [3] and so on. In this way it is easy to recognize when a bird has alternate songs in its repertoire. These numbers can be found both in the text and in the Book of Contents. Finally where there *are* alternate songs, reference is often made to these other songs, specifically, within each one of the entries or categories for that bird.

As a further aid to quick identification, I have also set in **bold type** what I consider to be key words describing the song, and have *italicized* key elements within the song which characterize it. In the latter case, it is usually the note(s) within the song that is (are) emphasized or highest in pitch, but it could also be a particularly noticeable or distinctive part of a song.

Finally, for each bird in this section I have outlined its summer and winter range in order to give an idea of what you can expect to see (hear) in your specific area, not only during the breeding season but also during the winter months.

PART II: HABITAT GUIDE

The second section of this book provides a listing of the same birds, using the same formula of song categories outlined in the first section. However, this time they are organized by *habitat*. For example, we can see a list of those birds which inhabit marshes and swamps, but we can also find out which bird in this habitat sings a song with two notes repeated. This should prove to be a useful cross-reference, when trying to identify a song that you are associating with a specific habitat. It could be another method of cutting down on search time. As in Part I (the songs section), I have set in **bold type** key descriptive words and have *italicized* elements within the songs listed. It should be pointed out though, that the emphasis in this section is on habitat and nesting preferences, and that the song descriptions do not always have the same detail as those in the first section, nor do they have the visual representation of the songs which is provided in the first section.

At the end of the habitat section I have included a quick summary or overview of all the songs, organized by habitat. Included in this listing are the songs of *all* the 125 birds dealt with in this book. It will provide a reference for quick analysis of basic quality or specific characteristics of a song, as well as allow for quick comparison of similar songs.

PART III: GOING FOR A WALK

In the final section of this book, entitled "Going for a Walk", I have tried to lead the reader (user) through each habitat, as if going out for a walk in that particular habitat, during the breeding season. The object in doing this is to represent a real-life situation, emphasizing what to listen for, where to look and what to expect, as you work your way through each habitat. Being able to identify bird songs in the field, while going for a walk in any of these habitats, can add much more pleasure and enjoyment to such an outing. It should be pointed out that some of the birds are more locally common than others and some of the "northern breeders" may only be seen during migration, in many areas.[1] Chances of seeing these birds will vary according to geographic location.[2] However, most of the birds listed are quite common and widespread in the East and should be fairly easy to see and hear.

PART IV: OTHER COMMON BIRD SONGS

This section outlines information for a further 25 birds in order to give a bit more depth beyond the original 100 birds which are the focus of this book.

1. I define "northern breeders" as those birds which all but abandon the U.S. or breed entirely in Canada. Throughout the book, these birds will be identified with an asterisk next to their names.
2. In addition to my range notes for each bird in Part I, it is also handy to consult the excellent range maps in some of the field guides available, in order to see what you can expect in your particular area. The Peterson field guide (east of the Rockies), fourth edition, has excellent, large range maps included at the back of the book, for individual species.

Part 1

Bird Songs

White-throated Sparrow

I VERY SHORT SONGS

1. RED-TAILED HAWK

One single **drawn-out** scream lasting a couple of seconds. A loud, raspy, "KEEAHHRR", slurring downward.

Summer – Throughout e. Canada and U.S. *Winter* – S. Ont. and e. U.S. to Panama.

Woodland areas and fields. Often seen sitting in trees and on fence posts along highways, if not soaring in the sky overhead.

2. AMERICAN WOODCOCK [1]

A sharp, nasal "PEENT" (with a slightly buzzy or raspy quality) **delivered from the forest floor**. It may be repeated with a generous pause in between. However the single "PEENT" call is diagnostic. The call suggests that of the Common Nighthawk but, unlike the Common Nighthawk, it is delivered while on the ground. Also, in flight display, a light twittering or trill, made by the wings, as the bird climbs, and a series of chirps or warbles as it descends to the ground.

Summer – C. Ont. to Newfoundland, south to the Gulf states. *Winter* – Gulf states to Missouri and up the Atlantic coast to Mass.

Moist woodland thickets and forest edges.

3. GREAT-CRESTED FLYCATCHER [1]

A very loud single "WHEEP", or a loud burry "FRREEEP" (each **rising** and on a fairly high pitch). The latter note has a rolling of the "R" which gives it a trilled effect. It is often repeated a few times in succession. The "WHEEP" is often repeated with a generous pause between each delivery.

Summer – S.Ont. and Que., east into N.S. and throughout e. U.S. *Winter* – S. Fla. and Texas coast to Colombia.

Woodlands and orchards, usually higher up in the tree.

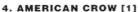

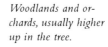

4. AMERICAN CROW [1]

A loud raspy nasal "CAW". A common call of woodlands, farmlands, fields, parks and shorelines, where many birds may congregate, except during the nesting period.

Summer – Throughout e. U.S. and Canada (except n. Que. and n. Nfld). *Winter* – S. Ont,. the Atl. provinces and all the e. U.S.

A common bird of woodlands, farmlands, shorelines, fields and parks.

5. COMMON RAVEN [1]

A deep nasal "GRONK" or "CRUK" – a grunting or croaking sound which is **lower in pitch than the "CAW" of the American Crow**. Also other harsh or croaking notes.

Canyons, forests, cliffs and rugged coastal areas.

Summer – Locally in Texas and the Appalachians, but generally in the most northern states and all e. Can. (except s. Ont.). *Winter* – Same.

Red-tailed Hawk

1. RING-NECKED PHEASANT

A **very loud**, harsh and croaking "KROOOK-OOK" (sometimes emphasized on the first syllable and sometimes on the second). It has something of the quality of a "rooster call" horn on an old or antique car.

Farmlands, fields, open woods and brushy areas.

Summer – Atl. states N.J. to Nova Scotia; also s. Ont. and states bordering the Grt. Lakes (except nw. portions). *Winter* – Same.

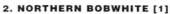

2. NORTHERN BOBWHITE [1]

A clearly whistled, medium-pitched "BOB – *WHITE*", the second note starting on the same pitch, but rising sharply higher in exclamation. It sometimes gives a three-note version "BOB – BOB – *WHITE*", which simply repeats the first note. When either version is repeated, there is a generous pause between each delivery.

Farmlands, fields, open brushy areas and wood margins. It often sings from a post or some other favourite perch.

Summer – S. Ont. and most of the e. U.S. s. of the w. Grt. Lakes, c. Penn., and Cape Cod. *Winter* – Same.

Common Loon

* 1. COMMON LOON [2]

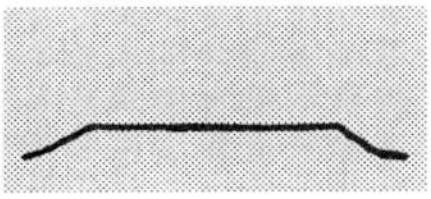

A fairly long, mournful or wailing call (2-3 seconds), with similarities to a **howling wolf**. It tends to rise in pitch and is prolonged on the second syllable, and then drops on the last syllable – "oh-OOOOO-ooo". The three syllables are definitely slurred together as in the howl of a wolf. This is one common call in the Loon's repertoire, and it will often be heard along with its characteristic tremolo laughing calls.

Usually heard on deep lakes in the northern regions, with suitable shoreline for nesting.

Summer – Throughout e. Can. and in extreme n. states. *Winter* – Atl. and Gulf coasts.

2. NORTHERN BOBWHITE [2]

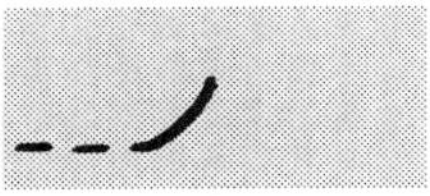

The Northern Bobwhite's common song is a clearly whistled, medium-pitched "BOB – *WHITE*", the second note starting on the same pitch, but **rising sharply higher in exclamation**. It sometimes gives a three-note version "BOB – BOB – *WHITE*", which simply repeats the first note. When either version is repeated, there is a generous pause between deliveries.

Farmlands, fields, open brushy areas and wood margins. It often sings from a post or some other favourite perch.

Summer – S. Ont. and most of the e. U.S. s. of the w. Grt. Lakes, c. Penn., and Cape Cod. *Winter* – Same.

3. MOURNING DOVE [1]

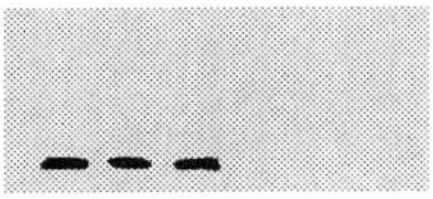

At a distance the song sounds like a **slow**, sad "OOO–OOO–OOO". This three-note song is often repeated with a generous pause in between each delivery. At close range the full song can be heard, "OH-*WOOO* (one long note slurred upward, and then briefly downward at the end) OOO–OOO–OOO". Many people are fooled by this song, thinking it to be that of an owl.

Open woodlands, fields, as well as in towns, in suburbs and at backyard feeders.

Summer – S. Ont. to N.S. and all e. U.S. *Winter* – S. Ont. and all of e. U.S. except the extreme n. states.

4. RED-WINGED BLACKBIRD [1]

A squeaky, gurgling "COY-LA-*REE*". The first note is down-slurred and squeaky, the second, quicker, and a bit higher, and the third note, continuing **up the scale**, is a harsh, raspy, trill. It is a very common sound in and around swamps and marshes. Often all that is heard is the two-note "LA-REE", or even simply the raspy trill "REE". Calls include "CHECK" or "CHUCK" notes and a high-pitched "TSEE-ER". When repeated, there is a long pause between each delivery.

In swamps and marshes, but also in dry fields and in bushy areas.

Summer – N. Ont., c. Que. to Nfld. and all the e. U.S. *Winter* – S. Ont. and s.of the Grt. Lakes (not the N.E. and Appalachians).

5. BROWN-HEADED COWBIRD [1]

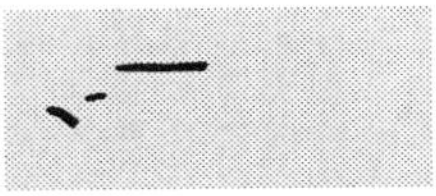

A quick little song – 2 very short, bubbly, gurgling sounds, followed by a thin, high-pitched, short whistle. "GLUG-LA-*SEEE*". The last note has a thin sharp quality like someone sucking air between their two front teeth. Calls include a "CHUCK" note and a loud, harsh rattle or chatter. The song can be repeated, with a long pause in between each delivery.

Farms, roadsides, open woodlands, parks, and also in suburban areas.

Summer – C. Ont., s. Que. to Nfld. and all of the e. U.S. except Fla. and part of the S.E. *Winter* – S. Ont. and south of the Grt. Lakes.

II REPEATED NOTES

SINGLE NOTE REPEATED / Chatter or trill

DISTINCT SINGLE NOTE REPEATED / Slower (measured notes)

DISTINCT SINGLE NOTE REPEATED / Faster (less deliberate)

TWO NOTES REPEATED / Slower (measured notes)

TWO NOTES REPEATED / Faster (less deliberate)

THREE NOTES REPEATED

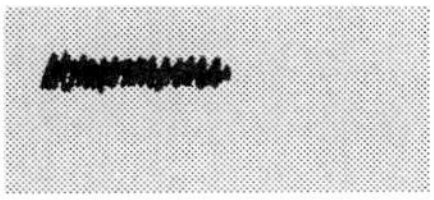

1. CHIMNEY SWIFT

A high-pitched, rapidly repeated and noisy " twittering" usually discloses their presence in the sky over towns and cities.

Summer – Throughout e. U.S. and Can., except s. Fla. and Texas. *Winter* – S. Am.

Chimneys, barns, and quite common in flocks over cities and towns, rapidly "winging it" after insects. Its distinctive rapid wingbeats also invite the description "twittering".

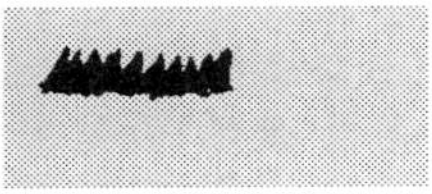

2. BELTED KINGFISHER

A **loud**, sharp, yet dry, **rattling** series of notes sometimes given in short bursts, and usually delivered in flight.

Summer – Throughout e. Can and U.S. *Winter* – S. Ont. and Nova Scotia, and U.S. south of New Eng. and Grt. Lakes.

Over or near water (swamps, marshes, rivers and streams), where it fishes from wires, posts or tree branches.

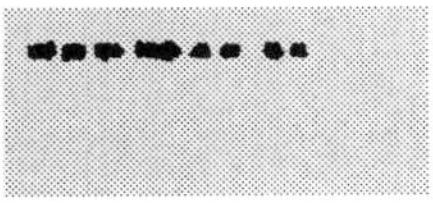

3. EASTERN KINGBIRD [1]

A high-pitched rapid "twittering" **(raspy and sharp**) which **sputters** and changes speed. "ZEE-ZEE-ZEE-ZEEE-TEE-ZEE-TEE-ZEE". It also sings a slower repeated "ZEET–ZEET–ZEET..." , as well as a slurred two-note "KIT-*ZEE*" (second syllable emphasized and rising sharply, and sounding like one slurred note), which can be repeated fairly quickly, but is not rushed.

Summer – N. Ont. and c. Que. to Nova Scotia, and throughout the e. U.S. *Winter* – S. Am.

Wood edges, open country, orchards and roadsides, often near water. It is easily spotted, either flitting about in trees, or perched on a fence, or on some overhead wires.

4. MARSH WREN

A **squeaky chatter**. It is a jerky, sharp, rattling series of notes that sounds like a squeaky sewing machine. The quick phrases vary slightly in pitch.

Summer – S. Ont. and most of the northern half of the U.S., as well as along the Atl. and Gulf coasts. *Winter* – Atl. coast and Gulf states to Mex.

Tall grass and cattail marshes, as well as along marshy inlets and rivers.

5. CEDAR WAXWING [1]

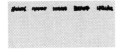

A very high-pitched, **thin trill**, or trilled note. It is high-pitched but has more the quality of a raspy, trilled whistle, than a sweet or musical sound. It sounds like a fairly short, buzzy "SREEEE" or "TREEEE". It is quite weak and does not carry far. Also, as A. C. Bent states, it can run into "almost a long clear whistle" at times. Both of these can be repeated, with variable pauses between deliveries.

Summer – N. half of the U.S. and throughout e. Can. (n. Ont. to Newfoundland).
Winter – S. Can.and throughout the e. U.S.

Open woodlands, orchards, and shrubs. It likes to feed on berries.

6. YELLOW-RUMPED WARBLER [3]

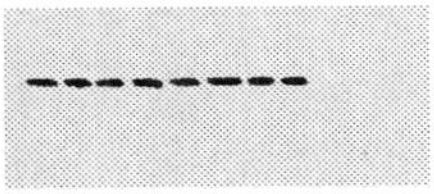

A **sweet**, slow **trill**, not particularly loud. "WHEE-WHEE-WHEE-WHEE..." or a slightly sharper, sibilant "SWEE-WHEE-WHEE-WHEE-WHEE...". The speed varies from a rapid series of notes to a slow trill. Also, the ending sometimes rises or drops in pitch.

Summer – Extreme n. states to the far north across e. Can. *Winter* – S. Grt. Lakes to the Gulf and also along the Atl. coast.

Coniferous and mixed woodlands, in open areas or woodland edges.

7. WORM-EATING WARBLER

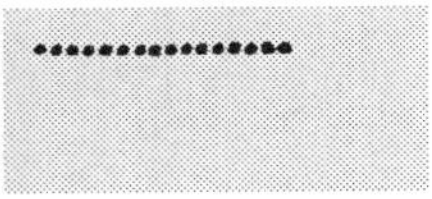

A rapid, **dry**, buzzy trill. It is similar to the Chipping Sparrow's trill but is more rapid, dry and buzzy as well as weaker.

Summer – From the Gulf states to south of the Grt. Lakes, and casual to sw. Ont.
Winter – West Indies to Panama.

Deciduous slopes covered with dead leaves, and also with dense undergrowth.

8. PINE WARBLER

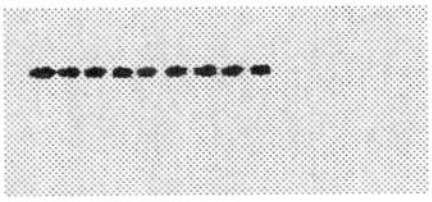

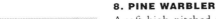

A soft, high-pitched, **musical chirping** or trill. It is sweeter, fuller and usually slower than the Chipping Sparrow's trill and lacks its gusto or strength.

Summer – S. Ont. and the n. Grt. Lakes states; also the more eastern and Gulf states. (Largely absent from the central/western portion of E. U.S.) *Winter* – Gulf, s. Atl. states and casual up the coast..

Open pine woods.

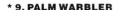

* 9. PALM WARBLER

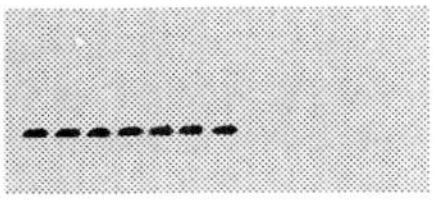

A dry, slow trill with a slightly buzzy or husky quality. It sounds like "ZWEET-ZWEET-ZWEET-ZWEET-ZWEET-ZWEET". The notes are fairly weak, unmusical, and on the same pitch, although they can waver slightly (alternately up and down). A.C. Bent points out that the song has been described as sounding like a "debilitated Chipping Sparrow" (Walter Faxon).

Woodland edges, marshes and in open areas of brushland in migration, but it nests in northern spruce bogs and in scattered trees around muskeg.

Summer – From the extreme northern states to n. Ont., c. Que. and Newfoundland.
Winter – U.S. Atl. coast and the Gulf states.

10. CHIPPING SPARROW

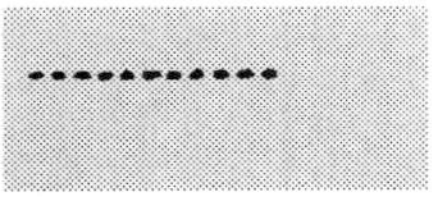

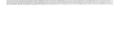

A dull, unmusical (yet to me slightly sweet) twitter or trill, consisting of rapidly repeated, **sharp chips** in the same cadence as a rapidly running sewing machine. It is the standard of comparison for many other trills.

Open woodlands, orchards, parks and gardens.

Summer – Throughout e. Can. and U.S. (except Fla.). *Winter* – Atl. coast (s. of R.I.) and the extreme southern and Gulf states.

11. SWAMP SPARROW [2]

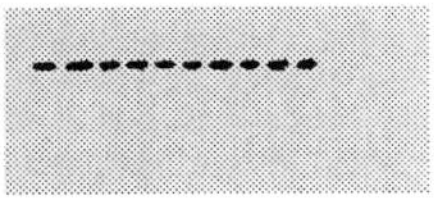

A slow, **sweet trill** like a musical, rich Chipping Sparrow – definitely sweeter, slower and louder than the Chipping Sparrow. It also sings a slow, sweet, and deliberate "SWEET-SWEET-SWEET-SWEET-SWEET-SWEET-SWEET".

Swamps, bogs, marshes and the edges of marshy streams or lakes, as well as in wet meadows.

Summer – Throughout e. Can. and south to W. Va. and n. Mo.
Winter – S. Ont. and most of the e. U.S. south of L. Huron.

Chipping Sparrow

1. KILLDEER [3]

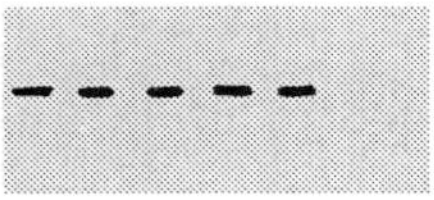

A sharp, fairly high-pitched "DEE—DEE—DEE—DEE..." repeated many times. This series of notes can be delivered as slower, measured notes, as shown here, but it can also be a rapid series of "DEE-DEE-DEE-DEE-DEE" notes. The Killdeer becomes **very noisy** when disturbed and is therefore hard to miss (or, for that matter, to mistake).

Gravelly or sandy areas, usually near water, and open areas with little growth.

Summer – All e. U.S. (except s. Fla.), to n. Ont., s. Que. and Nova Scotia. *Winter* – S. half of U.S. but n. to Cape Cod and Ohio.

2. AMERICAN WOODCOCK [2]

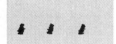

A raspy, nasal "PEENT", **delivered from the forest floor,** and repeated with generous pauses in between. This call suggests that of the Common Nighthawk but the Woodcock delivers its call while on the ground. Also, in flight display, a light twittering or trill, made by the wings, as the bird climbs, and a series of chirps or warbles as it descends to the ground.

Moist woodland thickets and forest edges.

Summer – C. Ont. to Newfoundland, south to the Gulf states. *Winter* – Gulf states to Missouri and up the Atl. coast to Mass.

3. RUFFED GROUSE

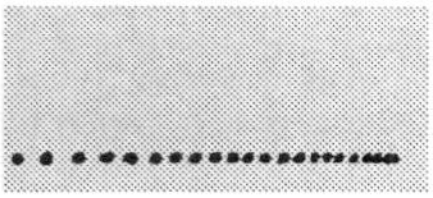

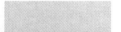

Not a song, but a beating or thumping of the wings that starts slowly and **speeds up**, ending in a rapid flurry. It has a soft, muffled, thumping quality – "THUMP.... THUMP.... THUMP... THUMP... THUMP.. THUMP..THUMP THUMPTHUMPTHUMPTHUMP....", speeding up to a rapid "PRRRR".

Thick, dry, mixed woodland areas, on, or close to the ground.

Summer – N. Ont. and c. Que. to Nfld., through New Eng. to n. Geo., and in the n. Grt. Lakes states. *Winter* – Same.

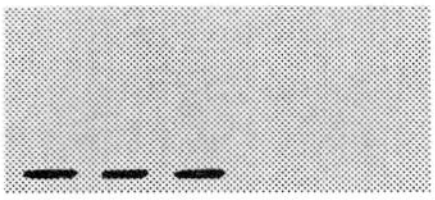

4. MOURNING DOVE [2]

At a distance the song sounds like a **slow**, sad "OOO–OOO–OOO". It has been included here under the heading, "Single Note Repeated", because of the obvious repetition of the single "OOO" note. However, it is also listed under "Three Notes Repeated", since it often repeats this grouping of three notes after a generous pause. Closer up you can hear the full 4-note song: "OH-*WOOO* (one long note slurred upward, and then briefly downward at the end) OOO–OOO–OOO ". Many people mistake this song for that of an owl.

Summer – S. Ont. to N.S. and all of the e. U.S. *Winter* – S. Ont. and all of e. U.S. except the extreme n. states.

Open woodlands, fields, as well as in towns, suburbs and at backyard feeders.

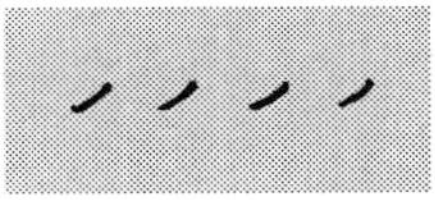

5. COMMON NIGHTHAWK

A sharp, nasal "BEEK – BEEK – BEEK...", repeated with short pauses in between. It sometimes sounds like a quick two-syllabled "*BEE*-ICK" (emphasized on the first syllable), which is repeated with short pauses in between.

Summer – Throughout e. U.S. and Can. *Winter* – S. Am.

Found in country and city, and, although it is active day and night, it is very often seen (like the Chimney Swift) chasing insects in the evening sky over cities and towns.

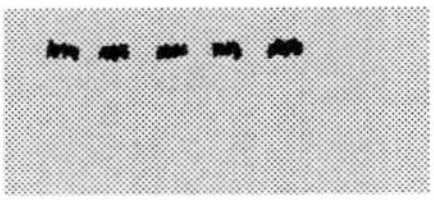

6. EASTERN KINGBIRD [2]

A single, high-pitched, **raspy and sharp** "ZEET" which is repeated with a short pause between each note. It also has a slurred, two-note "KIT-*ZEE*" (second syllable emphasized and rising sharply, and sounding like one slurred note), as well as a high-pitched, rapid twittering of "ZEET" notes which sputters and changes speed.

Summer – N. Ont. and c. Que. to Nova Scotia and throughout the e. U.S. *Winter* – S. Am.

Wood edges, open country, orchards and roadsides, often near water. It is easily spotted, either flitting about in trees, or perched on a fence, or on some overhead wires.

7. GREAT CRESTED FLYCATCHER [2]

A series of loud burry "FRREEEP" calls (each **rising** and on a fairly high pitch), or a very loud "WHEEP" repeated slowly. Each of these may also be heard as one single note, with the same qualities as described above.

Woodlands and orchards, usually higher up in the tree.

Summer – S. Ont. and Que., east into Nova Scotia and throughout the e. U.S.
Winter – S. Fla. and Texas coast to Colombia.

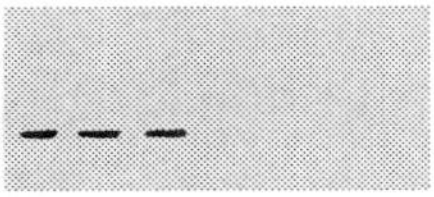

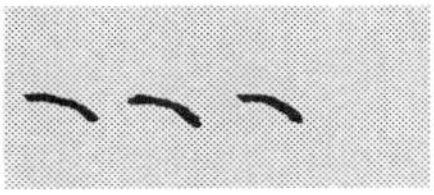

8. BLUE JAY [1]

A **harsh**, piercing and 'steely' "JAAY–JAAY–JAAY..." or a down-slurred, screeching "JEEAH–JEEAH–JEEAH...", both **very loud** and repeated several times. Its two- and three-note songs are more musical, especially its bell-like "TULL-ULL" notes. It also mimics Red-shouldered and Broad-winged Hawks, some suggest, to scare off predators; others, playing on its nasty reputation, say it is a practical joke to terrify other birds.

Forests, mixed woodland (especially oak and pine), parks and city gardens.

Summer – C. Ont. to Newfoundland and throughout the e. U.S. *Winter* – Same

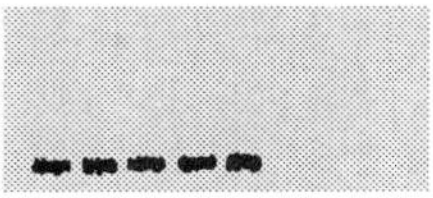

9. AMERICAN CROW [2]

A loud, raspy, nasal "CAW" repeated several times. A common call of woodlands, fields or shorelines, where many birds may congregate, except during the nesting period.

A common bird of woodlands, farmlands, shorelines, parks and fields.

Summer – Throughout e. U.S. and Canada (except n. Que. and n. Nfld.). *Winter* – S. Ont., the Atl. provinces and all of the e. U.S.

10. COMMON RAVEN [2]

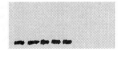

A deep, nasal "GRONK" or "CRUK", repeated several times. It is a grunting or croaking sound which is **lower in pitch than the "CAW" of the American Crow.** Also other harsh or croaking notes.

Canyons, forests, cliffs and rugged coastal areas.

Summer – Locally in Texas and the Appalachians, but generally in the extreme northern states and all e. Can. (except s. Ont.).
Winter – Same

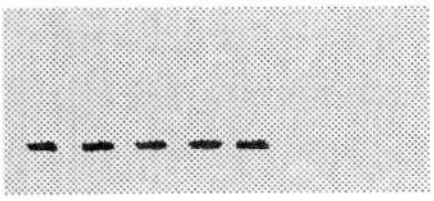

11. RED-BREASTED NUTHATCH

A series of nasal, twangy notes which are more nasal, higher-pitched and weaker than the White-breasted Nuthatch. "KNG–KNG–KNG–KNG–KNG–KNG..." (like a nasal "KING"). A.C. Bent describes the nasal call as sounding like "a blast on a tiny tin trumpet".

Conifer forests.

Summer – E. Can. (except s. Ont.), n. Grt. Lakes states, ne. states and down the Appalachians. *Winter* – E. Can. and e. U.S. (except s. Fla.).

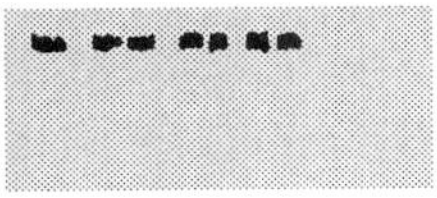

12. BLUE GRAY GNATCATCHER [2]

A **weak**, high-pitched and rough "SEE" or "SEE-SEE" or "SEE – SEE-SEE" repeated with varying pauses in between. It also has a **very weak**, rapid series of both **squeaky** and raspy notes that represents its song.

Varies from scrub to wooded swamp to thick woodland, but quite often near water.

Summer – S. Ont. and all e. U.S. except the most northerly states. *Winter* – Fla., s. Atl. and Gulf states southward.

13. CEDAR WAXWING [2]

A very high-pitched, **thin, trilled note** which can be repeated with variable pauses between deliveries. It is high-pitched but has more the quality of a raspy, trilled whistle, than a sweet or musical sound. It sounds like a buzzy "SREEEE – SREEEE – SREEEE...". At times it almost sounds like a long, high-pitched, clear whistle. It is a weak song and does not carry far.

Open woodlands, orchards and shrubs. It likes to feed on berries.

Summer – N. half of the U.S. and throughout e. Can. (n. Ont. to Newfoundland).
Winter – S. Can. and throughout e. U.S.

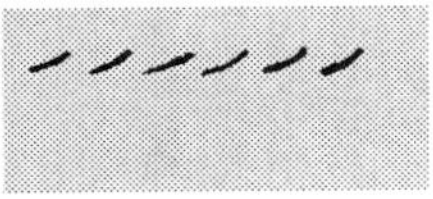

14. PROTHONOTARY WARBLER

Several clear, sweet, **emphatic notes**, all on one pitch and delivered at a moderate pace. It is a loud "TWEET-TWEET-TWEET-TWEET-TWEET-TWEET".

Wooded swamps where the nest is built not far over water in a tree cavity.

Summer – Atl. states (c. Fla. to New Jersey), and Gulf states to L. Mich., L. Erie and s. Ont. (not in the Appalachians). *Winter* – Mexico to S. Am.

*15. CAPE MAY WARBLER

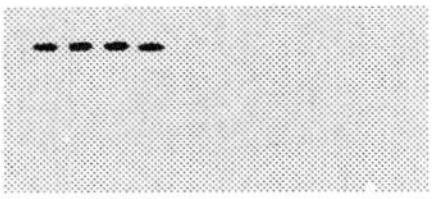

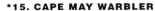

A very high-pitched and **weak** series of notes (commonly 4-6 notes but as many as 11-12) which are all on the same pitch. "SEE-SEE-SEE-SEE".

Spruce and fir forests, usually near the edge or near an open area.

Summer – C. Ont., s. Que. to Nova Scotia (not s. Ont.), and only the extreme n. states (the Great Lakes and N.E. areas).
Winter – Tip of Fla. and the West Indies.

*16. BLACKPOLL WARBLER

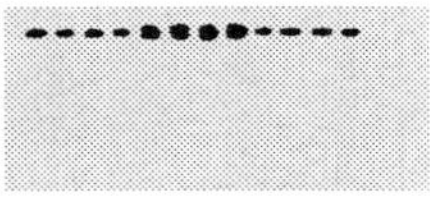

A series of single, high-pitched and weak "TSEE" notes that **get louder toward the middle** and then weaker again toward the end. "TSEE-TSEE-TSEE-*TSEE-TSEE-TSEE*-TSEE-TSEE-TSEE". These tinny or tinkling notes are quite weak and can be overlooked, but with practice in the field, they become quite distinctive. These distinctive notes, along with the stronger middle section of the song, become second nature to identifying this bird.

Fond of low conifer forests (especially spruce) in its northern breeding grounds.

Summer – Local areas in the ne. states and maritime provinces, but mainly in far northern Ontario, Quebec and Newfoundland.
Winter – S. Am.

Cape May Warbler

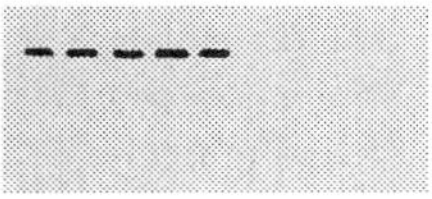

17. AMERICAN REDSTART [2]

A **high-pitched** and **variable** song consisting of weak, yet emphatic, single notes. It is sometimes delivered as a single note, repeated several times, at moderate speed, and on the same pitch, "TSEET-TSEET-TSEET-TSEET-TSEET". However, it is more often delivered with the last note higher or lower than the rest and it often alternates these two songs. "TSEET-TSEET-TSEET-TSEET-*TSEEE*" (last note higher) and "TSEET-TSEET-TSEET-TSEE-O" (last note lower). It can also sing slurred or two-note phrases ("TSEETA-TSEETA-TSEETA-TSEETA") with similarities to the song of the Black and White Warbler. Its song is notorious for fooling even experienced birders. I often detect a pumping or pulsating quality to the delivery, especially up close.

Deciduous woods, thickets and bush, often near water. Also wood edges, and young second growth woods, as well as roadside trees, gardens and parks.

Summer – N.c. Ont. (James Bay) to Nfld. and south to the Gulf states (not Fla. and the s. Atl. coast). *Winter* – Tip of Fla. and Texas

18. NORTHERN CARDINAL [1]

A **very loud**, rich and drawn-out "TWEEER-TWEEER-TWEEER-TWEEER...", with each note sliding downward, or a quicker "WHOIT-WHOIT-WHOIT-WHOIT...", each note rising, and also "CHET-CHET-CHET-CHET..." like a chatter (all versions repeated up to 7-8 times or more). It also gives combinations: "TWEEER-TWEEER-TWEEER...WHOIT-WHOIT-WHOIT-WHOIT...". Two-note songs repeated are common too. "*BIRDY-BIRDY-BIRDY-BIRDY*..." (accented on the first syllable) or "TU-*WEET* TU-*WEET* TU-*WEET* TU-*WEET*..." (accented on the last syllable) are two examples.

Open woodlands, wood edges, gardens and stream-side thickets. The Cardinal likes to sing from high perches, such as the top of a high tree or a rooftop antenna, from which it will definitely attract your attention with its very loud and very persistent singing.

Summer – S. Ont. and throughout the e. U.S. (c. Maine and c. Wisc. south). *Winter* – Same.

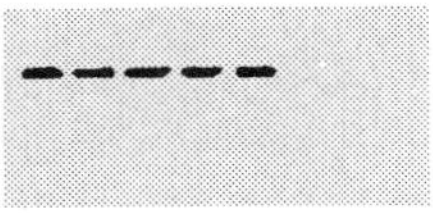

19. SWAMP SPARROW [1]

A slow, sweet, distinct and deliberate "SWEET-SWEET-SWEET-SWEET-SWEET-SWEET". It also has a slow trill similar to the Chipping Sparrow's but definitely sweeter, slower and louder than the Chipping Sparrow.

Marshes, swamps, streams and bogs, as well as in wet meadows.

Summer – Throughout e. Can. and south to W. Va. and n. Mo. *Winter* – S. Ont. and most of the e. U.S. south of L. Huron.

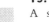

Northern Cardinal

1. KILLDEER [3]

Description under "Slower Delivery" above.

2. RUFFED GROUSE

Description under "Slower Delivery" above.

3. BLACK-BILLED CUCKOO

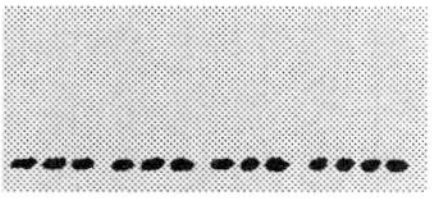

This is a **long song** with several series of rapid "COO-COO-COO" notes (given 2, 3 or 4 to a series). The notes have a fairly nasal and **ringing quality**, unlike the soft "COO"s of the Mourning Dove.

In open woods, shrubs, thickets, and in streamside groves.

Summer – C. Ont., s. Que. to Nova Scotia. Northern half of the U.S., but as far south as n. Ala. and Ga. *Winter* – S. Am.

4. NORTHERN FLICKER [1]

To me, it sometimes sounds like a long, rapid repetition of "KEE-KEE-KEE-KEE-KEE-KEE-KEE...", **loud and ringing**. A. C. Bent describes it as "WICK-WICK-WICK-WICK-WICK..." It also has a squeaky two-note call, with emphasis on the first syllable, a **jerky or snappy** "*WEE*KA-*WEE*KA-*WEE*KA-*WEE*KA-*WEE*KA...". The call note is a loud, sharp "KEE-YER" or "KLEER".

Open woodlands and suburban areas. The Flicker is often seen feeding on ants on the ground.

Summer – All of the e. U.S. and Can. (to the far north). *Winter* – S. Ont. to Fla.

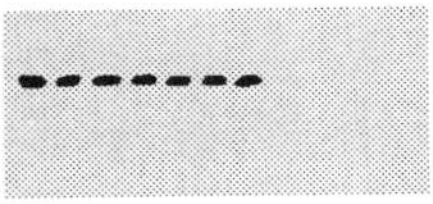

5. BLACK-CAPPED CHICKADEE [3]

A **cheerful, bright** and quickly repeated "DEE-DEE-DEE-DEE-DEE-DEE-DEE...". This rapid series of repeated notes is often introduced by a squeaky and higher-pitched "CHICKA" or "SICKA". Its two-note song is a clear, whistled "*FEEE*-BEE" – the first note higher and longer – repeated after a brief pause (sometimes a three-note "*FEEE*-BEE-BEE"). Its southern cousin, the Carolina Chickadee, has a distinctive four-note song ("*FEE*-SU BEE-SU") instead of two, and it also sings a quicker and higher-pitched version of the first series of notes described here.

Open woodlands, clearings and also in suburban areas. Common at feeders in winter.

Summer – N. Ont. to Nfld; mainly n. states but south to W. Va. and s. Ill. *Winter* – Same.

6. TUFTED TITMOUSE [2]

A loud, clear and **whistled** "PEEER-PEEER-PEEER" repeated fairly quickly, with each note rising slightly toward the end. Some squeaky notes suggesting the Chickadee or Blue Gray Gnatcatcher may also be heard as well as the common "WHEEDLE-WHEEDLE-WHEEDLE-WHEEDLE". This common song which consists of two notes repeated several times, fairly quickly, is also loud and clearly whistled.

Likes deciduous woodlands, orchards, suburban areas and feeders.

Summer – S. Ont. and all of the e. U.S. (except the extreme n. states and s. Fla.). *Winter* – Same.

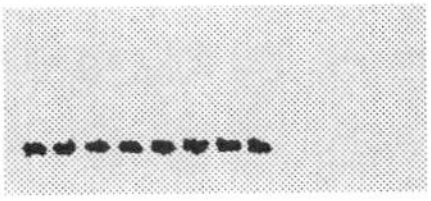

7. WHITE-BREASTED NUTHATCH

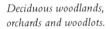

A rapid series of nasal, low-pitched notes, "WA-WA-WA-WA-WA-WA..." or "KANK-KANK-KANK-KANK-KANK-KANK-KANK..." (a bit rough and burry).

Deciduous woodlands, orchards and woodlots.

Summer – S. Ont. and Que. to N.S. and all of the e. U.S. except s. Fla. *Winter* – Same.

4. EASTERN KINGBIRD [3]

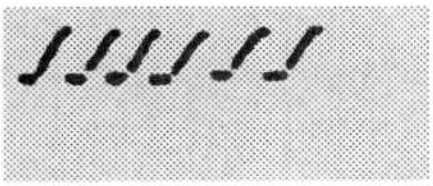

A common call is the "KIT-*ZEE*" call (second syllable emphasized and rising sharply, and sounding like one slurred note). It can be repeated slowly or fairly quickly, and it is also combined with other Kingbird calls. Other Kingbird calls include a single, repeated "ZEET–ZEET–ZEET–ZEET...", as well as a rapid high-pitched twittering of "ZEET" notes, which sputters and changes speed. All of its notes have a **harsh** quality, are high-pitched and are delivered quite emphatically.

Open country, wood edges, orchards and roadsides, often near water. It is easily spotted, flitting about in trees, or perched on a fence, or on some overhead wires.

Summer – N. Ont. and c. Que. to Nova Scotia, and throughout the e. U.S.
Winter – Same.

5. EASTERN PHOEBE

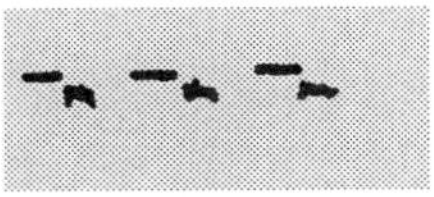

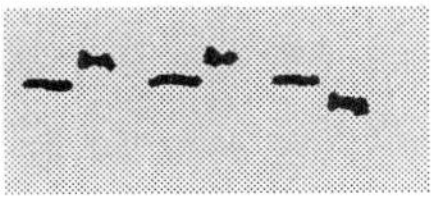

An **emphatic**, repeated, two-note song that sounds like "*FEE*-BEE" or "*FEE*-BREE", with the second note sometimes higher, but more often lower, than the first. The second note, also, is often more raspy or burred than the first note, which is whistled. A. C. Bent points out that the song despite being "uttered emphatically" and "sharply accented at the start...is never loud. It is, in fact, only a forceful, whistled whisper."

Open woodlands and near bridges and farm buildings. The nest is often built under a bridge or in a farm building, on a protected beam.

Summer – C. Ont. and s. Que. to New Brunswick, south to Virginia and the northern Gulf states. *Winter* – Southern half of the U.S. (Virginia and Tenn. south).

6. EASTERN WOOD-PEWEE [2]

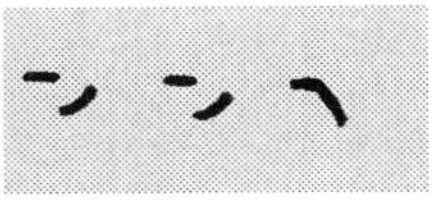

A slow, **drawn-out**, "PEEE-*WEEE*", the second note lower, but with an upward inflection. It is repeated often, with a generous pause between each phrase, and it also "works in" a drawn out "PEEE-YURR" every so often, with a downward inflection on the second syllable. It is also described as a three-note song since the "PEEE-*WEEE*" usually sounds more like a slurred "PEEE-A-*WEEE*". In general it is a clear sweet whistle, with the notes in each phrase moving slowly and easily together, with what could be described as a **melancholy** or **plaintive** quality. It sometimes sings other versions of these songs which have the last note highest.

Deciduous and mixed woodlands; also orchards and shade trees.

Summer – C. Ont. to N.S. and all the e.U.S. except Fla. pen. *Winter* – Cen. and S. Am.

7. BLACK-CAPPED CHICKADEE [1]

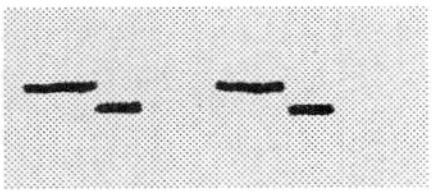

A clear, sweet, whistled "*FEEE*-BEE" – the first note higher and longer – repeated after a brief pause. It also has a three-note song repeated "*FEEE*-BEE-BEE", which quickly repeats the second note. Calls include the common, **very bright and cheerful** "CHICKA-DEE-DEE-DEE". Its southern cousin, the Carolina Chickadee sings a quicker and higher-pitched version of this, and has a distinctive four-note song ("*FEE*-SU BEE-SU") instead of two.

Open woodlands, clearings, and in suburban areas. It is quite common at feeders in winter.

Summer – N. Ont. to Nfld; mainly n. states but south to W Va. and s. Ill. *Winter* – Same.

8. BLUE-WINGED WARBLER

A short two-note song, with the first note higher and buzzy and the second note a lower raspy trill. A slow "ZEEE-ZREEE", repeated after a generous pause The distinctive buzzy quality gives it an almost **insect-like sound**.

Open woodlands and forest edges, brushy meadows, swamps and along the edges of small streams.

Summer – S. Ont. to n. Gulf states (w. of Appal.) and, in the east, from s. Vt. and Mass. to N.J. and Va. *Winter* – Mex. to Pan.

9. RUFOUS-SIDED TOWHEE [2]

The characteristic song is a three-note, "DRINK-YOUR-*TEA-EE-EE-EE-EE*", with the last note prolonged, higher, and trilled. The two-note version, referred to here, sounds like, "DRINK-*TEA-EE-EE-EE-EE*", again, with the last note prolonged, higher, and trilled. The song is delivered at a fairly slow, measured pace, and is also quite musical. It is repeated after a fairly generous pause.

Open woodlands, areas with dense undergrowth and thickets, where it is seen scouring the ground in search of food.

Summer – C. Ont., s. Que. and all of the e. U.S. *Winter* – Sw. Ont. to the Gulf and from Va. up the Atl. coast to Cape Cod.

Rufous-sided Towhee

1. NORTHERN FLICKER [2]

A squeaky two-note call, with the first note emphasized, and higher-pitched. It is a **jerky or snappy** "*WEE*KA-*WEE*KA-*WEE*KA-*WEE*KA-*WEE*KA-*WEE*KA..." - repeated many times. Its single-note song is a long, rapid, repetition of "KEE-KEE-KEE-KEE-KEE..." or "WICK-WICK-WICK-WICK..." (as A.C. Bent describes it). The call note is a loud, sharp "KEE-YER" or "KLEER".

Open woodlands and suburban areas. The Flicker is often seen on the ground, feeding on ants.

Summer – All of the e. U.S. and Can. (to the far north). *Winter* – S. Ont. to Fla.

2. LEAST FLYCATCHER

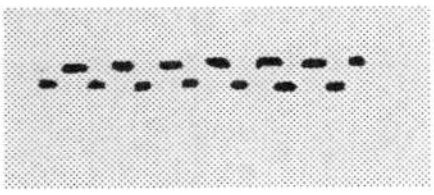

Two sharp, dry notes, repeated quickly, over and over. A snappy, emphatic "CHE-*BEK* CHE-*BEK* CHE-*BEK* CHE-*BEK*...", the second syllable higher and strongly accented.

In forests, open woods, wood margins, and orchards.

Summer – N. Ont., s. Que. to N.S., south to Penn. and down the Appalachians to n. Geo. *Winter* – Mexico to Panama.

3. BLUE JAY [2]

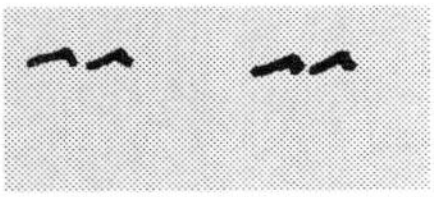

Two (sometimes three) quick bursts "WHEEDLE-WHEEDLE", repeated after a pause. The length of the pause varies, although it is usually generous – a few seconds. This song is pleasant and musical, but still has the sharp, "**creaking wheelbarrow**" quality of its three-note "WHEEL-DE-LEE" song. Both are unlike its harsh, single-note "cries" or its soft bell-like calls ("TULL-ULL" or "TWIRL-ERL"). It also mimics various hawks.

Forests, mixed woodland (especially oak and pine), parks and city gardens.

Summer – C. Ont. to Newfoundland and throughout the e. U.S. *Winter* – Same.

4. TUFTED TITMOUSE [1]

A series of loud, **clear**, two-note **whistles**, fairly quickly repeated: "WHEEDLE-WHEEDLE-WHEEDLE-WHEEDLE" or "PETER-PETER-PETER-PETER". Some squeaky notes, suggesting the Chickadee or Blue-gray Gnatcatcher, may also be heard, as well as its repeated single-note song, a clear, whistled "PEEER-PEEER-PEEER".

Deciduous woodlands, in suburban areas and at feeders.

Summer – S. Ont. and all e. U.S. (except extreme n. states and s. Fla.) *Winter* – Same

5. CAROLINA WREN [2]

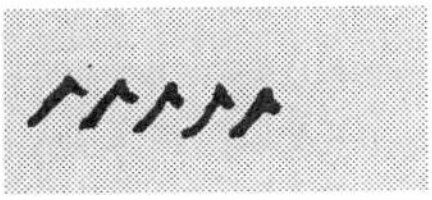

A **very loud**, **rich** and sweet song, "TWEEDLE-TWEEDLE-TWEEDLE" sung rapidly. It also has a three-note version, a rolling "*TWEE*DLE-DEE *TWEE*DLE-DEE *TWEE*DLE-DEE" (or "TEA-KETTLE TEA-KETTLE TEA-KETTLE"), with the emphasis on the first note of each three-note phrase. It also has a rich chatter. The Tufted Titmouse above has a **clear**, whistled song; however, the key word with the Wren is definitely **rich** – it has a sweet, **rich**, whistled song.

In moist woodland areas with tangled undergrowth and thick brush; also along streams and swamps with sufficient cover, as well as in gardens.

Summer – S. Ont. and e. U.S. south of Cape Cod in the east and Wisc. in the west. *Winter* – Same.

6. BLACK AND WHITE WARBLER

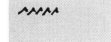

A high, **thin** (even squeaky), two-note phrase repeated fairly quickly. It sounds like "*WEE*SEE-*WEE*SEE-*WEE*SEE-*WEE*SEE..." – first note higher and emphasized, and giving it a rhythmic quality.

Deciduous and mixed woodlands. It creeps along branches and tree trunks like a nuthatch.

Summer – N. Ont., s. Que. and Nfld., south to the Carolinas and n. Gulf states. *Winter* – Fla., s. Atl. and Gulf coasts.

*7. BAY-BREASTED WARBLER

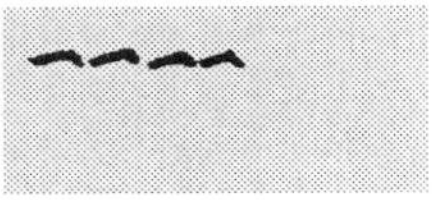

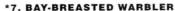

A **thin**, high-pitched, **short** song, delivered rapidly. This repeated two-note song is similar to the song of the Black and White Warbler, but, as R.T. Peterson points out, it is "thinner, shorter, more on one pitch." It sounds like "TEESI TEESI TEESI".

Coniferous and mixed woodlands in the more open areas.

Summer – N. and c. Ont., and s. Que. to Nova Scotia and the ne. corner of the U.S. *Winter* – Panama and n. S. Am.

8. OVENBIRD

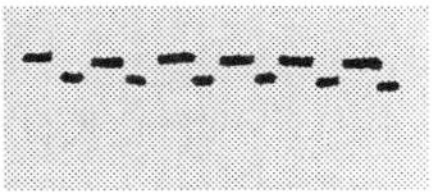

A loud, clear, "*TEACH*ER-*TEACH*ER-*TEACH*ER...", accented on the first syllable, and repeated many times in quick succession. It also **gets louder** as it progresses.

Deciduous woods with leafy cover, but sparse undergrowth, on or near the ground.

Summer – N. Ont., c. Que. and Nfld. south to n. Gulf states. *Winter* – Gulf coast, Fla., Mex. and n. S. Am.

9. KENTUCKY WARBLER

A **very loud**, emphatic, and **rich** song, consisting of several two-note, whistled phrases, "CHUR-*EE* CHUR-*EE* CHUR-*EE* CHUR-*EE* CHUR-*EE*", each emphasized on the second syllable. It is very similar to the Carolina Wren's song; however, the Kentucky's song would be heard from near, or on the ground, whereas the Carolina Wren tends to sing from a more elevated perch.

Moist woodlands with dense undergrowth, where it spends its time on, or near the ground.

Summer – All of the e. U.S. s. of L. Mich. (except Fla. and the extreme S.E.). *Winter* – Mex. and n. S. Am.

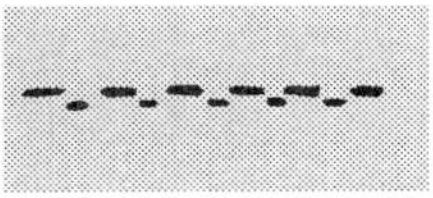

***10. CONNECTICUT WARBLER [2]**

A **very loud**, clear series of two-syllable phrases that **speeds up** as it progresses and sounds like "*BEE*CHER-*BEE*CHER-*BEE*CHER-*BEE*CHER-*BEECH*" with the first note higher and emphasized. A very loud, emphatic, and rich song, it does not have a smooth delivery, but has a jerky or **hesitant** quality, as it starts up. Other adjectives which could be used to describe its song are resonant and even explosive. It also has a repeated three-syllable song which sounds like "CHICH-U-*EE* CHICH-U-*EE* CHICH-U-*EE*", with all the same characteristics as the two-note song, but with the last note emphasized and higher.

A northern breeder, it is found near the ground in open poplar woods in its western range, but in spruce and tamarack bogs in its eastern range.

Summer – From the northern Grt. Lakes states (Minn., Wisc. and Mich.) to nc. Ont. (James Bay) *Winter* – N. S. Am.

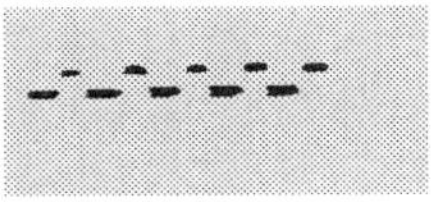

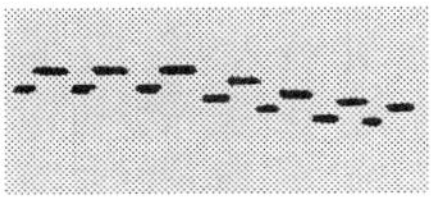

11. NORTHERN CARDINAL [2]

A **very loud**, **rich** song. "*BIR*DY-*BIR*DY-*BIR*DY-*BIR*DY...", accented on the first syllable, or "TU-*WEET* TU-*WEET* TU-*WEET*...", accented on the last syllable, and sometimes sliding slowly down the scale. Both versions are repeated many times and can be combined, often in mid-song, with other Cardinal notes or phrases. (These variations would be found under "Long Songs–Varying Notes".) Example: "TWEEER-TWEEER-*BIR*DY-*BIR*DY-*BIR*DY...".

Open woodlands, gardens and in streamside thickets. The Cardinal likes to deliver its very loud and persistent song from a high perch, such as the top of a tree or a rooftop antenna.

Summer – S. Ont. and throughout the e. U.S. (c. Maine and c. Wisc. south). *Winter* – Same

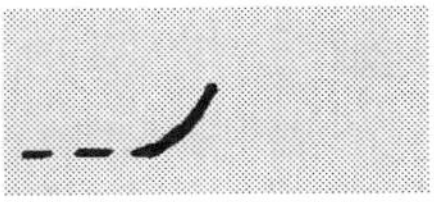

1. NORTHERN BOBWHITE [4]

The Northern Bobwhite's common song is a clearly whistled, medium-pitched "BOB – *WHITE*", the second note starting on the same pitch but **rising sharply higher in exclamation**. It sometimes gives a three-note version which simply repeats the first note "BOB – BOB – *WHITE*". When either version is repeated, there is a generous pause in between each delivery.

Farmlands, fields, open brushy areas and wood margins. It often sings from a post or from some other favourite perch.

Summer – S. Ont. and most of the e. U.S. south of the Grt. Lakes, south of c. Penn. and Cape Cod on the coast. *Winter* – Same.

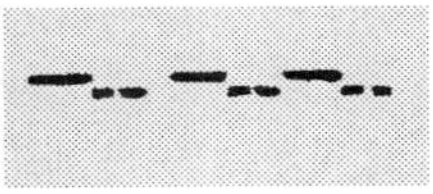

2. KILLDEER [2]

A sharp, fairly high-pitched, "*DEEE*-DEE-DEE...*DEEE*-DEE-DEE...", repeated many times. The first note is emphasized, longer and higher. The second and third notes are both on the same pitch, but lower than the first note and quicker. The Killdeer becomes **very noisy** when disturbed and is therefore hard to miss.

Gravelly or sandy areas, usually near water, and open areas with little growth.

Summer – All e. U.S. (except s. Fla.) to n. Ont., s. Que. and Nova Scotia. *Winter* – S. half of U.S. but n. to Cape Cod and Ohio.

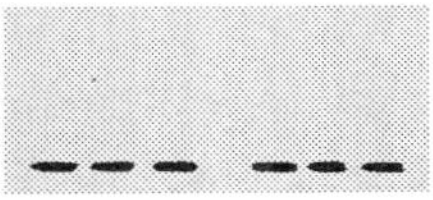

3. MOURNING DOVE [3]

At a distance the song sounds like a **slow**, sad "OOO–OOO–OOO". This three-note song is repeated after a generous pause. At close range the full song can be heard, "OH-*WOOO* (one long note slurred upward, and then briefly downward at the end) OOO–OOO–OOO". Many people mistake this song for that of an owl.

Open woodlands, fields, as well as in towns, in suburbs and at backyard feeders.

Summer – S. Ont. to N.S. and all of e. U.S. *Winter* – S. Ont. and all of e. U.S. except the extreme n. states.

4. WHIP-POOR-WILL

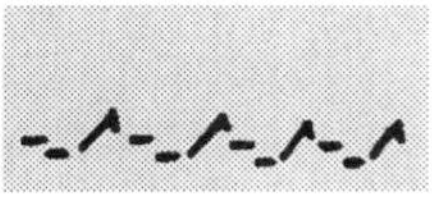

This bird gives an excellent rendition of its name "*WHIP*-POOR-*WILL*" over and over again, from its hiding place on the forest floor. Its snappy or **whippy** song is given **at night** and is repeated for long stretches of time with almost no pause between each phrase. The first note is emphasized and higher than the second. The last note, as well as emphasized most, is also the highest and longest and rises in pitch. This emphasis on the first and last notes gives the song its whippy or snappy rhythm. It is replaced in the south by the equally snappy four-notes repeated, of the Chuck-will's-widow.

Usually seen in the drier areas of deciduous and mixed woodlands where it is fairly open, and where there is a floor covering of dead leaves.

Summer – C. Ont., s. Que. to Nova Scotia, south to Va. and over to the n. Gulf states. *Winter* – Fla., Gulf and s. Atl. coast to C. Am

5. EASTERN WOOD-PEWEE [1]

Two-note version

A slow, **drawn-out** and whistled "PEEE-A-*WEEE*" sliding lower on the second note and then upward on the third. This is repeated with a generous pause between each phrase. It also "works in" a drawn-out "PEEE-YURR", every so often, with a downward inflection on the second syllable. It often sounds to me like a two-note song – a slow, drawn-out "PEEE-*WEEE*" (the last note starting lower and rising, as illustrated in the second song representation). It sometimes sings other versions of these songs which have the last note highest. In general, it is a clear sweet whistle, with the notes in each phrase moving slowly and easily together, with what could be described as a **melancholy** or **plaintive** quality.

Deciduous and mixed woodlands; also orchards and shade trees.

Summer – C. Ont. to N.S. and all e. U.S. except Fla. pen. *Winter* – Cen. and S. Am.

*6. OLIVE-SIDED FLYCATCHER

One of the more easily recognized bird songs. It sounds like a whistled "QUICK-*THREE*-BEERS" – a quick intro note; the second note, the highest; and the last note, drawn out, and sliding slightly downward. The song is repeated often.

Summer – Mainly n. Ont., c. Que. and Nfld. south to the extreme northern U.S., but there are local populations south of this.
Winter – S. Am.

Open coniferous woodlands (deciduous and mixed on migration). It will repeatedly dart out after insects and return to the same dead branch at the top of a tree.

7. BLUE JAY [3]

A musical, rolling "WHEEL-DE-LEE", repeated after a short pause. The first note rises slightly. The second and third are on the same pitch. It has a sharp quality to it that has led to it being described as sounding like a "**creaking wheelbarrow**". This song may be heard in combination with the Blue Jay's other songs, the harsh "JAAY" or "JEEAH" or the more pleasant "WHEEDLE-WHEEDLE", or its soft bell-like calls ("TULL-ULL" or "TWIRL-ERL"). It also mimics various hawks.

Summer – C. Ont. to Newfoundland and throughout the e. U.S. *Winter* – Same.

Forests, mixed woodland (especially oak and pine), parks, and city gardens.

8. BLACK-CAPPED CHICKADEE [2]

A clear, sweet, whistled "*FEEE*-BEE-BEE" – first note higher and longer than the second and third, which are both on the same pitch. The song is repeated after a brief pause. It also has a two-note version "*FEEE*-BEE". These may be heard in combination with its **bright and cheerful** "DEE-DEE-DEE-DEE..." or "CHICKA-DEE-DEE-DEE" calls. In the south, the Carolina Chickadee sings a higher, faster version of this, but it has its own distinctive four-note song ("*FEE*-SU BEE-SU").

Summer – N. Ont. to Nfld; mainly n. states, but south to W. Va. and s. Ill. *Winter* – Same.

Open woodlands, clearings and in suburban areas. It is quite common at feeders in winter.

9. CAROLINA WREN [1]

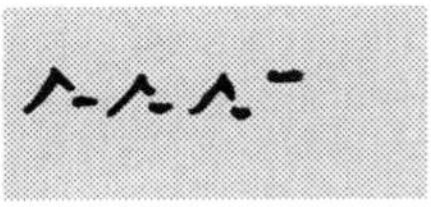

A **very loud** song. It gives a rolling, **rich** "*TWEE*DLE-DEE *TWEE*DLE-DEE *TWEE*DLE-DEE-*DEE* (or "TEA-KETTLE TEA-KETTLE TEA-KETTLE").The song rolls along, with the emphasis on the first note of each three-note phrase, and on the final note, when present, as shown here. It also has a rapid two-note version "TWEEDLE-TWEEDLE-TWEEDLE", with all the same qualities. Its loud, rich chatter may also be heard.

In moist woodland areas with tangled undergrowth and thick brush; also along streams and swamps with sufficient cover, as well as in gardens.

Summer – S. Ont. and e. U.S. south of Cape Cod in the east and Wisc. in the west. *Winter* – Same.

*10. CONNECTICUT WARBLER [1]

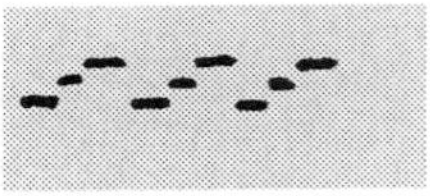

A **very loud**, clear series of three-syllable phrases that **speeds up** as it progresses and sounds like "CHICH-U-*EE* CHICH-U-*EE* CHICH-U-*EE*", with the last note higher and emphasized. A very loud, emphatic, and rich song, it does not have a smooth delivery, but has a jerky or **hesitant** quality, as it starts up. Other adjectives which could be used to describe its song are resonant and even explosive. It also has a two-syllabled song which sounds like "*BEE*CHER-*BEE*CHER-*BEE*CHER-*BEE*CHER-*BEECH*". It has the same qualities as the above song, including the hesitant start and the more rapid follow-through (speeding up), but the first note is higher and emphasized in this case.

A northern breeder, it is found near the ground in open poplar woods in its western range, but in spruce and tamarack bogs in its eastern range.

Summer – From the northern Grt. Lakes states (Minn., Wisc. and Mich.) to nc. Ont. (James Bay). *Winter* – N. S. Am.

11. COMMON YELLOWTHROAT

One of the more common and easily recognized bird songs. It is a loud and clear "*WIT*CHITY-*WIT*CHITY-*WIT*CHITY-*WITCH*", usually sung at a moderate speed. In each phrase, usually the first note is higher and accented, with the next two notes lower, and both on the same pitch. Although the song can vary considerably, the characteristic up and down "**whippy**" rhythm is always present.

Found in swamps, marshes, moist grass or shrubby areas. It likes to skulk low among the reeds and tangles, but it is also seen on the branches of shrubs and bushes, at a higher elevation.

Summer – N. Ont. and c. Que. to Nfld. and south throughout the e. U.S. *Winter* – All Gulf states and up the Atl. coast.

12. RED-WINGED BLACKBIRD [2]

A squeaky, gurgling "COY-LA-*REE*". The first note is down slurred and squeaky, the second, quicker, and a bit higher, and the third note, continuing **up the scale**, is a harsh, raspy, trill. It is a very common sound in and around swamps and marshes. Often all that is heard is the two-note "LA-REE", or even simply the raspy trill "REE". Calls include "CHECK" or "CHUCK" notes and a high-pitched "TSEE-ER". Song is repeated after a generous pause.

In swamps and marshes, but also in dry fields and in bushy areas.

Summer – N. Ont., c. Que. to Nfld. and all the e. U.S. *Winter* – S. Ont. and s.of the Grt. Lakes (not the N.E. and Appalachians).

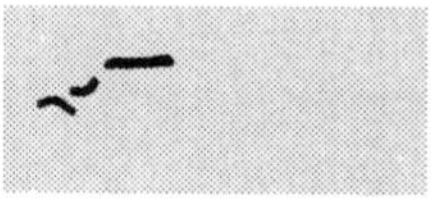

13. BROWN-HEADED COWBIRD [2]

A quick little song – 2 very short, bubbly, gurgling sounds, followed by a thin, high-pitched, short whistle. "GLUG-LA-*SEEE*". The last note has a thin sharp quality like someone sucking air between their two front teeth. Calls include a "CHUCK" note and a loud, harsh rattle or chatter. Song is repeated after a generous pause.

Farms, roadsides, open woodlands, parks, and also in suburban areas.

Summer – C. Ont., s. Que. to Nfld. and all of the e. U.S. except Fla. and part of the S.E. *Winter* – S. Ont. and south of the Grt. Lakes.

14. RUFOUS-SIDED TOWHEE [1]

The characteristic three-note song sounds like "DRINK-YOUR-*TEA-EE-EE-EE-EE*" – last note prolonged, higher and trilled. The first two notes are whistled clearly, with the second note lower than the first. There is also a two-note version "DRINK-*TEA-EE-EE-EE-EE*" as well as a four-note version "DRINK-AT-YOUR-*TEA-EE-EE-EE-EE*". The song is delivered at a fairly slow, measured pace, and is also quite musical. It is repeated after a fairly generous pause.

Open woodlands, areas with dense undergrowth and thickets, where it is seen scouring the ground in search of food.

Summer – C. Ont., s. Que. and all e. U.S.
Winter – Sw. Ont. and s. of L. Erie to Gulf and from Va. to Fla. Also up Atl. coast to Cape Cod.

Red-winged Blackbird

Carolina Wren

III SHORT SONGS – VARYING NOTES

SEVERAL VARYING NOTES / Slower (measured notes)

SEVERAL VARYING NOTES / Faster (less deliberate)

CONTAINING A DISTINCT REPEATED NOTE OR PHRASE

1. AMERICAN ROBIN [1]

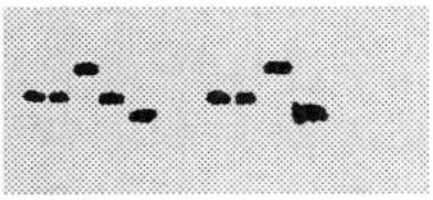

A loud, **rolling**, "cheerful" song, consisting of short, sweet phrases, rising and falling: "CHEERI*LY*-CHEERY-CHEERI*LY*-CHEER" or "TWEEDLE-*DEET*-DEEO TWEEDLE-*DEET*-DEE" (last note a bit hoarse) – often repeated many times, with a brief pause between each delivery. The final note of the "CHEERI*LY*" phrase (or the "*DEET*" note) is accented and higher. When the pauses between deliveries are less distinct, it sounds like one long carolling song. Common calls include a series of "TUT-TUT-TUT..." notes, a sharp "PEEK" and a quick series of rising notes referred to as the Robin's "laugh".

Common in woodlands, parks, and gardens, as well as on the lawns of cities and towns.

Summer – Throughout e. Canada and the U.S. except Fla. and the extreme S.E.
Winter – S. Ont. and most of e. U.S. (not N.E. or Alleghenies); the Atl. coast to Nfld.

2. HERMIT THRUSH

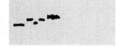

Listen for the distinct, **long, introductory, flute-like note** (usually **lower**) followed by several, clear, rising and falling, reedy notes, in a slow, yodelling cadence. There are several phrases, very similar in form, but sung at different pitches, each with that distinct introductory note. It sounds like the same song being repeated over and over but in a different key each time. Two examples of these sound like, "HEY-BREVITY-BREE" (last note higher) or "HEY-BREVITY-BREVITY" (on same pitch). Hearing the clear, sweet notes of this song has been described as almost a religious experience by some and the Hermit Thrush has been referred to as the most gifted singer of all North American birds.

Coniferous and mixed woodlands, where it is found in thickets and on the forest floor.

Summer – N. Ont. south into Minn., Wisc. and Mich. and c. Que. to Nfld., south to W. Va. *Winter* – Ohio south; also n. to C. Cod.

3. WOOD THRUSH

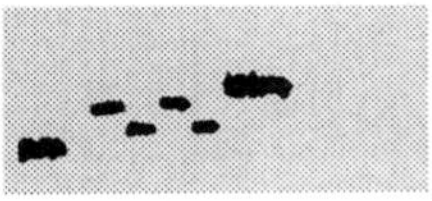

Although some phrases are sung quickly, in general, the pace of the Wood Thrush song is measured and in no hurry. It has a distinctive "*EO-LAY*" sound (or "*EO-EO-LAY*") that gives it a "**yodelling**" quality. It is a loud, liquid song, with each phrase ending in a trill (sometimes higher, sometimes lower) and it is further characterized by its hollow, flute-like thrush sound. Each phrase is also introduced by a very brief little chatter. Distinctive call, a loud, rapid "WHIP-PIP-PIP-PIP-PIP-PIP-PIP-PIP".

Moist woodlands (mainly deciduous) in the lower canopy and floor of the forest, and also in swamps.

Summer – C. Ont., s. Que. south to n. Fla. and the Gulf. *Winter* – Mexico to Panama.

4. BLACK-THROATED GREEN WARBLER [1]

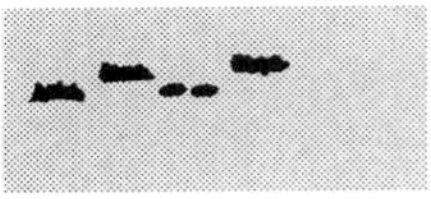

A slow, buzzy "ZOO-*ZEE*-ZOO-ZOO-*ZEE*" ("TREES-*TREES*-MURMURING-*TREES*"). The third and fourth notes are clearer (not buzzy) and quicker. The "*ZEE*" notes are accented and higher-pitched, and the "ZOO" notes are all on the same pitch and lower. Another song is clearer and quicker: "ZEE-ZEE-ZEE-ZEE-ZEE-ZOO-ZEE" (the "ZOO" lower).

Coniferous or predominantly coniferous forests.

Summer – N. Ont., c. Que. and Nfld. to the extreme n. states, the Appalachians and s. Atl. coast. *Winter* – S. Fla., Tex. to Pan.

5. BLACK-THROATED BLUE WARBLER [1]

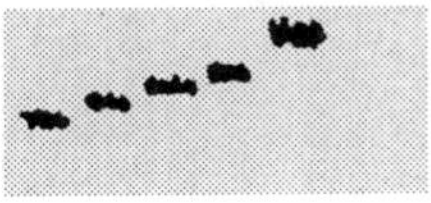

This song consists of 3-5 evenly spaced, **buzzing notes** sliding up the scale, with the last note noticeably higher. "ZEEP-ZEEP-ZEEP-ZEEP-*ZEEE*". The song proceeds at an even, **measured pace**. It is commonly given as one single note repeated, with only the last note noticeably higher.

Mixed conifer and hardwood forest with heavy undergrowth.

Summer – C. Ont., s Que. to Nova Scotia, the extreme n. states and down the Appalachians. *Winter* – S. Fla., the West Indies and S. Am.

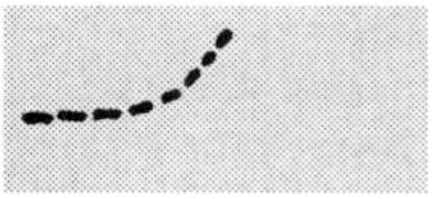

6. PRAIRIE WARBLER

A series of thin, raspy, or buzzy notes (6-10) **climbing** up the scale, and often speeding up toward the end. "ZEE-ZEE-ZEE-ZEE-ZEE-ZEE...", (rising and getting faster). The song itself varies in speed. It can be given quickly or slowly, but the notes are usually separate – no slurs or trills.

Summer – Scattered populations s. Ont., Mich. and N.E. states, but mainly well south of the Grt. Lakes to Fla. *Winter* – Fla. to the West Indies and Cen. Am.

Open woodlands, brushy fields, forest edges, as well as burned-over areas.

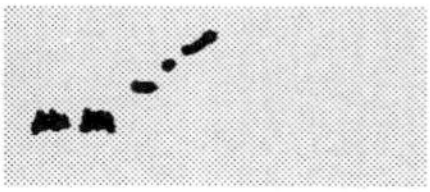

7. COMMON GRACKLE

A short, forced, or hesitating series of **harsh clucks**, ending in a high-pitched, **squeaky note**. The notes tend to get higher in pitch as they proceed. "CHACK–CHACK–KEEK-A-LEEK".

Summer – Throughout e. Can. and the U.S. *Winter* – S. Ont. and all e. U.S. south of this.

In fields, marshes, open woodlands and in suburbs. It nests, in colonies, in shrubs and in small trees (especially conifers) and marsh vegetation.

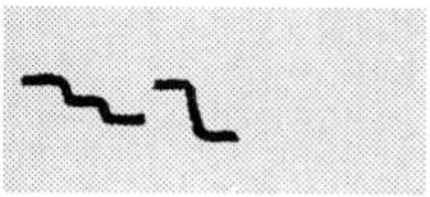

8. EASTERN MEADOWLARK

A sweet, clear, **slurred whistle**, given at a leisurely pace. A 5-note version sounds like "SEE-YOU-SOON NOT-NOW", with the first three notes slurring downward. The fourth and fifth notes start high again, and also slur downward. There is a 4-note version too, which is the same, but leaves out the third note, "SEE-YOU NOT-NOW". The Meadowlark also has a dry trill or rattle at the end of its song.

Summer – C. Ont., s. Que. to N.B. and throughout the e. U.S. *Winter* – Around L. Ont. and L. Erie and all e. U.S. south of L. Mich., as well as up Atl. coast to Maine.

Grassy fields and meadows, where it builds its nest on the ground. It can be seen singing from a stump or a rock, but it might also be seen during its rather heavy-winged flights (alternately flapping and gliding) to or from the nest.

9. INDIGO BUNTING

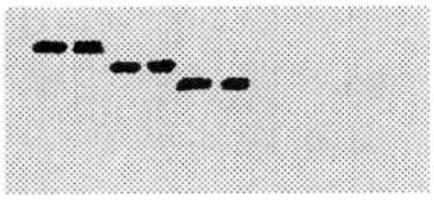

This song is characterized by high-pitched "**pairs**" of notes, sharp, and rhythmic, often with each pair at a lower pitch down the scale. It commonly consists of three or four pairs of notes and is delivered fairly quickly, but it is definitely not rushed.

Open woodlands, brushy areas and clearings.

Summer – C. Ont., s. Que. and throughout the e. U.S. (except the Gulf coast and Fla.).
Winter – West Indies and Mex. to Pan.

*10. WHITE-CROWNED SPARROW

There are 2-3 clear, sweet, introductory notes (sounding like a White-throated Sparrow), followed by raspy (or husky) notes moving **down the scale**, and ending in a low trill. "ZWEE-ZA-ZA-ZOO-ZEE-ZOO". The first note is a little longer than the other introductory note(s). The last note is a low trill (sometimes a buzzy note), and the overall song is given at a moderate speed.

It breeds in the open, stunted woodlands and scrub of the far north. In winter it likes open woodlands, grasslands, roadsides and tangles, where it feeds at ground level.

Summer – Extreme n. Ont., Que. and Nfld.
Winter – S. Ont. south to the Gulf (not in the N.E., the Appal's, the s. Atl. coast or Fla.).

Black-throated Blue Warbler

*1. COMMON LOON [1]

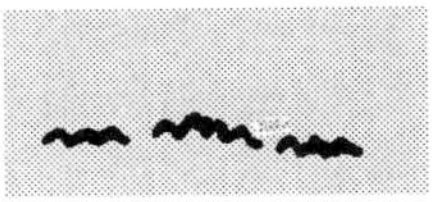

Tremolo or wavering quality

A series of repeated, tremolo, **laughing calls**. A quick "YOODLE-OODLE-OO". This is often heard along with other Loon calls, notably the longer, drawn-out wailing call, which has similarities to a howling wolf "oh-OOOOO-ooo" (rising and emphasized on the second syllable, and then dropping on the last).

Usually heard on deep lakes, with good shoreline for nesting.

Summer – Throughout e. Can. and in extreme n. states. *Winter* – Atl. and Gulf coasts.

2. EASTERN BLUEBIRD [1]

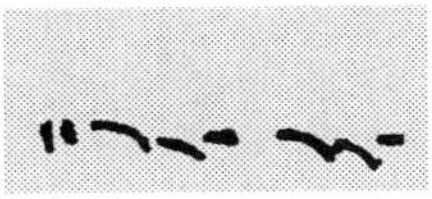

A short, sweet, gentle, and variable warble, sometimes introduced by a couple of "CHICK" notes. "CHICK–PEEER-CHUR-WEE... PEEER-CHUR-WEE". The first note slurs downward, and the second note slides down slightly into the third (both on a similar pitch and lower than the first). The call is a 2-note, sweet "CHUR-WEE". This gentle warble can also be strung together into a series of phrases to create a longer song.

Open woodlands, orchards and any open country with a few trees or posts (for perches and nesting) and areas of open grass and fields.

Summer – C. Ont., s. Que. to N.S. and all the e. U.S. *Winter* – The e. U.S., from c. Ohio south, and up the coast to Cape Cod.

*3. SWAINSON'S THRUSH

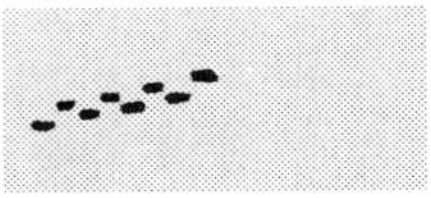

The song is the opposite of the Veery in that it is an **ascending**, rapid spiral of hollow, flute-like notes, rolling up the scale. "I'M-*GOING*-TO-*WEAR*-MY-*BOOTS*-TO*DAY*", accenting every second syllable on the way up the scale, gives an idea of the length of the song, and the rhythm, but the song is quite variable. It is sweet and musical but not as pleasant as the Hermit or Wood Thrush and it is delivered with a slightly wheezy or windy quality. A.A. Saunders described it as "WHAO-WHAYO-WHIYO-WHEYA-WHEEYA".

Moist, coniferous woodlands and streamside thickets.

Summer – Extreme n. states to n. Ont. (not s. Ont.), c. Que. and Nfld. (local s. of Grt. Lakes). *Winter* – S. Mex. to Argentina.

4. VEERY

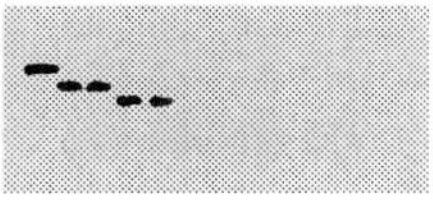

A **descending** series of flute-like, hollow notes."VA-VEER-VEER-VEER-VEER", down the scale.The emotion evoked is not so much of joy, but holier, like a hymn (to A.C. Bent).

Moist forest floors and thickets.

Summer – C. Ont., s. Que. to Nfld., the Grt. Lakes and ne. states and down the Appalachians. *Winter* – Cen. and S. Am.

5. WHITE-EYED VIREO

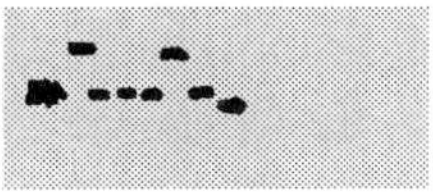

A **variable**, **snappy** song that begins with an introductory "CHICK" or "CHICK-SEE". It is quite **variable** but one common version follows this immediately with what sounds like "PUT-THE-GA*ZE*BO-UP" (strongly accented and rising on the "*ZE*" and dropping on the last two notes). An alternative version that I have heard leaves the last note off, and it sounds like "CHICK-BUILD-THE-GA*ZE*BO". R.T. Peterson describes another common rendition as "a sharply enunciated CHICK'-A-PER-*WEE*OO-CHICK'." It also utters a rapid "CHICK-*THREE*-BEERS" (rising and emphasized on the "*THREE*").

In wood margins, dense moist thickets, and tangles.

Summer – Sw. Ont. and throughout the e. U.S. south of L. Erie. *Winter* – Fla., the Gulf and s. Atl. coasts.

6. WARBLING VIREO [2]

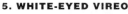

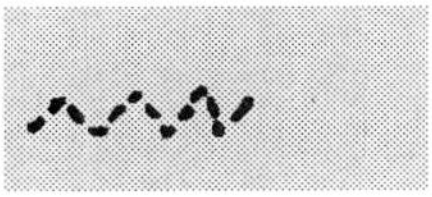

Shows rhythm

The characteristic song of the Warbling Vireo is a long, rambling, warbling, up and down song, that **ends on an upswing**, and is delivered with a slightly "**burry**" quality. However it sometimes gives a shorter version of this song with all of the same qualities mentioned above except the length. It is a persistent singer and its undulating or "roller-coaster" delivery is a common sound of open woodlands.

Open deciduous and mixed woodlands, usually in the upper branches. Also orchards and shade trees. Often found near human habitation.

Summer – S. Ont. to N.B. and south to Miss., Tenn. and N.C. (absent from the S.E.). *Winter* – Mexico to Nicaragua.

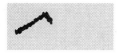

7. NORTHERN PARULA WARBLER [1]

A buzzy trill which **rises** and then **snaps** at the end. "DSEEEEEEEEE-UH". It also sings several buzzy notes, on the same pitch with the last buzzy note higher and usually rising, "TSWEE-TSWEE-TSWEE-*TSWEEEE*".

Coniferous, and mixed woodlands, preferring Usnea, or old man's beard, in the north, for nesting, and Spanish moss in the south.

Summer – C. Ont., s. Que. to N.S. and all e. U.S. except s. Fla., parts of the N.E. and large areas of the states bordering L. Huron and L. Mich. *Winter* – Fla., Mex., Cen. Am. and W. Indies.

8. CANADA WARBLER

Key to identifying this bird is the sharp "CHIP" or "CHICK" opening note, which is followed immediately by a short, **rapid warble** of varied notes (**up and down in pitch**). The loud song is highly variable but its basic characteristics remain the same – short, quick, sweet, and fidgety (moving quickly up and down in pitch).

Dense woodland undergrowth, brush, and thickets.

Summer – N. Ont., c. Que. to N.S., the n. Grt. Lakes states, the ne. states and down the Appalachians. Winter – N. S. Am.

9. NORTHERN ORIOLE [1]

Highly variable. Rich one- and two-note phrases with some harsh notes mixed in, quick changes in pitch and a whippy or snappy rhythm.

A highly variable song characterized by short, distinct phrases of one or two notes each, usually delivered fairly quickly. A loud series (4-16 notes) of clear, **rich whistles** (some prolonged), with **harsh chicks** and burred notes thrown in (mainly in longer versions), as well as rapid changes in pitch, which give it a jerky delivery. Many birds have a distinct **whippy rhythm** in their song. A rough or harsh chatter may also be heard as well as a series of repeated notes. Its two-note call is often repeated between song deliveries.

Open woodlands, orchards, shade trees and suburbs.

Summer – C. Ont. and s. Que. to N.S., south to Md. and inland from n. Va. to n. Geo., over to c. La. (not the s. Atl or S.E.). *Winter* – Atl. and Gulf coasts; Mex. to Col.

10. SCARLET TANAGER

A series of short, sweet, Robin-like phrases, that are delivered with a **burry** or **raspy** quality, and move briskly (but not rapidly) up and down in pitch."TWEER-TWEER-TUWEET-TUWEET-TWEER" or combinations of notes that sound like "TUWEET-TWEER" (1-2 syllable notes in short phrases).The 2-note call is also diagnostic – a chip with a burry, lower-pitched second note:"KEEP-GOING" or "CHIP-CHURR".

Deciduous or pine-oak woodlands, orchards, parks and shade trees.

Summer – C. Ont., s. Que. to N.B., south to Va., n. Geo. and Ala. *Winter* – N. S. Am.

11. HOUSE FINCH [2]

High-pitched, rapid and varied notes, as well as the characteristic harsh "CHURRR" ending.

A bubbly, loud, high-pitched and musical series of notes delivered very quickly. Often at or near the end a burry or **harsh "CHURR"** (or a more biting "VEEER" or "JEEER") which is longer than the other notes and slides downwards. Overall, it is variable and irregular with sharp changes in pitch. Sometimes this abbreviated version replaces the longer song.

Open woodlands, farms, cities and suburbs. It is very much at home in cities and around human habitation.

Summer – S. Ont. and the e. U.S. south of the Grt. Lakes to Ala. and Geo. (and spreading). *Winter* – Same.

12. AMERICAN GOLDFINCH [2]

Flight song

This song can be a long song (usually in the spring) or a fairly short song (usually in the summer, after the start of nesting), but in either case it is a **canary-like** series of clear, sweet notes, combined with trills (less in summer) and characteristic **drawn-out squeaky notes** ("SWEEE" rising). The diagnostic flight song is a clear and whippy "PER-*CHICK*-O-REE" (or "CHEE-*CHI*-CHI-CHEE"), emphasized on the second note. It is delivered on the uprise of its undulating flight or along with its regular song.

In weedy fields, open woodlands, and farmlands and along roadsides. The Goldfinch is fond of thistles and weeds, which it uses for food, as well as for nesting materials.

Summer – C. Ont., s. Que. to Nfld. and the e. U.S., south to Va. and into the n. Gulf states. *Winter* – S. Ont., s. Que. and N.S. and all of the e. U.S.

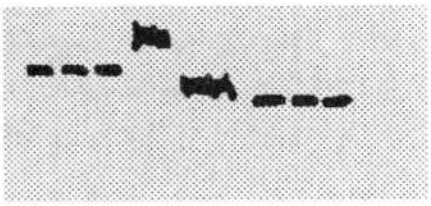

13. SONG SPARROW

This song is introduced by 2-3 repeated, sweet notes, followed by a short, buzzy, "*ZREE*", a lower liquid trill, and ending with a lower, buzzy note (sometimes 2-3 notes).
"SWEET'N-SWEET'N-*ZREE*-SUGAR-IT"
or
"SWEET-SWEET-SWEET-*ZREE*-SUGAR-IT-IT-IT".
It is quite variable in form.

Marshes, gardens and roadsides, as well as streamside thickets.

Summer – N. Ont., s. Que to Nfld., the n. half of the e. U.S. and the Appalachians.
Winter – S. Ont. to N.S. and all of the e. U.S. except portions of the most northerly states.

Song Sparrow

1. MOURNING DOVE [4]

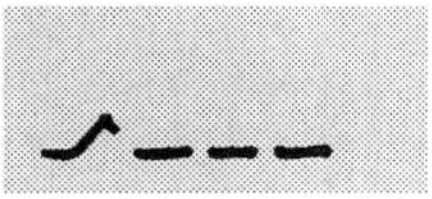

At a distance the song sounds like a simple, three-note song – a sad, **slow**, "OOO–OOO–OOO". At closer range, the full four-note song can be heard, and it sounds like "OH-*WOOO* (one long note slurred upward, and then briefly downward at the end) OOO–OOO–OOO". It is repeated after a generous pause. Many people mistake this song for that of an owl.

Open woods and fields, as well as in towns, in suburbs and at backyard feeders.

Summer – S. Ont. to N.S. and all e. U.S.
Winter – S. Ont. and all e. U.S. except extreme northern areas.

2. BLACK-CAPPED CHICKADEE [4]

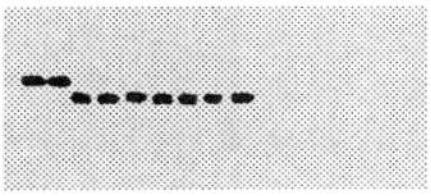

A snappy two-note introduction "CHICKA", followed immediately by a rapid series of "DEE-DEE-DEE-DEE-DEE..." notes, all with a squeaky, yet **bright and cheerful** quality. The two-note introduction is higher-pitched than the series of repeated notes. In the south, the Carolina Chickadee gives a quicker, higher-pitched version of this call. The Black-capped Chickadee's two-note song is a clear, whistled "*FEEE*-BEE" – the first note higher and longer – repeated after a brief pause (sometimes a three-note song). The Carolina Chickadee has a distinctive four-note song "*FEE*-SU BEE-SU".

Open woodlands, clearings, and also in suburban areas. It is a common visitor at feeders in winter.

Summer – N. Ont. to Nfld.; mainly n. states, but south to W. Va. and s. Ill. *Wnter*–Same

3. NORTHERN PARULA WARBLER [2]

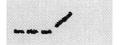

Several buzzy notes on the same pitch with the last buzzy note higher and usually rising. "TSWEE-TSWEE-TSWEE-*TSWEEEE*". Although similar in form to the Black-throated Blue Warbler's song, the Parula's notes are looser with a slight trilled effect. Its other common song is a buzzy trill which **rises** and then snaps at the end. "DSEEEEEEEEE-UH".

Coniferous, and mixed woodlands, preferring Usnea, or old man's beard, in the north, for nesting, and Spanish moss in the south.

Summer – C. Ont., s. Que. to N.S. and all e. U.S. except s. Fla., parts of the N.E. and large areas of the states bordering L. Huron and L. Mich.
Winter – Fla., Mex., Cen. Am. and W. Indies.

4. BLACK-THROATED GREEN WARBLER [2]

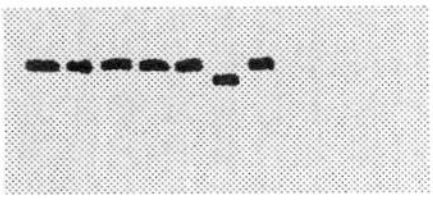

A quick series of short, clear, high-pitched notes."ZEE-ZEE-ZEE-ZEE-ZEE-ZOO-ZEE" (with the "ZOO" lower). This warbler's other song is a slow, buzzy "ZOO-*ZEE*-ZOO-ZOO-*ZEE*". The third and fourth notes are clearer (not buzzy) and quicker. The "ZEE" notes are accented and higher-pitched, and the "ZOO" notes are all on the same pitch and lower.

Coniferous or predominantly coniferous forests.

Summer – N. Ont., c. Que. and Nfld. to the n. states, down the Appalachians and s. Atl. coast. *Winter* – S. Fla. to Pan.

5. BLACK-THROATED BLUE WARBLER [2]

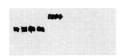

Several (3-5) evenly spaced, **buzzing notes** on one pitch, with the last note noticeably higher and often slurring upwards. "ZEEP-ZEEP-ZEEP-ZEEP-*ZEEE*". It is sung at an even, **measured pace**. The 3-5 buzzy notes sometimes slide up the scale, with the last note noticeably higher. The quality is husky, nasal and buzzing.

Mixed conifer and hardwood forest with heavy undergrowth.

Summer – C. Ont., s. Que. to N.S., into the n. states and down the Appalachians.
Winter – S. Fla., the West Indies and S. Am.

6. CERULEAN WARBLER

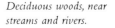

Several **rapid**, **buzzy** notes on one pitch, and then a final buzzy note which is higher-pitched. "ZREE-ZREE-ZREE-ZREE-ZREEEE" ("JUST-A-LITTLE-*SNEEZE*"). Some variations have a chirpy series of notes as an introduction (not buzzy), but the **buzzy, higher-pitched, final note** is diagnostic. It is similar in form to the Black-throated Blue Warbler's song, but the notes tend to be quicker, more wiry or looser, and the last note stays on one pitch.

Deciduous woods, near streams and rivers.

Summer – S. Ont. and the interior states south to La., Miss., Ala.; also N.Y. to N.C. in east.
Winter – S. Am.

7. MAGNOLIA WARBLER

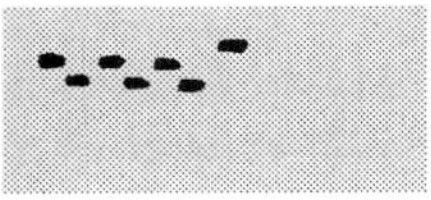

The song of the Magnolia Warbler is short (usually consisting of a few two-note phrases), rapid, and yet quite variable. One common version, delivered in its rather **thin**, or weak voice, sounds like a rapid, whistled, "WEETO-WEETO-WEETEE-*EET*" (last note rising), or "SEEYA-SEEYA-SEEYA-*SOON*". Another shorter version ends with the second last note emphasized, and the last note lower. It sounds like a thin, rapid, whistled "SEEYA-SEEYA-*SEAT*-YA" ("PRETTY-PRETTY-*RA*CHEL").

Low stands of coniferous forests, as well as along the edge of coniferous forests, in dense thickets of spruce and fir.

Summer – N. Ont. (not s. Ont.), c. Que. to Nfld., the n. Grt. Lakes states, the N.E. and down to W. Va. *Winter* – Tip of Fla., Mex. to Pan. and the W. Indies.

8. CHESTNUT-SIDED WARBLER

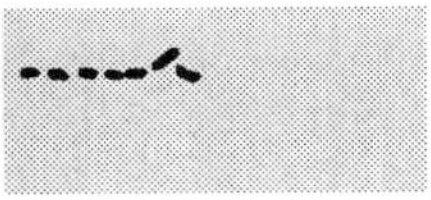

A fast series of introductory notes (3-5) on the same pitch, almost like a trill, and then a **"snappy" ending**. It sounds like "SWEET-SWEET-SWEET-SWEET-TO-*BEAT*-CHA", with the second last note accented and highest, and the last dropping.

Second growth deciduous forest with thickets, brush and bushes.

Summer – C. Ont., s. Que. to N.S., the n. Grt. Lakes states, the N.E. and down the Appalachians. *Winter* – Cen. Am.

9. BLACKBURNIAN WARBLER

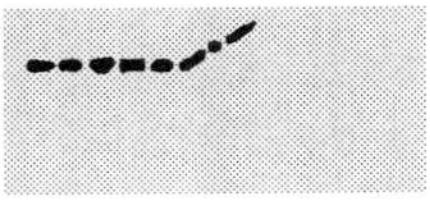

A **short**, **weak**, and **very high-pitched** song. It starts with a few single or double-note whistles, and ends on an even higher-pitched, slow, chirping trill. "SWEET-SWEET-SWEET-*TRRRR*". Another version goes "SEET-SEET-SEET-SEET-SEET-SEEDLEE-*SEET*", with the last note rising extremely high.

Coniferous and mixed forests (deciduous forests in the southern part of its range).

Summer – N. Ont., c. Que. to N.S., the n. Grt. Lakes states, the N.E. and down the Appalachians. *Winter* – Costa Rica to Peru.

10. AMERICAN REDSTART [1]

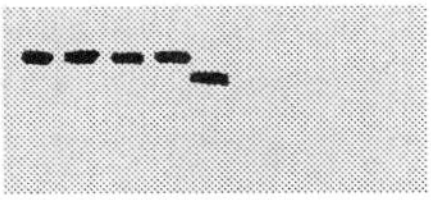

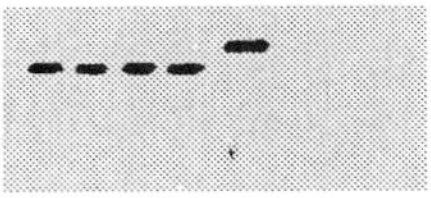

A **high-pitched** and **variable** song, consisting of weak, yet emphatic single notes (sometimes two-note phrases, similar to the Black and White Warbler's phrases). "TSEET-TSEET-TSEET-TSEET-*TSEEE*" (last note higher) and "TSEET-TSEET-TSEET-TSEE-O" (last note lower). It often uses both songs, and is the only wood warbler to alternate songs in this way. It also sings its song all on one pitch – a single note (or two-notes) repeated. The Redstart song can easily fool even experienced birders. I often detect a pumping or pulsating quality to the delivery, especially up close.

Deciduous woods, thickets, and bush, often near water. Also wood edges, and young second growth woods, as well as roadside trees, gardens and parks.

Summer – Nc. Ont. (James Bay) to Nfld. and south to the Gulf states (not Fla. and the s. Atl. coast). *Winter* – Tip of Fla. and Texas coast southward.

11. YELLOW WARBLER

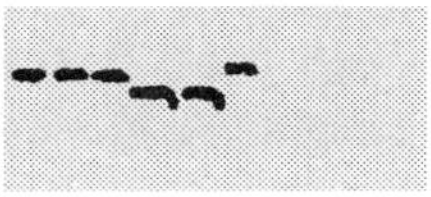

Several, clear, **sweet** notes. The first 3-4 notes are on the same pitch. The song is a **rapid** "TWEET-TWEET-*TWEET*-TWEEDLE-DEEDLE-*DEET*", or "TWEET-TWEET-*TWEET*-TWEEDLE-DE-*DEET*", both with the last note rising. It has been described as a quick "SWEET-SWEET-*SWEET*-SWEETER-THAN-*SWEET*".

Open woodlands with small trees, brush and bushes especially where they border wet or swampy areas. Also hedgerows and orchards.

Summer – N. Ont., n. Que. to Nfld. and south to n. Gulf states. *Winter* – W. Indies and Mex. to S. Am.

*12. WILSON'S WARBLER

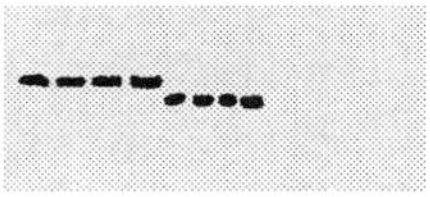

A rapid chatter of **staccato** notes, **dropping** in pitch, and **speeding up** at the end. It is more "ringing" than sweet or musical. "CHEE-CHEE-CHEE-CHEE CHE-CHE-CHE".

Thickets and shrubs. It is found on or close to the ground in wet or boggy areas, and along streams.

Summer – C. and n. Ont., c. and n. Que. to Nfld. and in the extreme ne. states. *Winter* – Mexico to Panama.

13. HOODED WARBLER

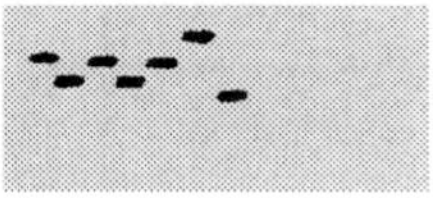

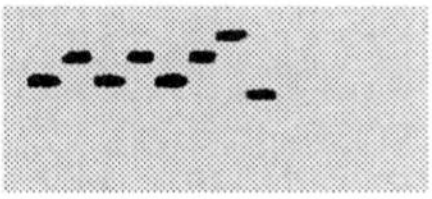

A **very loud**, **rich**, and clear song, given at moderate speed. In form, it is similar to the Magnolia Warbler's song. "WITTA-WITTA-WI-*TE*-O". The song consists of 2 two-note phrases (first note emphasized) as introduction. The third phrase starts the same, but the second note breaks higher in pitch, and volume, and the last note drops much lower - the characteristic **"TE-O" ending**. An alternate song shifts the emphasis to the second note in each phrase, and thus starts on a lower note: "TA-WIT TA-WIT TA-WI-*TE*-O".

In swamps, and in moist woodlands with good undergrowth.

Summer – S. Ont., N.Y. and Mich. south to the Gulf (not Fla. pen.); also up the coast to R.I. *Winter* – W. Indies and Mex. to Pan.

American Redstart

14. GOLDEN-WINGED WARBLER

A raspy, **buzzing song** of four notes, the first note long, and the last three, shorter, and on a lower pitch. A lazy "*ZEEE*-ZREE-ZREE-ZREE".

Open woodlands, brushy meadows, and forest edges.

Summer – S. Ont., the Grt. Lakes states, Mass. and down the Appalachians.
Winter – Guatemala to Colombia.

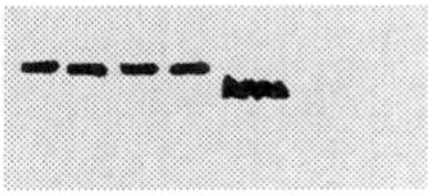

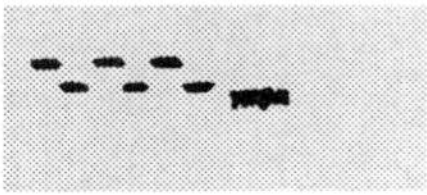

15. NASHVILLE WARBLER

A loud, repeated series of high-pitched notes, followed by a **short trill, on a lower pitch**. "SWEET-SWEET-SWEET-SWEET-TRRRR", or "SEEWEE-SEEWEE-SEEWEE-TRRRR". The song is delivered at a moderate speed.

In thickets along swamps, spruce bogs, forest edges and second growth woods.

Summer – N. Ont., c. Que. to N.S., the n. Grt. Lakes states, the ne. states and down to n. W. Va.. *Winter* – Texas coast to Guatemala.

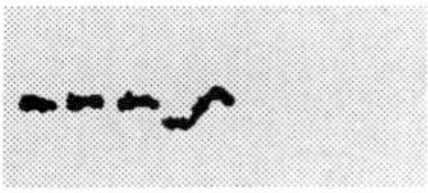

16. MOURNING WARBLER

A **loud**, rich, **musical** and short song which has considerable variation. One version sounds to me like "CHEE-CHEE-CHEE CHURR-*E*-AH" (rising higher on the "E" and then dropping), and sometimes like "CHEE-CHEE-CHEE CHURR-AH" (dropping at the end). Peterson describes it as "CHIRRY, CHIRRY, CHORRY, CHORRY (CHORRY lower)". Still other versions sound like "CHEE-CHEE-CHEE CHO-CHO-CHO". Its loud, rich and musical song also has a slightly burry or husky quality.

Thickets, tangles, brushy areas and moist woodlands, on or close to the ground.

Summer – C. Ont., s. Que. to Nfld, the n. Grt. Lakes states, the ne. states and south to n. W. Va.. *Winter* – Nicaragua to Ecuador.

17. YELLOW-RUMPED WARBLER [2]

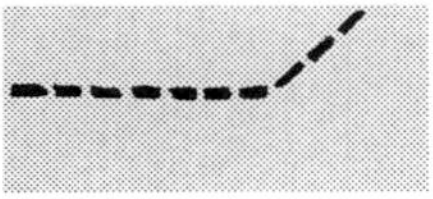

A sweet, slow, **trill**, not particularly loud, with the last part **rising or dropping** in pitch."WHEE-WHEE-WHEE-WHEE..." or a slightly sharper, sibilant "SWEE-WHEE-WHEE-WHEE...". The speed varies from a rapid series of notes to a slow trill and it can also be delivered with all notes on the same pitch.

Coniferous and mixed woodlands, in open areas and woodland edges, orchards and in evergreen thickets by streams or other waterways.

Summer – Extreme n. states, to the far north across e. Can. (not s. Ont.) *Winter* – S. Grt. Lakes to the Gulf and also up the Atl. coast.

18. WHITE-THROATED SPARROW

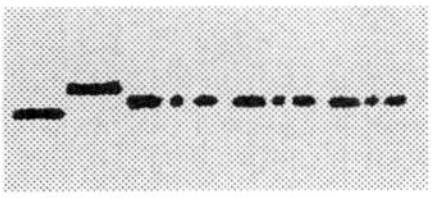

One (sometimes two) clear, whistled note(s), followed by **3 three-note phrases** ("CANADA-CANADA-CANADA") are characteristic. The whole song is sung at an easy, leisurely pace. "OH-*SWEET* CANADA-CANADA-CANADA". The first introductory note is lower than the repeated series of notes, and the second is slightly higher than the following phrases (sometimes the phrases are lower in pitch than the introductory notes). The three-note phrases are accented on the first note of each phrase and this gives it a **rhythmic** or rolling quality, much like the "WITCHITY-WITCHITY-WITCHITY" of the Common Yellowthroat. Often a three-note phrase is added between the two introductory notes. "OH-CANADA-SWEET-CANADA-CANADA-CANADA."

A more northerly breeding sparrow found in woodland edges, brushland, thickets, and roadsides. It feeds on the ground, foraging among the leaves.

Summer – N. Ont., n. Que to Nfld. and south to the n. Grt. Lakes states and the ne. states. *Winter* – S. Ont. and the e. U.S. except s. Fla. and the extreme ne. states.

American Robin

IV LONG SONGS – VARYING NOTES

MANY VARYING NOTES / Slower (measured notes)

MANY VARYING NOTES / Faster (less deliberate)

CONSISTING OF SHORT VARIABLE PHRASES

1. BROWN THRASHER

A long series of harsh and sweet whistles, each phrase commonly sung twice.

This is a fairly easy song to identify because each note or phrase is commonly **repeated** or **sung in couplets**. Its long series of notes and phrases ranges from harsh to sweet whistles, and is sung very deliberately. Each couplet is separated by a brief, but noticeable, pause. In general it is a loud, clear, rich song.

In thickets, brush, and tangles of open woods, woodland edges and open areas.

Summer – S. Ont., Que. and all e. U.S. except n. Maine. *Winter* – Atl. coast (s. of C. Cod), Gulf states and up the Miss. R. to Ind.

2. AMERICAN ROBIN [2]

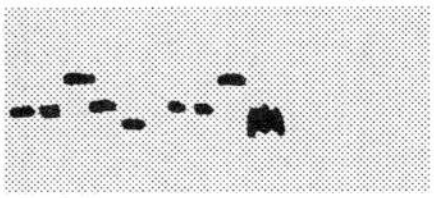

Its loud, **rolling**, "cheerful" song (consisting of a series of short, sweet phrases, rising and falling, "CHEERI*LY*-CHEERY-CHEERI*LY*- CHEER" or "TWEEDLE-*DEET*-DEEO TWEEDLE-*DEET*-DEE") usually has a brief pause between deliveries, but its early morning song is a bit quicker and this pause is not noticeable. It sounds like **one long carolling song**. Common calls include a series of "TUT-TUT-TUT..." notes, a sharp "PEEK" and also a quick series of rising notes referred to as the Robin's "laugh".

Common in woodlands, parks and gardens, as well as on the lawns of cities and towns.

Summer – Throughout e. Can. and the U.S. except Fla. *Winter* – S. Ont. and e. U.S. (not N.E. or Alleghenies); also Atl. coast n. to Nfld.

3. YELLOW-BREASTED CHAT

The sheer variety, the slow delivery, and the fairly long pauses between phrases are all diagnostic.

One of the more distinctive, and memorable of bird songs. It is a long series of notes, **slowly presented** (either a single note, or one note repeated several times) with a **distinct pause** between each note or short phrase. The notes include:

- whistles - clear, and sometimes *burry* "WHOIT" notes.
- harsh "caw"s and raspy Blue Jay-like cries ("JEAHH").
- "kek"s or "crick"s.

Dense thickets, tangles and brush on woodland edges, in overgrown pastures and also along streams and swamps.

Summer – Sw. Ont. and all of e. U.S. except Grt. Lakes states, the N.E. and Fla. pen. *Winter* – Texas Gulf coast and tip of Fla. to Panama.

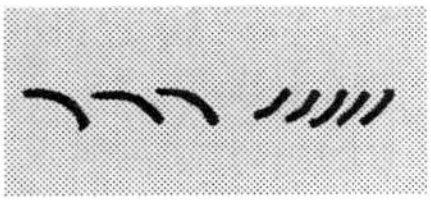

4. NORTHERN CARDINAL [3]

Its **very loud**, rich one- and two-note songs are often combined and thus are included in this category. One example is the following: "TWEEER-TWEEER-TWEEER (each note slurred downward) followed immediately by a quick "WHOIT-WHOIT-WHOIT..." (each note rising). Other combinations could include the "CHET-CHET-CHET..." like a chatter, or the two-note "*BIRDY-BIRDY-BIRDY-BIRDY*..." (accented on the first syllable), or "TU-*WEET*TU-*WEET*TU-*WEET*TU-*WEET*..." (accented on the last syllable).

Summer – S. Ont. and throughout the e. U.S. (c. Maine and c. Wisc. south). *Winter* – Same

Open woodlands, wood edges, gardens and streamside thickets. The Cardinal likes to deliver its very loud and persistent song from a high perch, such as the top of a tree or a roof-top antenna.

Brown Thrasher

A rolling rhythm and sweet, Robin-like notes, with a hint of tremolo.

5. ROSE-BREASTED GROSBEAK

A long series of short, **Robin-like whistles**, that are sweeter and higher-pitched than a Robin, and have a hint of **tremolo** (wavering quality) that the Robin lacks, making it sound like a more "professional" singer. The song is sung fairly quickly, although not rushed, and it also has a fairly jerky (rising and falling) progression to it. Compared to the Robin, it has a very short pause after each phrase, and thus it sounds more like a continuous delivery. Its distinct call note is a "high-pitched, short and squeaky 'KINK'", as described by A.A. Saunders, and it can also be heard mixed in with its regular song.

Deciduous woods, orchards, bushes, by a stream or a clearing.

Summer – C. Ont. and s. Que. to Nova Scotia, south to the Grt. Lakes states, the N.E. and down the Appalachians. *Winter* – W. Indies and Mexico to Peru.

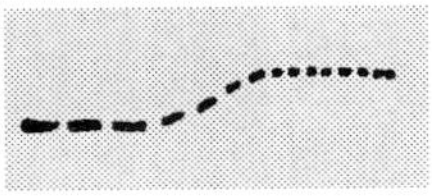

6. FIELD SPARROW

A few, slow, sweet, introductory notes, **accelerating** and flowing smoothly into a very rich, sweet, high-pitched song, and then ending in a **beautiful trill**. The song starts slowly, and then speeds up progressively into a rich trill. It can rise slowly as it speeds up, but it can also stay on the same pitch, or even drop.

Open woodland, brush, and fields.

Summer – S. Ont. and most of e. U.S. except Fla. and portions of the most northerly states. *Winter* – S. Ont. and south of the Grt. Lakes to the Gulf states.

1. YELLOW-BILLED CUCKOO

Characterized by the repeated, chattering "KEK-KEK-KEK..." intro and the slowing "KUT-A-KOWP" ending.

A rapid, chattering, "KEK-KEK-KEK-KEK-KEK", turning into "KYOLP-KYOLP-KYOLP", and ending with a few "KUT-A-KOWP"s. The delivery also **slows down** toward the end.

Summer – S. Ont. and all but the most northerly portions of the e. U.S.
Winter – S. Am.

Open woods, orchards, thickets, and stream-side groves.

2. HOUSE WREN

From rushed, squeaky sounds, to a rich, sweet, lower trill.

A rapid, exuberant burst of **squeaky**, **rising notes**, that ends in a slightly **lower sweet trill**. It begins as a distinctly rushed, squeaky sound and proceeds to a short, but rich trill, on a lower pitch. The House Wren will appear on a nearby bush or branch to deliver this song or to scold an intruder with its harsh, grating chatter.

Summer – C. Ont., s. Que. to New Brunswick and the e. U.S. south to n. Geo.
Winter – Atl. coast to Maryland and all Gulf states.

Brush, shrubs or tangles in open woods, and also in nest boxes.

3. RUBY-CROWNED KINGLET

Three parts: Several high-pitched squeaky notes and a sweet chatter followed by three-note phrases (sometimes two-note phrases).

A **loud**, clear 3-part song, consisting of a series of high-pitched, sweet, **three-note phrases**, introduced by several high-pitched squeaky notes and a musical chatter. The **three-note phrases** sound like "TWIDDLE-*DEE* TWIDDLE-*DEE* TWIDDLE-*DEE*" with each one rising and emphasized on the last syllable. Two-note phrases are also used and sound like "HEDGY-HEDGY-HEDGY" with the emphasis on the first syllable.

Summer – C. and n. Ont., Que. to Nfld. and the most northerly states. *Winter* – Sw. Ont. and all of the e. U.S. south of L. Ont. except the Appalachians.

Common in woodlands, especially conifers, where it is easily recognized by its small size, and its habit of constantly flicking its wings.

4. BLUE-GRAY GNATCATCHER [1]

A thin rapid series of squeaky notes.

A **thin**, rapid series of both **squeaky** and raspy notes, which is quite faint and **easily overlooked** even in the breeding season. The call is a high-pitched, rough and repeated "SEE-SEE-SEE-SEE...", with varying pauses in between. A. A. Saunders described this song as "more curious than beautiful", which hints at its lack of musical appeal, and its very faint, squeaky delivery.

Summer – S. Ont. and all e. U.S. except the most northerly states. *Winter* – Fla., s. Atl. and Gulf states southward.

Woodlands and thickets, quite often near water.

5. GRAY CATBIRD

No repetition of notes and a raspy, cat-like "mew".

A **loud** jumbled **mixture** of squeaky, nasal, and sweet notes, interrupted every so often by a distinctive, **cat-like "mew" call**. This call is a downward-slurred, raspy, or squeaky, note, and it is very distinctive simply because it is so different, and so much slower, than the other notes. In general, it has a pleasant, whistled quality, some birds even comparing to the Robin's sweet tone. However, the Catbird's song is less rich than the Brown Thrasher or Northern Mockingbird with which it is often compared. Also, unlike these two birds, the Catbird has **no repetition** of notes or phrases in its song.

Summer – S. Ont., s. Que. to N. S. and all e. U.S. except Fla. and the s. Gulf states.
Winter – Fla. and Gulf to Cuba and Pan.

Low in dense thickets, or underbrush (often along marshes or waterways), and in similar heavy vegetation in woodlands and in suburban areas.

6. NORTHERN MOCKINGBIRD

A collection of different notes and calls, with each repeated many times.

A **very loud,** rich series of various notes and phrases, each **repeated several times** (6 or more) in its very long delivery. This very distinctive repetition of each is the key to identification. The Mockingbird is a noted mimic of other birds (often improving on the original) as well as animals and even of such man-made sounds as squeaking wheelbarrows and whistles.

Summer – S. Ont., into Que. and N.S. and all the e. U.S. except the extreme n. states
Winter – Same

Thickets or woodland edges in the country, but also common in towns and suburbs, often seen singing high in a tree, or on top of a lamp post.

7. EASTERN BLUEBIRD [2]

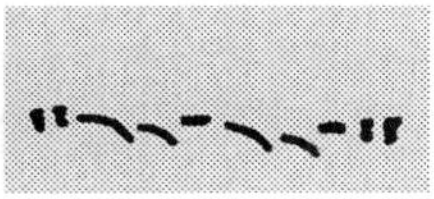

A short, sweet, gentle and variable warble, sometimes introduced by a couple of "CHICK" notes. "CHICK–PEEER-CHUR-WEE...PEEER- CHUR-WEE". The first note slurs downward, and the second note slides down slightly into the third (both on a similar pitch and lower than the first note). The call is a two-note, sweet "CHUR-WEE". This gentle warble can be strung together into a series of phrases to create the longer song referred to here.

Summer – C. Ont., s. Que. to N.S. and all the e. U.S. *Winter* – The e. U.S. north to s. Ind. and Ohio and up to C. Cod.

Open woodlands, orchards, areas of open grass and fields, and any open country with a few trees or posts.

8. WARBLING VIREO [1]

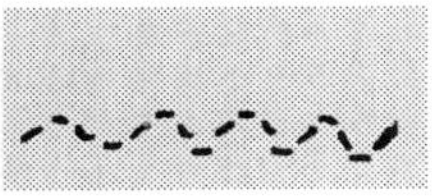

Shows rhythm.

A long, rambling, warbling, up and down song, **that usually ends on an upswing**, and is delivered with a slightly "**burry**" quality. The Warbling Vireo is a persistent singer and its undulating or "roller-coaster" song is a common song of open woodlands.

Summer – S. Ont. to N.B. and south to Miss., Tenn. and N. C. (absent from the S.E.). *Winter* – Mexico to Guatemala.

Open deciduous and mixed woodlands, usually in the upper branches. Also orchards and shade trees. Often found near human habitation.

*9. TENNESSEE WARBLER

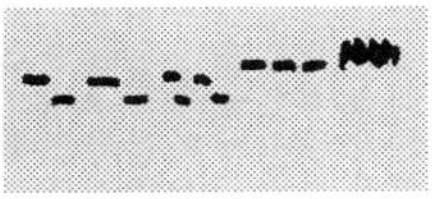

A loud, staccato, 3-part song, more sharp and **dry**, than musical. It starts slowly, and **gets faster**, as well as **louder**, ending in a trill. The notes within each part are on the same pitch, although the overall song can be variable – rising or falling. "CHICKA----CHICKA--CHICKA--CHICKA-SWEET-SWEET-SWEET TRRRRR". An active bird and a persistent singer.

Summer – C. and n. Ont., and c. Que. to Nfld and N.S., into n. Mich. and n. areas of New Eng. *Winter* – Mex. to S. Am.

Deciduous and mixed woodlands, and forest edges. It is often found high up in large trees.

10. EUROPEAN STARLING

Characterized by high-pitched squeaky notes and twittering, and especially by the down-slurred "WHEEEE-ERR".

A series of chips, raspy, and squeaky notes, and sharp twitterings, combined every so often with the characteristic drawn-out and down-slurred "*WHEEEE-ERR*". Starlings also mimic many other birds as they deliver their own personal repertoire.

Summer – Throughout the e. U.S. and north to n. Ont., c. Que. and Nfld. *Winter* – Slight movement south, from northern regions.

In cities, and in the country in parks, fields, and farms. Most often seen in flocks on the ground, foraging for insects, but also seen in trees feeding on fruits and berries.

11. NORTHERN ORIOLE [2]

Highly variable. Rich one- and two-note phrases, some harsh notes mixed in, quick changes in pitch and a whippy or snappy rhythm.

A highly variable song characterized by short, distinct phrases of one or two notes each, usually delivered fairly quickly. A loud series (4-16 notes) of clear, **rich whistles** (some prolonged), with **harsh chicks** and burred notes thrown in, as well as rapid changes in pitch which give it a jerky delivery. Brief pauses between groups of notes add to this jerky, emphatic delivery. Many birds have a distinct, **whippy rhythm** in their song. A rough or harsh chatter may also be heard as well as a series of repeated notes. Its two-note call is often repeated between song deliveries.

Summer – C. Ont. and s. Que. to N.S., south to Md. and inland from n. Va. to n. Geo., over to c. La. (not the s. Atl. or S.E.). *Winter* – Atl. and Gulf coasts; Mex. to Col.

Open woodlands, orchards, shade trees and suburbs.

12. HOUSE FINCH [1]

High-pitched, rapid and variable notes, as well as the characteristic, harsh "CHURRR" ending.

A bubbly, loud, high-pitched and musical series of notes delivered very quickly. Often at or near the end a burry or **harsh "CHURR"** (or a more biting "VEEER" or "JEEER") which is longer than the other notes and slides downwards. Overall, it is variable and irregular with sharp changes in pitch.

Summer – S. Ont. and the e. U.S. south of the Grt. Lakes to Ala. and Geo. (and spreading). *Winter* – Same.

Open woodlands, farms, cities and suburbs. It is very much at home in cities and around human habitation.

13. AMERICAN GOLDFINCH [1]

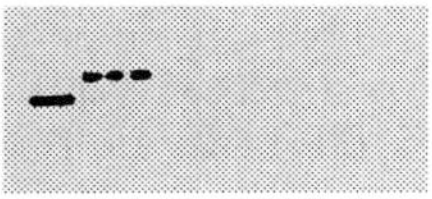

A long, **canary-like** (bubbly and high-pitched) series of clear, sweet notes, combined with trills (less in summer) and characteristic **drawn-out squeaky notes** ("SWEEE", rising). The diagnostic flight song is a clear and whippy "PER-*CHICK*-O-REE", (or "CHEE-*CHI*-CHI-CHEE") emphasized on the second note, and given by the bird on the uprise of its undulating flight. This is also worked into its regular song. The Goldfinch song can be a long song as described here (usually in the spring), but it can also be a fairly short song (usually in the summer, after the start of nesting) with the same characteristics–just less trills.

In weedy fields and in open woodlands and roadsides. The Goldfinch is fond of thistles and weeds, which it uses for food, as well as for nesting materials.

Summer – C. Ont., s. Que. to Nfld. and the e. U.S., south to Va. and into the n. Gulf states. *Winter* – S. Ont., s. Que. and N.S. and all of the e. U.S.

American Goldfinch

1. RED-EYED VIREO

Many short, sweet phrases, each separated by a definite pause.

Short, sweet, **emphatic**, **Robin-like phrases** (2-3 notes), with brief pauses between, repeated over and over. The phrases are variable, but almost sound like questions and answers sometimes, as the short phrases end with upward and then downward inflections. It should be noted, however, that most phrases do end with an upward inflection. The Red-eyed Vireo is also known to include phrases of the Great-crested Flycatcher, the Olive-sided Flycatcher and the Eastern Bluebird in its repertoire.

Summer – N. Ont., c. Que. to N.S. and all e. U.S. except s. Fla. *Winter* – N. S. Am.

A very common bird of woodlands and deciduous forests, with a thick undergrowth of saplings.

2. YELLOW-THROATED VIREO

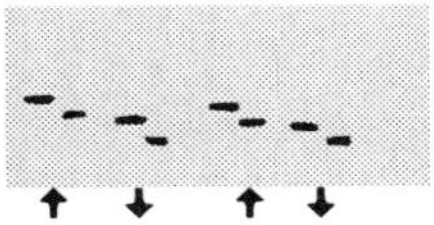

Its song is similar to the Red-eyed Vireo's, but it is slower, lower-pitched, and has a rough, or **hoarse** quality. The **pauses are longer** and more obvious. One common combination of notes sounds like a burry, whistled, "EE-LAY..........OH-LAY", (with the "EE-LAY" higher than the "OH-LAY"). The first note of each phrase is higher than the second also. These two phrases are repeated with a similar long pause between deliveries.

Summer – S. Ont. and all e. U.S. except extreme northerly portions and s. Fla. *Winter* – Mexico to Venezuela.

A fairly common bird of open woodlands, forest edges, orchards and shade trees; also mixed woodlands and deciduous forests.

3. SOLITARY VIREO

Short phrases – simpler, slower and sweeter than the Red-eyed.

Its short, sweet, emphatic, Robin-like phrases are also similar to the Red-eyed Vireo's, but each phrase is **simpler** and more to the point. It is also **slower**, higher, and **sweeter**. The less common Philadelphia Vireo (a northern breeder) may be seen in migration. Its phrases are also slower and higher-pitched than the Red-eyed Vireo's, but not as sweet as either of these two.

Summer – C. and n. Ont., s. Que. to Nfld., south to the n. Grt. Lakes states, the N.E. and down the Appalachians. *Winter* – S. Atl. and Gulf states to C. Am.

A common bird of northern mixed woodlands.

Part 2

Habitat Guide

Introduction

I have chosen six basic habitats in order to classify the one hundred birds dealt with in this book. There are some complications in defining six specific habitats. It is not always easy to draw definite lines and neat boundaries for each habitat and its bird life, since one habitat tends to blend into another. Nevertheless, each habitat does have its own special attraction for certain species of birds and I have organized the habitats and the specific birds accordingly.

Another consideration in organizing birds into specific habitats arises during migration. Many migrating birds are less fussy about their surroundings during the northward trip and are seen outside of the type of habitat that they would characteristically choose on the breeding grounds. This would apply particularly to those "northern breeders", who pass right through the United States and southern Canada on the way to their summer homes. Since my charts group birds according to their nesting habitat, more scope should be given to the habitat described, when looking for these "transients", during the spring migration. For this reason, I have placed an asterisk next to the name of any bird which could be considered a "northern breeder", or any bird which generally would be seen only during migration, in the eastern United States and parts of southern Canada. Basically these birds all but abandon the U.S. and nest anywhere from this border area all the way up to Canada's far northern regions.

I have organized the habitat guide in the form of a chart in order to show, at a glance, as much information as possible. It presents the birds using the same system of song categories as outlined in Part I. This time however, the priority is habitat, and each habitat section will deal only with the bird songs associated with that specific habitat. This should cut down on the possibilities and the search time when trying to identify a particular bird song. It may also help in distinguishing birds with very similar songs, if their habitats are quite different. Finally, it provides a handy list of birds which you would be likely to see or hear in a given habitat.

The following is a list and brief explanation of the six habitats used in this section:

I MARSHES AND SWAMPS

Wetland areas characterized, on the one hand by having marshy borders (cattails, rushes, reeds and grasses) and a scattering of bushes or small trees, and on the other, by having an area of flooded forest. While sometimes marshes and swamps merge and share the same general area (and some species of birds), each one also has its own distinct vegetation, and its own variety of birdlife.

II STREAMSIDE GROVES AND THICKETS

Any place along streams where there are small stands of trees and also areas along streams where there are tangles, vines and thickets. This streamside location provides many birds with the food and cover they require, as well as a wide choice of potential nesting sites.

III DECIDUOUS FORESTS

In the east, the hardwood forests cover a large part of southern Canada and the United States. These forests provide a wide variety of different habitats within them, ranging from wet, lowland areas and moist, leaf-covered forest floors, to shrubby growth and tangles with smaller trees, right up to the rarified air in the upper levels of some of the older stands of trees. This general habitat also includes those birds which are commonly found along the edges or openings of deciduous forests.

IV EVERGREEN FORESTS

The evergreen forests dominate the landscape south of the tundra in Canada and continue southward into the northern United States. In the east they run south into the United States, following the Appalachian mountains. The birds dealt with here are those which inhabit the conifer forests or the edges of those forests. Many of these birds are warblers and several of them I classify as "northern breeders", meaning that they breed anywhere from the most northerly portions of the eastern U.S. into the far northern reaches of eastern Canada.

V GRASSLANDS, FIELDS AND MEADOWS

This habitat includes those birds which inhabit open, grassy areas with very little other growth (shrubs or trees). I have also included in this category the more urban type of grasslands such as parks, lawns and golf courses.

VI OPEN WOODLANDS AND BRUSHY AREAS

This habitat includes those areas that have trees, but the trees are spread out in an open or scattered fashion (orchards or parks for example). It also includes brushy areas that adjoin woodlands, or that are found along roadsides, fencerows or in clearings. Basically it deals with birds that shun the dense forests and prefer the more open areas of brush and woodlands.

NOTE ON RANGES

It should be noted that, although most of the birds dealt with in this book are quite common throughout the eastern United States and southern Canada, there are some which are more locally common than others. Also some of the birds, as has been mentioned above, are "northern breeders" and may only be seen during migration by many of us. In addition to my notes on summer and winter ranges provided in Part I, an excellent aid in confirming exactly what you can expect to see in your particular locality are the range maps which are provided in the more popular field guides.

HABITAT OVERVIEWS

At the end of the habitat section, I have included a quick overview of the songs for each of the habitats. In these overviews I have included the songs of *all* of the 125 birds dealt with in this book. It will provide a ready reference for quick analysis of the quality and basic characteristics of a given song, as well as allow for quick comparison when there are other similar songs.

I MARSHES AND SWAMPS

I VERY SHORT SONGS

Single-note song

Three-note song

II REPEATED NOTES

Chatter or trill

One note repeated

Two notes repeated

Three notes repeated

III SHORT SONGS

Several varying notes

III SHORT SONGS

Containing a distinct repeated note or phrase

IV LONG SONGS

Many varying notes

Northern Orioles

SINGLE-NOTE SONG

I Very short songs

AMERICAN WOODCOCK

It is found in the scrubby edges of forests, second growth woodlands or alder stands, and in swampy thickets, on the ground and near water. A very simple nest is built among the leaves, and the moist ground provides a supply of earthworms.

A sharp, nasal "PEENT" (with a slightly buzzy or raspy quality) **delivered from the forest floor**. It may be repeated after a generous pause. Flight displays – a light twittering or trill while climbing and a series of chirps or warbles on the descent.

THREE-NOTE SONG

I Very short songs

*** COMMON LOON**

Usually nests on land, at or very near the water, in fresh water lakes. The nest can be located in marshy or reedy areas but also on bare or sandy shorelines.

A fairly long, mournful or wailing call with similarities to a **howling wolf** "oh-OOOOO-ooo". This common call will often be heard along with its characteristic tremolo laughing calls.

RED-WINGED BLACKBIRD

Seen clinging to reeds or cattails, or in a smaller tree not far overhead. The nest is usually built in wet or marshy areas, but also in dry fields, bushy areas and in small trees. The nest is found from ground or water level up to 15 ft. (4.5 m.) high.

A squeaky, gurgling "COY-LA-*REE*" with each note rising higher, and the last note a harsh, raspy trill (longer than the first two quick notes). Commonly repeated after a long pause.

CHATTER OR TRILL

II Repeated notes

BELTED KINGFISHER

Usually seen over or near water, sitting on a branch or other favourite perch. The nest is burrowed into a bank or cliff, near the top, and is usually located near water (lakes, rivers, streams, ponds or marshes).

A **loud**, sharp, **rattling** series of notes, sometimes given in short bursts and usually in flight.

MARSH WREN

On or among cattails singing or scolding intruders. The nest is built a few feet (1 m.) above the water or ground, and is attached to several stems of the surrounding reeds or rushes. The male will also build several "dummy" nests in the area.

A **squeaky chatter**. It is a jerky, sharp, rattling series of notes that sounds like a squeaky sewing machine.

CHATTER OR TRILL (continued)

II Repeated notes

***PALM WARBLER**

A ground-loving warbler of the northland that nests on the ground in sphagnum and spruce bogs and among scattered trees around muskeg. It will also nest in a spruce sapling up to 4 ft. (1.3m.) off the ground. In migration it is found in woodland edges, marshes and in open areas of brushland.

A dry, **slow trill** with a slightly buzzy quality. The notes are fairly weak, unmusical and on the same pitch, although they can waver slightly (alternately up and down).

SWAMP SPARROW

It nests and is usually found low among the reeds or vegetation of swamps and marshes, and along the edges of marshy streams and lakes, as well as in wet meadows.

A slow **sweet trill** like a musical, rich Chipping Sparrow. It also sings a slow, sweet, distinct and deliberate "SWEET-SWEET-SWEET-SWEET-SWEET-SWEET".

ONE NOTE REPEATED

II Repeated notes

KILLDEER

It nests on the ground in an open, flat area, often around a pond, a marsh or a swamp. It is also found on golf courses, in plowed fields, gravel pits and almost any open, gravelly or stony area.

A sharp, fairly high-pitched "DEE – DEE – DEE – DEE..." delivered slowly or quickly. It also gives the characteristic repeated "KILL-*DEE* KILL-*DEE* KILL-*DEE*...", as well as a three-note "*DEEE*-DEE-DEE", also repeated many times.

AMERICAN WOODCOCK

(see above)

BLUE-GRAY GNATCATCHER

Varied habitat ranging from scrub to wooded swamps to thick woodland, but quite often near water. It nests from a few feet (1 m.) above the ground to very high – 70-80 ft. (21.3-24.4 m.).

A **weak**, high-pitched and rough "SEE", or "SEE-SEE", or "SEE – SEE-SEE" repeated with varying pauses in between. These are examples of its very distinctive call notes. Its song is represented by a **thin**, rapid series of both **squeaky** and raspy notes, which is even more **difficult to hear** than its call notes.

PROTHONOTARY WARBLER

In wooded swamps, it nests in a tree cavity not far above the water, usually about 3-4 ft. (1-1.5m.).

Several clear, sweet, **emphatic notes**, all on one pitch, and delivered at a moderate pace. A loud "TWEET-TWEET-TWEET-TWEET-TWEET-TWEET"

SWAMP SPARROW

(see above)

TWO NOTES REPEATED

CANADA GOOSE

Nests on beaver houses or clumps of vegetation in the water or along the shore of ponds, lakes and marshes, as well as in grassy fields.

Two syllables, the second higher and longer, "KA-HONK KA-HONK KA-HONK...". A nasal and resonant **bugling** that breaks slightly like the "changing voice" of an adolescent boy.

KILLDEER

(see above)

CAROLINA WREN

In moist woodland areas characterized by thick brush and tangles, and along streams and swamps with sufficient cover. The nest is usually less than 10 feet (3m.) off the ground in some kind of cavity, natural or man-made: woodpecker hole, tree stump or crotch, in stone walls, and around buildings or bridges.

A **very loud**, **rich** and sweet song, "TWEEDLE-TWEEDLE-TWEEDLE" or a three-note song, "*TWEE*DLE-DEE *TWEE*DLE-DEE *TWEE*DLE-DEE", both sung quickly.

BLUE-WINGED WARBLER

Found in overgrown, brushy meadows, open woodlands and forest edges, as well as in swamps and along the edges of small streams. The nest is built on, or just above the ground.

A two-note buzzy or raspy trill, with the second note lower and rougher than the first. A slow, **almost insect-like** "ZEEE-ZREEE".

KENTUCKY WARBLER

Feeds on or near the ground in moist deciduous woods and is often found in swampy thickets and along waterways with dense undergrowth. The nest is concealed among the foliage, on or just above the ground, often at the base of a tree or shrub, or in a mound of vegetation.

A **very loud**, emphatic and **rich** song, consisting of several two-note, whistled phrases. "CHUR-*EE* CHUR-*EE* CHUR-*EE* CHUR-*EE* CHUR-*EE*" (each emphasized on the second syllable).

***CONNECTICUT WARBLER**

Found in bogs or wooded swamps with thick undergrowth, where it nests on the ground among the foliage. In its western range it can be found in moist woodlands and open poplar woods.

A **very loud**, clear series of two-syllable phrases that **speeds up** as it progresses – an emphatic, ringing "*BEE*CHER-*BEE*CHER-*BEE*CHER-*BEE*CHER-*BEECH*". Also a three-syllable song which sounds like "CHICH-U-*EE* CHICH-U-*EE* CHICH-U-*EE* CHICH-U-*EE*".

THREE NOTES REPEATED

II Repeated notes

KILLDEER
(see above)

CAROLINA WREN
(see above)

***CONNECTICUT WARBLER**
(see above)

COMMON YELLOWTHROAT
Often seen low in marsh reeds or in surrounding bushes, where the nest is built among the vegetation on or near the ground.

A loud, clear "*WIT*CHITY-*WIT*CHITY-*WIT*CHITY-*WITCH*" delivered with a characteristic up and down "**whippy**" rhythm.

RED-WINGED BLACKBIRD
(see above)

SEVERAL VARYING NOTES

III Short songs

***COMMON LOON**
Usually nests on land, at or very near the water, in fresh water lakes. The nest can be located in marshy or reedy areas but also on bare or sandy shorelines.

A series of repeated, tremolo, laughing calls. A quick "YOODLE-OODLE-OO". Also heard with its fairly long, mournful or wailing call "oh-*OOOOO*-ooo" which has similarities to a **howling wolf**.

WOOD THRUSH
Moist woodlands in the lower canopy and floor of the forest, usually near water (a swamp or stream). The nest can be up to 50 ft. (15.2 m.) high, but is usually about 10 ft. (3 m.) off the ground.

A loud, liquid song with each phrase ending in a trill. Characterized by the hollow, flute-like thrush sound and its distinctive "*EO-LAY*" sound (or "*EO-EO-LAY*") that gives it a "**yodelling**" quality.

CANADA WARBLER
Thick deciduous and mixed woodlands with dense undergrowth and damp brushland and thickets, usually near streams and bogs. The nest is built on or near the ground.

A sharp "CHIP" or "CHICK" introductory note, which is followed immediately by a short, **rapid warble** of varied notes (moving quickly **up and down in pitch**). Variable but characteristically short, quick, sweet and fidgety (quickly up and down in pitch).

SEVERAL VARYING NOTES (continued)

III Short songs

COMMON GRACKLE

It feeds, like Starlings and Robins, on the ground in fields and on lawns. It usually nests in colonies in the shrubs and small trees (especially conifers) of suburbs or open woodlands, or in the vegetation around a marsh or swamp. The nest is most often built quite low, but it can be as high as 60 ft. (18.3 m.).

A short, forced, or hesitating series of **harsh clucks**, ending in a high-pitched, **squeaky note**. "CHACK–CHACK–KEEK-A-LEEK".

SONG SPARROW

Likes moist or swampy areas in woodland edges, stream-side thickets, shrubby meadows and cattail swamps. However, it is also found in drier locations such as along country roads and fences. The nest is built on, or fairly close to the ground, among the brush or tangles.

Consists of 2-3 repeated, sweet notes, followed by a short, buzzy "*ZREE*", a lower liquid trill, and ending with a lower, buzzy note (sometimes 2-3 notes). "SWEET-SWEET-SWEET-*ZREE*-SUGAR-IT" (last note may be repeated).

CONTAINING A DISTINCT REPEATED NOTE OR PHRASE

III Short songs

YELLOW WARBLER

Likes areas with scrub or brush or small trees, especially where they border marshes, swamps or other waterways. Also fond of brushy fences, hedgerows and roadside thickets, as well as apple orchards. The nest usually ranges from 2-12 ft. (0.6-3.7 m.) above the ground and is built in a small tree, shrub or tangle.

Several clear, **sweet** notes. A **rapid** "TWEET-TWEET-*TWEET* TWEEDLE-DEEDLE-*DEET*" or "TWEET-TWEET-*TWEET* TWEEDLE-DE-*DEET*", both with the last note rising.

*WILSON'S WARBLER

Wet or boggy areas and wooded swamp edges, among willow or alder stands, as well as in streamside thickets. The nest is built on the ground, very well concealed by the surrounding grass or vegetation, and often at the base of a sapling or a bush.

A rapid chatter of **staccato** notes, **dropping** in pitch, and **speeding up** at the end. It is more "ringing" than sweet or musical. "CHEE-CHEE-CHEE-CHEE CHE-CHE-CHE".

HOODED WARBLER

Found close to the ground in wooded swampy areas, or in moist deciduous woodlands along streams with thickets and thick undergrowth. The nest is built just over the ground (usually no more than 6 ft. [1.8 m.]) among the thick undergrowth, in a sapling, vine or shrub.

A **very loud**, **rich** and clear "WITTA-WITTA-WI-*TE*-O" ("*TE*" louder and higher and the "O" much lower.) or with the emphasis on the second note "TA-WIT TA-WIT TA-WI-*TE*-O".

CONTAINING A DISTINCT REPEATED NOTE OR PHRASE (cont'd) — III Short songs

NASHVILLE WARBLER

Found in thickets along swamps, spruce bogs, forest edges and in second growth woodlands, usually close to the ground where it nests.

A loud, repeated series of high-pitched notes, followed by a **short trill, on a lower pitch**. "SWEET-SWEET-SWEET-SWEET-TRRRR", or "SEEWEE-SEEWEE-SEEWEE-TRRRR".

MOURNING WARBLER

It builds its nest on or close to the ground in the thickets and tangles of moist northern woodlands or in the thick undergrowth along the edge of swamps. However it is also found in dry brushy areas and in roadside shrubbery.

A **loud**, **musical** and short song which has considerable variation.

1. "CHEE-CHEE-CHEE CHURR-*E*-AH"
2. "CHEE-CHEE-CHEE CHURR-AH"
3. "CHIRRY, CHIRRY, CHORRY, CHORRY (CHORRY lower)" according to R.T. Peterson.
4. "CHEE-CHEE-CHEE CHO-CHO-CHO".

MANY VARYING NOTES — IV Long songs

BLUE-GRAY GNATCATCHER

Varied habitat ranging from scrub to wooded swamps to thick woodland, but quite often near water. Its dainty, hummingbird-like nest is built on a fairly small branch (often at a vertical fork), from a few feet (1 m.) above the ground, to very high – 70-80 ft. (21.3-24.4 m.).

A **thin**, rapid series of both **squeaky** and raspy notes, which is quite faint, and **easily overlooked**. The call is a high-pitched, rough and repeated "SEE-SEE-SEE-SEE..", with varying pauses in between.

GRAY CATBIRD

Found in tangles or thickets often along woodland edges, marshes or waterways, where the nest is concealed among the vines and tangles, usually 3-10 ft. (0.9-3 m.) off the ground.

A **loud** jumbled **mixture** of squeaky, nasal, and sweet notes, interrupted every so often by a distinctive, **cat-like "mew" call**, which is different and much slower than the other notes.

YELLOW-BREASTED CHAT

Dense tangles, thickets and brush on woodland edges, in overgrown pastures, and also along streams or swamps in similar heavy growth. The nest is built about 2-6 ft. (0.6-1.8 m.) above the ground.

A long series of notes, **slowly presented** (some single notes, some repeated several times) with **distinct pauses** between each phrase. The notes include:

- whistles - clear, and sometimes burry "WHOIT" notes
- harsh "caw"s and raspy Blue Jay-like cries ("JEAHH")
- "kek"s or "crick"s

II STREAMSIDE GROVES AND THICKETS

I VERY SHORT SONGS

Single-note song

II REPEATED NOTES

Chatter or trill

One note repeated

Two notes repeated

Three notes repeated

III SHORT SONGS

Several varying notes

Containing a distinct repeated note or phrase

IV LONG SONGS

Many varying notes

Hooded Warbler

SINGLE-NOTE SONG

I Very short songs

AMERICAN WOODCOCK

It is found in the scrubby edges of forests, second growth woodland or alder stands and in swampy thickets, on the ground and near water. A very simple nest is built among the leaves, and the moist ground provides a supply of earthworms.

A sharp, nasal "PEENT" (with a slight buzzy or raspy quality) **delivered from the forest floor**. It may be repeated with a generous pause in between. Flight displays include a light twittering or trill as the bird climbs and a series of chirps or warbles as it descends to the ground.

CHATTER OR TRILL

II Repeated notes

BELTED KINGFISHER

Usually seen over or near water, sitting on a branch or other favourite perch. The nest is burrowed into a bank or cliff, near the top, and is usually located near water (lakes, rivers, streams, ponds or marshes).

A **loud**, sharp, **rattling** series of notes. This dry, rattling chatter is sometimes given in short bursts and usually in flight.

EASTERN KINGBIRD

Open country with scattered trees, wood edges and orchards, often near water. The nest is often built over water in a tree, or sometimes on a post standing in water. The height of the nest is usually between 10-20 feet (3-6 m.), but it can vary from 2-60 feet (0.6-18.3 m.).

A high-pitched rapid "twittering" (**raspy and sharp**) which **sputters** and changes speed. "ZEE-ZEE-ZEE-ZEEE-TEE-ZEE-TEE-ZEE". It also has a slower repeated "ZEET–ZEET–ZEET..." version, as well as a slurred two-note "KIT-*ZEE*" (second syllable emphasized and sounding like one sharp, rising note) which can be repeated fairly quickly.

WORM-EATING WARBLER

Prefers leaf-covered, shrubby hillsides or ravines, in deciduous forests, often near a stream. The nest is simply a hollow or cup, situated on the ground among the dead leaves. It is often at the base of a shrub or small tree.

A rapid, **dry**, buzzy trill, similar to the Chipping Sparrow's trill, but more rapid, dry and buzzy, as well as weaker.

SWAMP SPARROW

It nests and is usually found low among the reeds or vegetation of swamps and marshes, and along the edges of marshy streams and lakes, as well as in wet meadows.

A slow, **sweet trill** like a musical, rich Chipping Sparrow. It also sings a slow, sweet, distinct and very deliberate "SWEET- SWEET-SWEET-SWEET-SWEET- SWEET".

ONE NOTE REPEATED

AMERICAN WOODCOCK
(see above)

BLACK-BILLED CUCKOO
Prefers more wooded areas than the Yellow-billed Cuckoo, where it frequents shrubs and thickets, often near water. The nest is built in a tree or a bush, usually fairly low – about 6 ft. (1.8 m.) – although it can range from 2-20 ft. (0.6-6.1 m.).

This is a **long song** with several series of rapid "COO-COO-COO" notes (given 3-4 to a series). The notes have a fairly nasal and **ringing quality**, unlike the soft "COO"'s of the Mourning Dove.

EASTERN KINGBIRD
(see above)

BLUE-GRAY GNATCATCHER
Varied habitat ranging from scrub to wooded swamps to thick woodland, but quite often near water. Its dainty, humming-bird-like nest is built on a fairly small branch (often at a vertical fork), from a few feet (1 m.) above the ground, to very high – 70-80 ft. (21.3-24.4 m.).

A **thin**, rapid series of both **squeaky** and raspy notes, which is quite faint and **easily overlooked**. The call is a high-pitched, rough and repeated "SEE-SEE-SEE-SEE...", with varying pauses in between.

AMERICAN REDSTART
Open deciduous and mixed woodlands, young second growth woods and in the thick growth of smaller trees or bushes on the edge of a larger forest, as well as in road-side trees, gardens and parks. It also likes wil-low thickets along streams or ponds. The nest is usually no more than 10 feet (3m.) off the ground in a sapling, tree, shrub or vine tangle.

A **high-pitched** and **variable** song, consist-ing of weak, yet emphatic, single notes (sometimes two-note phrases, similar to the Black and White Warbler's song.). It is some-times a repeated "TSEET-TSEET-TSEET-TSEET-TSEET", delivered at moderate speed. More often though it is delivered with the last note higher or lower. "TSEE-TSEET-TSEET-TSEET-TSEET-*TSEEE*" (last note higher) or "TSEET-TSEET-TSEET-TSEE-O" (last note lower).

SWAMP SPARROW
(see above)

ONE NOTE REPEATED (continued)

NORTHERN CARDINAL

Woodland edges and in the brush and tangles of open woodlands, gardens and streamside thickets. It is often seen flitting in and out of tangles and thickets where its nest is built (if not in a small nearby tree), usually 3-10 ft. (1-3 m.) off the ground. The Cardinal also likes to sing from high perches, such as the top of a high tree or a roof-top antenna, from which it will definitely attract your attention with its very loud and persistent singing.

A **very loud**, rich and drawn-out "TWEEER– TWEEER– TWEEER– TWEEER...", or a quicker "WHOIT-WHOIT-WHOIT-WHOIT..." or "CHET-CHET-CHET-CHET..." like a chatter (all repeated up to 7-8 times or more). Two-note songs include "*BIR*DY-*BIR*DY-*BIR*DY-*BIR*DY..." (accented on the first syllable) or "TU-*WEET* TU-*WEET* TU-*WEET* TU-*WEET*..." (accented on the last syllable).

TWO NOTES REPEATED

EASTERN KINGBIRD

(see above)

EASTERN PHOEBE

Open woodlands and around farm buildings and bridges. The nest is often built under a bridge on a protected beam (also in a similar location in barns and other farm buildings).

An **emphatic**, repeated, two-note song that sounds like "*FEE*-BEE" or "*FEE*-BREE", with the second note most often lower than the first and also raspy or burry.

BLUE WINGED WARBLER

Found in overgrown, brushy meadows, open woodlands and forest edges, as well as in swamps and along the edges of small streams. The nest is built on, or just above the ground.

A two-note buzzy or raspy trill, with the second note lower and rougher than the first. A slow, **almost insect-like** "ZEEE-ZREEE".

CAROLINA WREN

In woodland areas characterized by thick brush and tangles, and along streams and swamps with sufficient cover. The nest is usually less than 10 ft. (3 m.) off the ground in some kind of cavity, natural or man-made: woodpecker hole, tree stump or crotch, in stone walls, and around buildings or bridges.

A **very loud**, **rich** and sweet song, "TWEEDLE-TWEEDLE-TWEEDLE", or a three-note song, "*TWEE*DLE-DEE *TWEE*DLE-DEE *TWEE*DLE-DEE", both sung quickly.

TWO NOTES REPEATED (continued)

II Repeated notes

KENTUCKY WARBLER

Feeds on or near the ground in moist deciduous woods and ravines and is often found along waterways with thick undergrowth and thickets. The nest is concealed among the foliage, on or just above the ground, often at the base of a tree or shrub, or in a mound of vegetation.

A **very loud**, emphatic, and **rich** song, consisting of several two-note, whistled phrases, "CHUR-*EE* CHUR-*EE* CHUR-*EE* CHUR-*EE* CHUR-*EE*" (each emphasized on the second syllable).

NORTHERN CARDINAL

(see above)

THREE NOTES REPEATED

II Repeated notes

CAROLINA WREN

(see above)

SEVERAL VARYING NOTES

III Short songs

***SWAINSON'S THRUSH**

Most common in smaller firs and spruce trees on the border of mature coniferous forests where there are some deciduous trees. It likes damp areas near streams, and the nest is usually fairly low – 2-7 ft. (0.6-2.1 m.) above the ground.

The song is the opposite of the Veery in that it is an **ascending**, rapid spiral of hollow, flute-like notes, rolling up the scale.

WOOD THRUSH

Moist woodlands in the lower canopy and floor of the forest, and usually near water (a swamp or stream). The nest can be up to 50 ft. (15.2 m.) high, but it is more likely to be found about 10 ft. (3 m.) off the ground, in a shrub or a sapling.

A loud, liquid song with each phrase ending in a trill. Characterized by the hollow, flute-like thrush sound and its distinctive "*EO-LAY*" sound (or "*EO-EO-LAY*") that gives it a "**yodelling**" quality.

WHITE-EYED VIREO

Thick shrub and undergrowth along woodland edges as well as among the thickets in moist areas, and along streams. The nest is usually built fairly low in the tangles or shrubbery – about 2-6 ft. (0.6-2 m.) off the ground.

A **variable**, **snappy** song that begins with an introductory "CHICK" or "CHICK-SEE". One common version follows this immediately with what sounds like "PUT-THE-GA*ZE*BO-UP" (strongly accented and rising on the "*ZE*" and dropping on the last two notes), or (with the last note off) "CHICK-BUILD-THE-GA*ZE*BO". It also utters a rapid "CHICK-*THREE*- BEERS" (the "*THREE*" rising and emphasized).

SEVERAL VARYING NOTES (continued)

III Short songs

CANADA WARBLER

Thick deciduous and mixed woodlands with dense undergrowth and damp brushland and thickets, usually near streams and bogs. The nest is built on or near the ground.

A sharp "CHIP" or "CHICK" introductory note, which is followed immediately by a short, **rapid warble** of varied notes (moving quickly **up and down in pitch**). Variable but characteristically short, quick, sweet, and fidgety (quickly up and down in pitch).

SONG SPARROW

Likes moist or swampy areas in woodland edges, streamside thickets, shrubby meadows and cattail swamps. However, it is also found in drier locations such as along country roads and fences. The nest is built on, or fairly close to the ground, among the brush or tangles.

Consists of 2-3 repeated, sweet notes, followed by a short, buzzy "*ZREE*", a lower liquid trill, and ending with a lower, buzzy note (sometimes 2-3 notes). "SWEET-SWEET-SWEET-*ZREE*-SUGAR-IT" (last note may be repeated).

CONTAINING A DISTINCT REPEATED NOTE OR PHRASE

III Short songs

CERULEAN WARBLER

Upper levels of tall deciduous trees, in forests and open woodlands with little ground cover, and often near streams and rivers. The nest is built quite high up, 20-50 ft. (6-15.2 m.), and sometimes even higher.

Several **rapid**, **buzzy** notes on one pitch, and then a **final buzzy note** which is higher-pitched. "ZREE-ZREE-ZREE-ZREE-*ZREEEE*"

.

AMERICAN REDSTART

(see above)

YELLOW WARBLER

Likes areas with scrub or brush or small trees that border marshes, swamps or other waterways. Also fond of brushy fences, hedgerows, and roadside thickets, as well as apple orchards. The nest usually ranges from 2-12 ft. (0.6- 3.7 m.) above the ground and is built in a small tree, shrub or tangle.

Several clear, **sweet** notes. A **rapid** "TWEET-TWEET-*TWEET* TWEEDLE-DEEDLE-*DEET*" or "TWEET-TWEET-*TWEET* TWEEDLE-DE-*DEET*", both with the last note rising.

***WILSON'S WARBLER**

Wet or boggy areas and wooded swamp edges among willow or alder stands, as well as in streamside thickets. The nest is built on the ground, very well concealed by the surrounding grass and vegetation, and often at the base of a sapling or bush.

A rapid chatter of **staccato** notes, **dropping** in pitch, and **speeding up** at the end. It is more "ringing" than sweet or musical. "CHEE-CHEE-CHEE-CHEE CHE-CHE-CHE".

CONTAINING A DISTINCT REPEATED NOTE OR PHRASE (cont'd) III Short songs

HOODED WARBLER

Found close to the ground in wooded swampy areas, or in moist deciduous woodlands along streams with thickets and thick undergrowth. The nest is built just over the ground (usually no more than 6 ft. [1.8 m.]) among the thick undergrowth, in a sapling, vine or shrub.

A **very loud**, **rich** and clear "WITTA-WITTA-WI-*TE*-O" ("*TE*" louder and higher and the "O" much lower), or with the emphasis on the second note "TA-WIT TA-WIT TA-WI-*TE*-O".

MANY VARYING NOTES IV Long songs

YELLOW-BILLED CUCKOO

Among the thickets of open woods, overgrown fields, streamside groves and in orchards. It is more common in the southern part of its range. The nest is built in a tree or in a shrub, usually about 4-10 ft. (1.2-3 m.) off the ground.

A rapid chattering "KEK-KEK-KEK-KEK-KEK", turning into "KYOLP-KYOLP-KYOLP', and ending with a few "KUT-A-KOWP"s. The delivery also **slows down** toward the end.

BLUE-GRAY GNATCATCHER

Varied habitat ranging from scrub to wooded swamps to thick woodland, but quite often near water. Its dainty, hummingbird-like nest is built on a fairly small branch (often at a vertical fork), from a few feet (1 m.) above the ground, to very high – 70-80 ft. (21.3-24.4 m.).

A **thin**, rapid series of both **squeaky** and raspy notes, which is quite faint and **easily overlooked**. The call is a high-pitched, rough and repeated "SEE-SEE-SEE-SEE...", with varying pauses in between.

GRAY CATBIRD

Found in tangles or thickets often along woodland edges, marshes or waterways where the nest is usually built up to 6 feet (2m.) off the ground.

A **loud** jumbled **mixture** of squeaky, nasal, and sweet notes, interrupted every so often by a distinctive, **cat-like "mew" call** (different and much slower than the other notes).

YELLOW-BREASTED CHAT

Dense tangles, thickets and brush on woodland edges, or in overgrown pastures, and also along streams and swamp edges in similar heavy growth. The nest is usually about 2-6 ft. (0.6-1.8 m.) above the ground.

A long series of notes (some single notes, some repeated several times), **slowly presented**, with **distinct pauses** between each phrase. The notes include:

- whistles – clear, and sometimes burry
- harsh "caw"s and raspy Blue Jay-like cries
- "kek"s or "crick"s

MANY VARYING NOTES (continued)

IV Long songs

NORTHERN CARDINAL

Woodland edges and in the brush and tangles of open woodlands, gardens and streamside thickets. It is often seen flitting in and out of tangles and thickets where its nest is built (if not in a small nearby tree), usually about 3-10 ft. (0.9-3 m.) off the ground. The Cardinal also likes to sing from high perches, such as the top of a high tree or a roof-top antenna, from which it will definitely attract your attention with its very loud and persistent singing.

Its **very loud**, rich, one-note and two-note songs are often combined to form a long song with varying notes. One example is the following: "TWEEER-TWEEER-TWEEER" (each note slurred downward), followed immediately by a quick "WHOIT-WHOIT-WHOIT..." (each note rising). Each note or pair of notes within these combinations can be repeated up to 7-8 times or more.

ROSE-BREASTED GROSBEAK

Second growth woods, scrub and bushes by streams and clearings. The nest is usually built in a shrub or small tree, about 10-15 ft. (3-4.6 m.) off the ground.

A long series of short, **Robin-like whistles**, that are sweeter and higher-pitched than a Robin, and have a hint of **tremolo** that the Robin lacks. It also has shorter pauses and therefore sounds more like a continuous delivery. A.A. Saunders described its call note as a "high-pitched, short and squeaky 'KINK'". This call can be mixed in with the regular song.

Red-eyed Vireo

I VERY SHORT SONGS

Single-note song

II REPEATED NOTES

Chatter or trill

One note repeated

Two notes repeated

Three notes repeated

III SHORT SONGS

Several varying notes

Blackburnian Warbler

SINGLE-NOTE SONG

I Very short songs

RED-TAILED HAWK

Woodland areas and fields. The nest is usually built in a tall tree, 35-90 ft. (10.7-27.4 m.) high, overlooking an open area. It can be found in heavy timber, but also in a fairly open area in a solitary tree.

One single, **drawn-out** scream lasting a second or two. A loud, raspy "KEEAHHRR", slurring downward.

AMERICAN WOODCOCK

It is found in the scrubby edges of forests, second growth woodlands or alder stands, and in swampy thickets, on the ground and near water. A very simple nest is built among the leaves, and moist ground provides a supply of earthworms.

A raspy nasal "PEENT" **delivered from the forest floor**. It may be repeated with a generous pause in between.

GREAT CRESTED FLYCATCHER

It nests in tree cavities in deciduous and mixed woodlands and in old orchards, anywhere from 10-70 ft. (3-21.3 m.) above the ground. It prefers areas near clearings or woodland borders.

A very loud single "WHEEP", or a loud burry "FRREEEP" (each **rising** and on a fairly high pitch). This single note is sometimes repeated a few times in succession.

AMERICAN CROW

A common bird of woodlands, farmlands, fields, parks and shorelines. It nests in deciduous and coniferous forests (with a preference for conifers) usually high in the tree. However, it is adaptable and will nest in shrubs, and even on telephone poles or on the ground at times.

A loud, raspy, nasal "CAW". This single note may be repeated several times in succession.

CHATTER OR TRILL

II Repeated notes

WORM-EATING WARBLER

Prefers leaf-covered, shrubby hillsides or ravines in deciduous forests, often near a stream. The nest is simply a hollow or cup, situated on the ground among the dead leaves. It is often at the base of a shrub or small tree.

A rapid, **dry**, buzzy trill, similar to the Chipping Sparrow trill, but more rapid, dry and buzzy, as well as weaker.

ONE NOTE REPEATED

AMERICAN WOODCOCK

(see above)

RUFFED GROUSE

Deciduous or mixed forest with thick undergrowth or cover, where a simple nest is built on the ground.

Not a song but a muffled beating or thumping of the wings that starts slowly and **speeds up**, ending in a rapid flurry.

GREAT CRESTED FLYCATCHER

(see above)

BLUE JAY

Forests, mixed woodlands (especially oak and pine), suburban areas, parks, and city gardens. The nest is usually built quite high in a tree, about 10-30 ft. (3-9.1 m.), and it also has a preference for conifers, where they are available.

A **harsh**, piercing, repeated and 'steely' "JAAY–JAAY–JAAY...", or a down-slurred, screeching "JEEAH–JEEAH–JEEAH...", both **very loud**. Also two quick bursts "WHEEDLE-WHEEDLE", repeated after a generous pause, as well as a three-note "WHEEL-DE-LEE" song, with its sharp, "creaking wheelbarrow" quality.

AMERICAN CROW

(see above)

BLACK-CAPPED CHICKADEE

Deciduous and mixed forests, and in more open areas, with scattered trees and bushes. The nest is built in tree cavities, 4-10 ft. (1.2-3 m.) off the ground.

A **cheerful, bright** and quickly repeated "DEE-DEE-DEE-DEE-DEE-DEE-DEE...", often introduced by a squeaky and higher-pitched "CHICKA" or "SICKA".

TUFTED TITMOUSE

Deciduous woodlands, orchards, suburban areas and feeders. The nest is built in a tree cavity, at variable heights, anywhere from 2-87 ft. (0.6-26.5 m.) off the ground.

A loud, clear and **whistled** "PEEER-PEEER-PEEER" repeated fairly quickly, with each note rising slightly toward the end. Its common two-note song sounds like "WHEEDLE-WHEEDLE-WHEEDLE", with the same qualities as the single-note song.

WHITE-BREASTED NUTHATCH

Deciduous woodlands, orchards and woodlots. The nest is built in a natural cavity or old woodpecker hole from very low to 50 ft. (15.2 m.) off the ground.

A rapid series of nasal, low-pitched notes, "WA-WA-WA-WA-WA..." or "KANK-KANK-KANK-KANK-KANK-KANK..." (a bit rough and burry).

ONE NOTE REPEATED (continued)

II Repeated notes

BLUE-GRAY GNATCATCHER

Varied habitat ranging from scrub to wooded swamps to thick woodland, but quite often near water. Its dainty, hummingbird-like nest is built on a fairly small branch (often at a vertical fork), from a few feet (1 m.) above the ground, to very high – 70-80 ft. (21.3-24.4 m.).

A **weak**, high-pitched and rough "SEE", or "SEE-SEE", or "SEE – SEE-SEE" repeated with varying pauses in between represents its distinctive call notes. It also has a **thin**, rapid series of **squeaky** and raspy notes that represents its song, and it is even more **difficult to hear** than its call notes.

AMERICAN REDSTART

Open deciduous and mixed woodlands, young second growth woods and in the thick growth of smaller trees or bushes on the edge of a larger forest, as well as in roadside trees, gardens and parks. It also likes willow thickets along streams and ponds. The nest is usually no more than 10 ft. (3m.) off the ground in a sapling, tree, shrub or vine tangle.

A **high-pitched** and **variable** song, consisting of weak, yet emphatic, single notes (sometimes two-note phrases, similar to the Black and White Warbler's song). It is sometimes a repeated "TSEET-TSEET-TSEET-TSEET-TSEET". More often though it is delivered with the last note higher or lower. "TSEET-TSEET-TSEET-TSEET-*TSEEE*" (last note higher) or "TSEET-TSEET-TSEET-TSEE-O" (last note lower).

TWO NOTES REPEATED

II Repeated notes

BLUE JAY

(see above)

BLACK-CAPPED CHICKADEE

Deciduous and mixed forests, and in more open areas with scattered trees and bushes. The nest is built in tree cavities 4-10 ft. (1.2-3 m.) off the ground.

A clear, sweet, whistled "*FEEE*-BEE" (the first note higher and longer) repeated after a brief pause. It also has a three-note song "*FEEE*-BEE-BEE", which quickly repeats the second note. This version is also repeated after a brief pause.

TUFTED TITMOUSE

(see above)

EASTERN WOOD-PEWEE

Deciduous and mixed woodlands, especially bordering fields and clearings, as well as in orchards and shade trees. It is usually found higher up in the tree, where the nest is built on a small horizontal branch, about 20 ft. (6.1 m.) off the ground. It can vary, however, anywhere from 8-45 ft. (2.4-13.7 m.) high.

A **slow**, **drawn-out** "PEEE-*WEEE*", with an upward inflection on the second note. It is repeated after a generous pause and it also "works in" a drawn out "PEEE-YURR" every so often, with a downward inflection on the second syllable. It is also described as a three-note song since the "PEEE-*WEEE*" usually sounds more like "PEEE-A-*WEEE*".

TWO NOTES REPEATED (continued)

II Repeated notes

BLACK AND WHITE WARBLER

Deciduous and mixed woodlands, showing preference for rocky hillsides. It is seen searching the bark of tree limbs and tree trunks for insects, much like a nuthatch. The nest, however, is built on the ground.

A high, **thin** (even squeaky), two-note phrase repeated fairly quickly. It sounds like "*WEE*-SEE *WEE*-SEE *WEE*-SEE...", the first note higher and emphasized.

KENTUCKY WARBLER

Feeds on or near the ground in moist deciduous woods; it is also found in swampy thickets as well as along waterways with dense undergrowth. The nest is concealed among the foliage, on or just above the ground, often at the base of a tree or shrub, or in a mound of vegetation.

A **very loud**, emphatic and **rich** song, consisting of several two-note, whistled phrases, "CHUR-*EE* CHUR-*EE* CHUR-*EE* CHUR-*EE* CHUR-*EE*" (each emphasized on the second syllable).

*CONNECTICUT WARBLER

In the east, it nests in northern bogs or wooded swamps with thick undergrowth, on the ground and among the foliage (moist woodlands and open poplar woods in the west). I mention it here because it can be seen during migration in the undergrowth of deciduous forests in favoured localities. It is a spring favourite at Canada's Point Pelee National Park.

A **very loud**, clear series of two-syllable phrases that **speeds up** as it progresses – an emphatic "*BEE*CHER-*BEE*CHER-*BEE*CHER-*BEE*CHER-*BEECH*". Also a three-note version that sounds like an accelerating "CHICH-U-*EE* CHICH-U-*EE* CHICH-U-*EE* CHICH-U-*EE*".

OVENBIRD

Deciduous woodlands with leafy cover, but sparse undergrowth. The nest is built on the ground among the leaves and is covered over by leaves and vegetation, forming a dome, or what looks like a miniature Dutch "oven".

A loud, clear "*TEACH*ER-*TEACH*ER-*TEACH*ER-*TEACH*ER...", accented on the first syllable, and repeated many times in quick succession. It also **gets louder** as it progresses.

THREE NOTES REPEATED

II Repeated notes

WHIP-POOR-WILL

Younger dry woodlands or woodland edges with little undergrowth, but with a covering of dead leaves providing a site for laying its eggs on the open ground.

Sings "*WHIP*-POOR-*WILL*" over and over again from its hiding place on the forest floor. This song is sung **at night** for long stretches of time, with almost no pause between each phrase. The emphasis on the first and last notes (with the last note rising) gives it a **whippy** or snappy rhythm.

THREE NOTES REPEATED (continued) — II Repeated notes

EASTERN WOOD-PEWEE
(see above)

BLUE JAY
(see above)

BLACK-CAPPED CHICKADEE
(see above)

***CONNECTICUT WARBLER**
In the east, it nests in northern bogs or wooded swamps with thick undergrowth, on the ground and among the foliage (moist woodlands and open poplar woods in the west). I mention it here because it can be seen during migration in the undergrowth of deciduous forests in favoured localities. It is a spring favourite at Canada's Point Pelee National Park.

A **very loud**, clear series of three-syllable phrases that **speeds up** as it progresses and sounds like "CHICH-U-*EE* CHICH-U-*EE* CHICH-U-*EE* CHICH-U-*EE*". Also a two-note "*BEE*CHER-*BEE*CHER-*BEE*CHER-*BEE*CHER-*BEECH*".

SEVERAL VARYING NOTES — III Short songs

WOOD THRUSH
Moist woodlands with undergrowth, in the lower canopy and floor of the forest, usually near water (a swamp or stream). The nest is built about 10 ft. (3 m.) high in a shrub or sapling, but sometimes in a tree as high as 50 ft. (15.2 m.) off the ground.

A loud, liquid song with each phrase ending in a trill. Characterized by the hollow, flute-like thrush sound and its distinctive "*EO-LAY*" sound (or "*EO-EO-LAY*") that gives it a "**yodelling**" quality.

VEERY
Moist forest floors and ravines. The nest is built on or close to the ground in a small shrub or sapling, or among tangles or fallen branches, or on a clump of vegetation.

A **descending** series of flute-like, hollow notes. "VA-VEER-VEER-VEER-VEER", down the scale.

BLACK-THROATED BLUE WARBLER
Mixed conifer and hardwood forest with second growth and shrubs, where the nest is built just above ground level – 1-3 ft. (0.3-0.9 m.). It is commonly constructed in conifer saplings, but may also be found in saplings of hardwoods, laurel and rhododendron thickets.

This song consists of 3-5 **evenly-spaced, buzzy notes**, sliding up the scale, with the last note noticeably higher and slurring upward. "ZEEP-ZEEP-ZEEP-ZEEP-*ZEEE*". Quite often these introductory notes are all on the same pitch.

SEVERAL VARYING NOTES (continued)

III Short songs

CANADA WARBLER

Thick deciduous and mixed woodlands, with dense undergrowth, damp brushland and thickets, usually near streams and bogs. The nest is built on or near the ground.

A sharp "CHIP" or "CHICK" introductory note, which is followed immediately by a short, **rapid warble** of varied notes (moving quickly **up and down in pitch**). Variable, but characteristically short, quick, sweet, and fidgety (quickly up and down in pitch).

SCARLET TANAGER

Nests in deciduous or pine-oak woodlands, orchards, parks and shade trees. It builds its nest fairly high up in the tree, usually about 15-45 ft. (4.6-13.7 m.) above the ground.

A series of short, sweet, Robin-like phrases, that are delivered with a **burry** or **hoarse** quality, and move briskly, (but not rapidly) up and down in pitch. "TWEER-TWEER-TUWEET-TUWEET-TWEER", or combinations of notes that sound like "TUWEET-TWEER" (1-2 syllable notes in short phrases).

CONTAINING A DISTINCT REPEATED NOTE OR PHRASE

III Short songs

BLACK-CAPPED CHICKADEE

Deciduous and mixed forests in more open areas with scattered trees and bushes. The nest is built in tree cavities 4-10 ft. (1.2-3 m.) off the ground.

A snappy two-note introduction "CHICKA", followed immediately by a rapid series of "DEE-DEE-DEE-DEE-DEE..." notes, all with a squeaky, yet **cheerful and bright** quality. The introduction is higher-pitched than the repeated notes.

BLACK-THROATED BLUE WARBLER

(see above)

CERULEAN WARBLER

Upper levels of tall deciduous trees, in forests and in open woodlands, with little ground cover and often near water. The nest is built quite high up, 20-50 ft. (6-15.2 m.), and sometimes even higher.

Several **rapid**, **buzzy** notes on one pitch, and then a **final buzzy note which is higher-pitched**. "ZREE-ZREE-ZREE-ZREE-*ZREEEE*".

CONTAINING A DISTINCT REPEATED NOTE OR PHRASE (cont'd) III Short songs

BLACKBURNIAN WARBLER

Although found mainly in coniferous forests, it is also found in deciduous forests (often oak) in the southern parts of its breeding range. The nest is usually built high in the tree.

A **short**, **weak**, and very high-pitched song. It starts with a few single- or double-note whistles, and ends on an even higher-pitched, slow chirping trill. "SWEET-SWEET-SWEET-*TRRRR*". Another version goes "SEET-SEET-SEET-SEET-SEET-SEEDLEE-*SEET*", with the last note rising extremely high.

AMERICAN REDSTART

(see above)

HOODED WARBLER

Found close to the ground in wooded swampy areas, or in moist deciduous woodlands along streams with thickets and thick undergrowth. The nest is built just over the ground (usually no more than 6 ft. [1.8 m.] high) among the thick undergrowth, in a sapling, vine or shrub.

A **very loud**, **rich** and clear "WITTA-WITTA-WI-*TE*-O" ("*TE*" louder and higher and the "O" much lower) or with the emphasis on the second note "TA-WIT TA-WIT TA-WIT-*TE*-O".

NASHVILLE WARBLER

Found in thickets along swamps, spruce bogs, forest edges and in second growth woodlands, usually close to the ground where it nests.

A loud, repeated series of high-pitched notes, followed by a **short trill, on a lower pitch**. "SWEET-SWEET-SWEET-SWEET-TRRRR" or "SEEWEE-SEEWEE-SEEWEE-TRRRR".

MANY VARYING NOTES IV Long songs

BLUE-GRAY GNATCATCHER

Varied habitat ranging from scrub to wooded swamps to thick woodland, but quite often near water. It nests from a few feet (1 m.) above the ground to very high – 70-80 ft. (21.3-24.4 m.).

A **thin**, **rapid** series of both **squeaky** and raspy notes, which is quite faint, and **easily overlooked**. The call is a high-pitched, rough, and repeated "SEE-SEE-SEE-SEE...", with varying pauses in between.

***TENNESSEE WARBLER**

Open edges of northern coniferous and deciduous forests, often in a moist area with second growth, small trees and brush, where the nest is built on the ground.

A loud, staccato, 3-part song, more sharp and **dry**, than musical. It starts slowly, and **gets faster**, as well as **louder**, ending in a trill. A persistent singer.

MANY VARYING NOTES (continued)

IV Long songs

ROSE-BREASTED GROSBEAK

Deciduous woods, second growth woods, orchards and bushes by streams and clearings. The nest is usually built in a shrub or small tree about 10-15 ft. (3-4.6 m.) off the ground.

A long series of short, **Robin-like whistles**, that are sweeter and higher-pitched than a Robin, and have a hint of **tremolo** that the Robin lacks. It also has shorter pauses and therefore sounds more like a continuous delivery. Its call, a "high-pitched, short and squeaky 'KINK'", (A.A. Saunders) can be mixed in with the regular song.

CONSISTING OF SHORT VARIABLE PHRASES

IV Long songs

RED-EYED VIREO

Favours deciduous woods with thick undergrowth of saplings about 6-10ft. (1.8-3 m.) high, where it builds its nest at about eye level. It is also found in open woodlands and near clearings and wood margins.

Short, sweet, **emphatic**, **Robin-like phrases** (2-3 notes each), with brief pauses in between, repeated over and over. Although most phrases end with an upward inflection, there is enough variation (up and down at the end of each phrase) that it gives the impression of questions and answers.

YELLOW-THROATED VIREO

Although formerly associated with deciduous and mixed forests, it is now primarily a bird of open woodlands, forest edges, orchards and shade trees.The nest is typically built fairly high up in a tree – over 20 ft. (6.1 m.) off the ground.

Its song is similar to the Red-eyed Vireo's, but it is **slower**, lower-pitched, and has a rough or **hoarse** quality (**also longer pauses**). One common combination of notes sounds like a burry, whistled, "EE-LAY.........OH-LAY", (with the "EE-LAY" higher than the "OH-LAY"). It is repeated slowly but often.

SOLITARY VIREO

In mixed woodlands the nest can be built in a conifer or a deciduous tree anywhere from 3-20 ft. (1-6.1 m.), but usually less than 10 ft. (3 m.) off the ground.

Short, sweet, emphatic, Robin-like phrases, similar to the Red-eyed Vireo's song, but it is **slower** higher and **sweeter**, as well as having each phrase **simpler** and more to the point.

IV EVERGREEN FORESTS

I VERY SHORT SONGS

Single-note song

II REPEATED NOTES

Chatter or trill

One note repeated

Two notes repeated

Three notes repeated

III SHORT SONGS

Several varying notes

Containing a distinct repeated note or phrase

IV LONG SONGS

Many varying notes

Consisting of short variable phrases

Solitary Vireo

SINGLE-NOTE SONG

I Very short songs

RED-TAILED HAWK

Woodland areas and fields. The nest is usually built in a tall tree, 35-90 ft. (10.7-27.4 m.) high, overlooking an open area. It can be found in heavy timber but also in a fairly open area in a solitary tree.

One single, **drawn-out** scream lasting a second or two. A loud, raspy, "KEEAHHRR", slurring downward.

AMERICAN CROW

A common bird of woodlands, farmlands, fields, parks and shorelines. It nests in deciduous and coniferous forests (with a preference for conifers) usually high in the tree. However it is adaptable and will nest in shrubs, and even on telephone poles or on the ground at times.

A loud, raspy, nasal "CAW". This single note may be repeated several times in succession.

COMMON RAVEN

The Common Raven commonly nests on rocky cliffs and ledges, but when trees are chosen, they are usually very tall conifers, and the nest is built quite high up, often near the top of the tree.

A deep nasal "GRONK" or "CRUK" – a grunting or croaking sound which is **lower in pitch than the "CAW" of the American Crow**. This note can be repeated several times. Also other harsh or croaking notes.

CHATTER OR TRILL

II Repeated notes

YELLOW-RUMPED WARBLER

In conifer and mixed forests, in open areas or woodland edges, and in evergreen thickets by a stream or in an orchard. The nest height varies from 4-50 ft. (1.2-15.2 m.), but is usually about 10-15 ft. (3-4.6 m.) off the ground.

A sweet, slow, **trill**, "WHEE-WHEE-WHEE-WHEE..." or a slightly sibilant "SWEE-WHEE-WHEE-WHEE...". The speed varies from a rapid series of notes to a slow trill. The slow trill can also rise or drop in pitch near the end.

PINE WARBLER

Open pine woodland, where the nest is built in a pine anywhere from 15-80 ft. (4.6-24.4 m.) above the ground, but usually averaging about 30-50 ft. (9.1-15.2 m.).

A soft, high-pitched, **musical chirping** or trill. It is sweeter, fuller and usually slower than the Chipping Sparrow's trill, and delivered with less gusto.

ONE NOTE REPEATED

II Repeated notes

AMERICAN CROW

(see above)

COMMON RAVEN

(see above)

ONE NOTE REPEATED (continued)

II Repeated notes

RED-BREASTED NUTHATCH

Nests in conifer forests, in tree cavities, usually 10-15 ft. (3.4-4.6 m.) off the ground, but sometimes up to 40 ft.(12.2 m.). The nest can be a natural cavity, an old woodpecker hole, or the bird may excavate it in a dead or rotting branch.

A series of nasal, twangy notes which are more nasal, higher-pitched, and not as loud as the White-breasted Nuthatch. It sounds like "KNG–KNG–KNG–KNG–KNG–KNG..." (like a nasal "KING").

***CAPE MAY WARBLER**

Nests high in a spruce or fir tree, usually along the forest edge, in its northern breeding range. The nests are usually about 30-60 ft. (9.1-18.3 m.) high, in the very uppermost spires of the tree, on the edge of the forest, or in an area of the forest that is fairly open.

A very high-pitched and **weak** series of notes (commonly 4-6 notes but as many as 11-12) which are all on the same pitch. "SEE-SEE-SEE-SEE".

YELLOW-RUMPED WARBLER

(see above)

***BLACKPOLL WARBLER**

Fond of low conifer forests (especially spruce) in its northern breeding grounds. The nest is often found low in young conifers, from ground level, to about 10 ft. (3 m.) off the ground.

A series of single, high-pitched and weak "TSEE" notes that **get stronger toward the middle** and then weaker again toward the end. "TSEE-TSEE-TSEE-*TSEE-TSEE-TSEE*-TSEE-TSEE-TSEE".

TWO NOTES REPEATED

II Repeated notes

***BAY-BREASTED WARBLER**

Coniferous and mixed woodlands, where the nest is usually built from 5-20 ft. (1.5-6.1 m.) above the ground, and often at the edge of a clearing or open area.

A **thin**, high-pitched, **short** song, delivered rapidly. R.T. Peterson points out that it is thinner, shorter, and more on one pitch than the Black and White Warbler. He describes it as "TEESI TEESI TEESI".

THREE NOTES REPEATED

II Repeated notes

***OLIVE-SIDED FLYCATCHER**

In conifer or mixed woodlands (deciduous and mixed on migration), where it likes the forest edges and clearings and more open areas. It is often seen on a dead branch at the top of a tree, taking flight after insects and returning to the same branch. The nest is usually built in a conifer, anywhere from 7-50 ft. (2.1-15.2 m.) off the ground.

It sounds like a whistled "QUICK-*THREE*-BEERS" – a quick intro note, the second note highest, and the third, drawn out and sliding slightly downward. It is repeated often.

SEVERAL VARYING NOTES

III Short songs

***SWAINSON'S THRUSH**

Most common in smaller firs and spruce trees on the border of mature coniferous forests, where there are some deciduous trees. It likes damp areas near streams and the nest is usually fairly low – 2-7 ft. (0.6-2.1 m.) above the ground.

The song is the opposite of the Veery in that it is an **ascending** rapid spiral of hollow, flute-like notes, rolling up the scale.

HERMIT THRUSH

Coniferous or mixed woodlands, where the nest is built on the ground under low brush or foliage.

A distinct, long, **introductory, flute-like note** (usually lower), followed by several, clear, rising and falling, reedy notes, in a slow, yodelling cadence. There are several similar phrases, sung at different pitches. Two examples are: "HEY-BREVITY-BREE" or "HEY-BREVITY-BREVITY".

NORTHERN PARULA WARBLER

Found in coniferous and mixed woodlands. The nest is often hidden in hanging lichens and mosses in trees (*Usnea*, or old man's beard, in the north, and Spanish moss in the south) and it varies from quite low to 40-50 ft. (12.2-15.2 m.) and higher.

A loud, buzzy trill which **rises** and then **snaps** at the end. "DSEEEEEEEEE-UH". It also sings several buzzy notes, on the same pitch, with the last buzzy note higher and usually rising. "TSWEE-TSWEE-TSWEE-*TSWEEEE*".

BLACK-THROATED GREEN WARBLER

Coniferous or predominantly coniferous forests, where the nest is built from almost ground level, up to 70 ft. (21.3 m.). However it is usually built fairly low. It also nests sometimes in deciduous trees and among shrubs and tangles.

A slow, buzzy "ZOO-*ZEE*-ZOO-ZOO-*ZEE*". The third and fourth notes are clearer (not buzzy) and quicker. The "*ZEE*" notes are accented and higher-pitched, and the "ZOO" notes are lower and all on the same pitch. Another song is clearer and quicker; "ZEE-ZEE-ZEE-ZEE-ZEE-ZOO-ZEE".

SEVERAL VARYING NOTES (continued)

III Short songs

BLACK-THROATED BLUE WARBLER

Mixed conifer and hardwood forest with second growth and shrubs, where the nest is built just above ground level – 1-3 ft. (0.3-0.9 m.). It is commonly constructed in conifer saplings, but may also be found in saplings of hardwoods, laurel and rhododendron thickets.

This song consists of 3-5 **evenly-spaced, buzzy notes**, sliding up the scale, with the last note noticeably higher and slurring upward. "ZEEP-ZEEP-ZEEP-ZEEP-*ZEEE*". Quite often these introductory notes are all on the same pitch.

CONTAINING A DISTINCT REPEATED NOTE OR PHRASE

III Short songs

NORTHERN PARULA WARBLER

(see above)

BLACK-THROATED GREEN WARBLER

(see above)

BLACK-THROATED BLUE WARBLER

(see above)

MAGNOLIA WARBLER

Open, low stands of conifer forest, or along the edges of conifer forests, in dense thickets of spruce and fir. The nest is usually found low in a small conifer, although sometimes as high as 25 ft. (7.6 m.) in larger trees.

Short (usually consisting of a few two-note phrases), rapid, and yet quite variable. One common version is a rather **weak**, rapid and whistled "WEETO-WEETO-WEETEE-*EET*" (last note rising), or "SEEYA-SEEYA-SEEYA-*SOON*". Another shorter version has the second last note emphasized, and the last note lower: "SEEYA-SEEYA-*SEAT*-YA".

YELLOW-RUMPED WARBLER

(see above)

BLACKBURNIAN WARBLER

Found mainly in coniferous forests (deciduous forests in its southern range), where the nest is usually built high in a conifer tree.

A **short**, **weak**, and very high-pitched song. It starts with a few single or double-note whistles, and ends on an even higher-pitched, slow chirping trill. "SWEET-SWEET-SWEET-*TRRRR*". Another version goes "SEET-SEET-SEET-SEET-SEET-SEEDLEE-*SEET*", with the last note rising extremely high.

MANY VARYING NOTES

IV Long songs

RUBY-CROWNED KINGLET

Coniferous forests where the nest is built from just above ground level to as high as 100 ft. (30 m.) above the ground in an evergreen.

A loud, clear three-part song, consisting of a series of high-pitched, sweet **three-note phrases**, introduced by several high-pitched squeaky notes and a musical chatter. The three-note phrases emphasize the last syllable: "TWIDDLE-*DEE* TWIDDLE-*DEE* TWIDDLE-*DEE*". The **two-note phrases** sound like "HEDGY-HEDGY-HEDGY", emphasizing the first syllable.

***TENNESSEE WARBLER**

Open edges of northern coniferous and deciduous forests, often in a moist area with second growth, small trees and brush, where the nest is built on the ground.

A loud, staccato, 3-part song, more sharp and **dry** than musical. It starts slowly, and **gets faster**, as well as **louder**, ending in a trill. It is a persistent singer.

CONSISTING OF SHORT VARIABLE PHRASES

IV Long songs

SOLITARY VIREO

In mixed woodlands, the nest can be built in a conifer or a deciduous tree, anywhere from 3-20 ft. (0.9-6.1 m.), but usually less than 10 ft. (3 m.) off the ground.

Short, sweet, emphatic, Robin-like phrases, similar to the Red-eyed Vireo's song, but it is **slower**, higher and **sweeter**, as well as having each phrase **simpler**, and more to the point.

Eastern Meadowlark

V GRASSLANDS, FIELDS AND MEADOWS

IV LONG SONGS

Many varying notes

SINGLE-NOTE SONG

I Very short songs

RED-TAILED HAWK

Woodland areas and fields. The nest is usually built in a tall tree, 35-90 ft. (10.7-27.4 m.) high, overlooking an open area. It can be found in heavy timber, but also in a fairly open area in a solitary tree.

One single, **drawn-out** scream lasting a second or two. A loud, raspy, "KEEAHHRR", slurring downward.

AMERICAN CROW

A common bird of woodlands, farmlands, fields, parks and shorelines. It nests in deciduous and coniferous forests (with a preference for conifers) usually high in the tree. However, it is adaptable and will nest in shrubs, and even on telephone poles or on the ground at times. It is common in fields and farmlands, where it feeds on insects, as well as on farm crops, the latter gaining it a bad reputation with farmers.

A loud, raspy, nasal "CAW". This single note may be repeated several times in succession.

TWO-NOTE SONG

I Very short songs

RING-NECKED PHEASANT

Farmlands, fields, brushy areas and open woods, where the nest is built on the ground.

A **very loud**, harsh, croaking "KROOOK-OOK" (sometimes emphasized on the first syllable and sometimes on the second). It has something of the quality of a "rooster call" horn on an old or antique car.

NORTHERN BOBWHITE

Farmlands, fields, open brushy areas and wood margins, where it often sings from a post or some other favourite perch. The nest is built on the ground.

A clearly whistled, medium-pitched "BOB – *WHITE*", the second note starting on the same pitch, but **rising sharply higher in exclamation**. It sometimes gives a three-note version "BOB – BOB – *WHITE*". This song can be repeated, and when it is, there is a generous pause between each delivery.

THREE-NOTE SONG

I Very short songs

NORTHERN BOBWHITE

(see above)

THREE-NOTE SONG (continued)

I Very short songs

RED-WINGED BLACKBIRD

Clinging to reeds or cattails, or in a small tree not far overhead. The nest is usually built in wet or marshy areas, but also in dry fields, bushy areas and in small trees. The nest is found from ground or water level up to 15 ft. (4.6 m.) high.

A squeaky, gurgling "COY-LA-*REE*". The first note is down-slurred and squeaky, the second, quicker, and a bit higher, and the third note, continuing **up the scale**, is a harsh, raspy trill. It is commonly repeated after a long pause.

BROWN-HEADED COWBIRD

Farmlands, fields, open woods, forest edges, roadsides, parks and suburbs. Being parasitic, it lays its eggs in any available nests (usually one egg per nest). However, certain species are more often victimized – finches, warblers, flycatchers and vireos.

A quick little song – 2 very short, bubbly, gurgling sounds, followed by a thin, high-pitched, short whistle: "GLUG-LA-*SEEE*". The last note has a thin, sharp quality like someone sucking air between their two front teeth. Calls include a "CHUCK" note and a loud, harsh rattle or chatter. The song can be repeated after a generous pause.

ONE NOTE REPEATED

II Repeated notes

KILLDEER

On the ground in an open, flat area, often around a pond, a marsh or a swamp. It is also found on golf courses, in plowed fields, gravel pits and almost any open, gravelly, or stony area. The nest is a slight depression on the open ground.

A sharp, fairly high-pitched "DEE–DEE–DEE–DEE..." repeated many times. It can also be a rapid series of "DEE-DEE-DEE-DEE-DEE" notes. This bird becomes **very noisy** when disturbed.

COMMON NIGHTHAWK

Plowed fields, open country and open pine woods. It is a common sight in the evening sky over towns and cities. Its eggs are laid on the ground in sparse, open or burned-over areas, or even on flat gravel rooftops in cities and towns.

A sharp nasal "BEEK – BEEK – BEEK...", repeated with a short pause in between. It sometimes sounds like a quick two-syllabled "*BEE*-ICK" (emphasized on the first syllable).

NORTHERN FLICKER

Although there are usually some trees or open woodlands nearby, the Northern Flicker can often be seen in city parks and lawns, as well as in country lanes and fields, where it feeds voraciously on the local ant population. The nest is excavated in a tree, pole or fence post, from near ground level to very high.

A long, rapid repetition of "KEE-KEE-KEE-KEE-KEE-KEE-KEE..." – also **loud and ringing**. A.C. Bent describes it as "WICK-WICK-WICK-WICK-WICK...". It also has a squeaky two-note call, with emphasis on the first syllable: a **jerky or snappy** "*WEE*KA-*WEE*KA-*WEE*KA-*WEE*KA-*WEE*KA...". Call note a loud, sharp "KEE-YER" or "KLEER".

ONE NOTE REPEATED (continued)

II Repeated notes

AMERICAN CROW
(see above)

TWO NOTES REPEATED

II Repeated notes

CANADA GOOSE

Nests on beaver houses or clumps of vegetation in the water, or along the shore of ponds, lakes and marshes, as well as in grassy fields.

Two syllables, the second higher and longer, "KA-HONK KA-HONK KA-HONK...". A nasal and resonant **bugling** that breaks slightly like the "changing voice" of an adolescent boy.

KILLDEER

On the ground in an open, flat area, often around a pond, a marsh or a swamp. It is also found on golf courses, in plowed fields, gravel pits and almost any open, gravelly, or stony area. The nest is a slight depression on the open ground.

A sharp, fairly high-pitched, repeated "KILL-*DEE* KILL-*DEE* KILL-*DEE*...", with the second syllable emphasized and higher-pitched. A three-note version goes "*DEEE*-DEE-DEE... *DEEE*-DEE-DEE..." repeated many times. The first note is emphasized, longer and higher. The second and third notes are on the same pitch, but lower than the first, and quicker. It becomes **very noisy** when disturbed.

NORTHERN BOBWHITE
(see above)

NORTHERN FLICKER
(see above)

THREE NOTES REPEATED

II Repeated notes

KILLDEER
(see above)

NORTHERN BOBWHITE
(see above)

RED-WINGED BLACKBIRD
(see above)

BROWN-HEADED COWBIRD
(see above)

EASTERN BLUEBIRD

Open woodlands, orchards and any open country with a few trees or posts (for perching and nesting) and areas of open grass and fields. The nest is built in a natural cavity or, frequently, in one of the many birdhouses that are being provided nowadays.

A short, sweet, gentle and variable warble, sometimes introduced by a couple of "CHICK" notes. "CHICK–PEEER-CHUR-WEE... PEEER-CHUR-WEE". The first note slurs downward, and the second note slides down slightly into the third (both on a similar pitch and lower than the first note). The call is a two-note sweet "CHUR-WEE". This gentle warble can also be strung together into a series of phrases to create a longer song.

AMERICAN ROBIN

Woodlands, parks, gardens and lawns. The nest is usually 5-25 ft. (1.5-7.6 m.) up in a tree or shrub, but is also found on porches or ledges of buildings, on a post or even sometimes on the ground. In cities and built-up areas the Robin is probably most closely associated with the lawns and parks which provide it with its daily supply of earthworms. However, it does eat other insects, as well as fruits and berries when they become available.

A loud, **rolling**, "cheerful" song, consisting of a series of short, sweet phrases, rising and falling. "CHEERI*LY*-CHEERY-CHEER-I*LY*-CHEER", or "TWEEDLE-*DEET*-DEEO-TWEEDLE-*DEET*-DEE" (last note a bit hoarse) – often repeated many times, with a brief pause between each delivery. The final note of the "CHEERI*LY*" phrase (or the "*DEET*" note) is accented and higher.

COMMON GRACKLE

It feeds, like Starlings and Robins and other birds in this category, on the ground in fields and on lawns. It usually nests in colonies, in the shrubs and small trees (especially conifers) of suburbs and open woodlands, or in the vegetation around a marsh or swamp. The nest is usually built quite low, but it can be as high as 60 ft. (18.3 m.).

A short, forced, or hesitating series of **harsh clucks**, ending in a high-pitched, **squeaky note**. The notes tend to get higher in pitch as they proceed. "CHACK–CHACK–KEEK-A-LEEK".

EASTERN MEADOWLARK

Open fields and meadows where the nest is built on the ground. If not seen singing from a stump or a rock, the next probable sighting would be during one of its heavy-winged flights (alternately flapping and gliding), as it leaves or returns to its nest in the meadow.

A sweet, clear, **slurred whistle**, given at a leisurely pace. A 5-note version sounds like "SEE-YOU-SOON NOT-NOW", with the first three notes slurring downward. The fourth and fifth notes start high again, and then also slur downward. There is also a 4-note version which just leaves out the third note; "SEE-YOU NOT-NOW".

SEVERAL VARYING NOTES (continued)

III Short songs

AMERICAN GOLDFINCH

Weedy fields, open woodlands, farmlands and roadsides, where the nest is usually built in a tree or a shrub 3-10 ft. (0.9-3 m.) above the ground.

This song can be a long song (usually in the spring) or a fairly short song (usually in the summer, after the start of nesting), but in either case it is a **canary-like** series of clear, sweet notes, combined with trills (less in summer) and characteristic **drawn-out squeaky notes** ("SWEEE", rising). The diagnostic flight song is a clear and whippy "PER-*CHICK*-O-REE", emphasized on the second note, and given by the bird on the uprise of its undulating flight. It is also worked into the regular song.

SONG SPARROW

Likes moist or swampy areas in woodland edges, streamside thickets, shrubby meadows and cattail swamps. However, it is also found in drier locations, such as along country roads and fences. The nest is built on, or fairly close to the ground, among the brush and tangles.

Consists of 2-3 repeated, sweet notes, followed by a short, buzzy "*ZREE*", a lower liquid trill, and ending with a lower, buzzy note (sometimes 2-3 notes). "SWEET-SWEET-SWEET-*ZREE*-SUGAR-IT" (last note may be repeated).

MANY VARYING NOTES

IV Long songs

EASTERN BLUEBIRD

(see above)

AMERICAN ROBIN

Woodlands, parks, gardens and lawns. The nest is usually 5-25 ft. (1.5-7.6 m.) up in a tree or a shrub, but it is also found on porches or ledges of buildings, on a post, or even sometimes on the ground. In cities and built-up areas the Robin is probably most closely associated with the lawns and parks which provide it with its daily supply of earthworms. However, it does eat other insects, as well as fruits and berries when they become available.

A loud, **rolling**, "cheerful" song, consisting of short, sweet phrases, rising and falling. "CHEERI*LY*-CHEERY-CHEERI*LY*-CHEER" or "TWEEDLE-*DEET*-DEEO-TWEEDLE-*DEET*-DEE" (last note a bit hoarse) – often repeated many times. The last note of the "CHEERI*LY*" phrase (or the "*DEET*" note) is accented and higher. There is usually a brief pause between deliveries, but its early morning song is quicker and this pause is not noticeable. It sounds like **one long carolling song**.

EUROPEAN STARLING

In cities and in the country, in parks, fields and farms, where there are orchards and scattered woods. It nests in any cavity (trees, buildings, bird houses) 10-25 ft. (3-7.6 m.) above the ground.

A series of chips, raspy, and squeaky notes, and sharp twitterings, combined every so often with the characteristic drawn-out, down-slurred and whistled "*WHEEEE-ERR*".

AMERICAN GOLDFINCH

Weedy fields, open woodlands, farmlands and roadsides, where the nest is usually built in a tree or a shrub 3-10 ft. (0.9-3 m.) above the ground.

A long **canary-like** series of clear, sweet notes, combined with trills and characteristic **drawn-out squeaky notes** ("SWEEE", rising). The diagnostic flight song is a clear and whippy "PER-*CHICK*-O-REE", (or "CHEE-*CHI*-CHI-CHEE") emphasized on the second note, and given on the uprise of its undulating flight. It is also worked into the regular song.

FIELD SPARROW

Woodland edges, overgrown pastures and brushy areas, meadows and clearings. Early nests are built near the ground and later nests are built a few feet (1 m.) higher.

A few slow, sweet, introductory notes, **accelerating** and flowing smoothly into a very rich, sweet, high-pitched song, and then ending in a **beautiful trill**. The song starts slowly, and then speeds up progressively into a rich trill. It can rise slowly as it speeds up, but it can also stay on the same pitch, or even drop.

VI OPEN WOODLANDS AND BRUSHY AREAS

I VERY SHORT SONGS

Single-note song

Two-note song

Three-note song

II REPEATED NOTES

Chatter or trill

One note repeated

Two notes repeated

IV LONG SONGS

Many varying notes

Consisting of short variable phrases

Rose-breasted Grosbeak

SINGLE-NOTE SONG

I Very short songs

RED-TAILED HAWK

Woodland areas and fields. The nest is usually built in a tall tree, 35-90 ft. (10.7-27.4 m.) high, overlooking an open area. It can be found in heavy timber but also in a fairly open area in a solitary tree.

One single, **drawn-out** scream lasting a second or two. A loud, raspy, "KEEAHHRR", slurring downward.

AMERICAN WOODCOCK

It is found in the scrubby edges of forests, second growth woodland or alder stands and in swampy thickets, on the ground and near water. A very simple nest is built among the leaves, and the moist ground provides a supply of earthworms.

A sharp, nasal "PEENT" (with a slightly buzzy or raspy quality) **delivered from the forest floor**. It may be repeated with a generous pause in between. Flight displays include a light twittering or trill as the bird climbs and a series of chirps or warbles as it descends to the ground.

GREAT-CRESTED FLYCATCHER

Nests in tree cavities in deciduous and mixed woodlands and in old orchards, anywhere from 10-70 ft. (3-21.3 m.) above the ground. It prefers areas near clearings or woodland borders.

A very loud single "WHEEP", or a loud burry "FRREEEP" (each note **rising** and on a fairly high pitch). This single note is sometimes repeated a few times in succession.

AMERICAN CROW

A common bird of woodlands, farmlands, fields, parks and shorelines. It nests in deciduous and coniferous forests (with a preference for conifers) usually high in the tree. However, it is adaptable and will nest in shrubs, and even on telephone poles or on the ground at times.

A loud, raspy, nasal "CAW". This single note may be repeated several times in succession.

TWO-NOTE SONG

I Very short songs

RING-NECKED PHEASANT

Farmlands, fields, brushy areas and open woods, where the nest is built on the ground.

A **very loud**, harsh, croaking "KROOOK-OOK" (sometimes emphasized on the first syllable and sometimes on the second). It has something of the quality of of a "rooster call" horn on an old or antique car.

TWO-NOTE SONG (continued)

I Very short songs

NORTHERN BOBWHITE

Farmlands, fields, open brushy areas and open woodlands, where it often sings from a post or some other favourite perch. The nest is built on the ground.

A clearly whistled, medium-pitched "BOB – *WHITE*", the second note starting on the same pitch, but **rising sharply higher in exclamation**. It sometimes gives a three-note version "BOB – BOB – *WHITE*". Each song may be repeated, and when it is, there is a generous pause in between each delivery.

THREE-NOTE SONG

I Very short songs

NORTHERN BOBWHITE

(see above)

MOURNING DOVE

Open woods, orchards, fields with trees or shrubs and suburban gardens. The nest is built in a tree (with a preference for evergreens), 10-25 ft. (3-7.6 m.) up, or in shrubs, or even sometimes on the ground.

At a distance, it sounds like a **slow**, sad "OOO–OOO–OOO" (a series of three notes which are repeated after a generous pause). Closer up you can hear the full four-note song (with the same qualities as above): "OH-*WOOO* (rising) OOO–OOO–OOO".

BROWN-HEADED COWBIRD

Farmlands, fields, open woods, forest edges, roadsides, parks and suburbs. Being parasitic, it lays its eggs in any available nests (usually one egg per nest). However, certain species are more often victimized – finches, warblers, flycatchers and vireos.

A quick little song – 2 very short, bubbly, gurgling sounds, followed by a thin, high-pitched, short whistle: "GLUG-LA-*SEEE*". The last note has a thin, sharp quality like someone sucking air between their two front teeth. The song can be repeated after a generous pause. Calls include a "CHUCK" note and a loud, harsh rattle or chatter.

CHATTER OR TRILL

II Repeated notes

CHIMNEY SWIFT

In the country, where there are hollow trees, wells or farm buildings (chimneys), or in cities and towns where there are many large chimneys. The nest is "glued" to the side of the chosen surface by the bird's saliva in a half-cup shape.

A high-pitched, rapidly repeated and noisy "twittering" usually discloses their presence in the sky over towns and cities.

CHATTER OR TRILL (continued)

II Repeated notes

EASTERN KINGBIRD

Open country with scattered trees, wood edges and orchards, often near water. The nest is often built over water in a tree, or sometimes on a post standing in water. The height of the nest is usually between 10-20 ft. (3-6 m.), but it can vary from 2-60 ft. (0.6-18.3 m.).

A high-pitched rapid "twittering" (**raspy and sharp**) which **sputters** and changes speed. "ZEE-ZEE-ZEE-ZEEE-TEE-ZEE-TEE-ZEE". It also has a slower repeated "ZEET–ZEET–ZEET..." version, as well as a slurred two-note "KIT-*ZEE*" (second syllable emphasized and sounding like one sharp rising note) which is repeated fairly quickly.

CEDAR WAXWING

Open woodlands, orchards and shrubbery. The nest can be built up to 50 ft. (15.2 m.) high in a tree, but it is usually about 5-20 ft. (1.5-6.1 m.) off the ground.

A high-pitched, **thin trill**, or trilled note which can be repeated. It is high-pitched but has a chirpy or buzzy quality (not sweet or musical). "SREEEE – SREEEE – SREEEE...", or "TREEEE – TREEEE – TREEEE...".

PINE WARBLER

Open pine woodland, where the nest is built in a pine anywhere from 15-80 ft. (4.6-24.4 m.) above the ground, but usually averaging about 30-50 ft. (9.1-15.2 m.).

A soft, high-pitched, **musical chirping** or trill. It is sweeter, fuller and usually slower than the Chipping Sparrow's trill, and delivered with less gusto.

CHIPPING SPARROW

Open woodlands, woodland edges, orchards and clearings, as well as in parks and gardens, in small trees and shrubs. The nest is built in a tree (often a conifer), a shrub or a vine, usually about 3-10 ft. (0.9-3 m.) off the ground.

A dull unmusical twitter or trill, consisting of rapidly repeated, **sharp chips** in the same cadence as a rapidly running sewing machine.

ONE NOTE REPEATED

II Repeated notes

AMERICAN WOODCOCK

(see above)

MOURNING DOVE

(see above)

BLACK-BILLED CUCKOO

Prefers more wooded areas than the Yellow-billed Cuckoo, where it frequents shrubs and thickets, often near water. The nest is built in a tree or in a bush, and though it is usually about 5-6 ft. (1.5-1.8 m.) off the ground, it can range anywhere from 2-20 ft. (0.6-6.1 m.).

This is a **long song** with several series of rapid "COO-COO-COO" notes (given 3-4 to a series). The notes have a fairly nasal and **ringing quality**, unlike the soft "COO"s of the Mourning Dove.

ONE NOTE REPEATED (continued)

COMMON NIGHTHAWK

Plowed fields, open country and open pine woods. It is a common sight in the evening sky over towns and cities. Its eggs are laid on the ground in sparse, open or burned-over areas, or even on flat gravel roof-tops in cities and towns.

A sharp nasal "BEEK – BEEK – BEEK...", repeated with a short pause in between. It sometimes sounds like a quick two-syllabled "*BEE*-ICK" (emphasized on the first syllable).

NORTHERN FLICKER

Open areas with scattered trees, orchards and suburban areas. The nest is excavated in a tree, pole or fence post. The height of the nest varies considerably from near ground level up to 60 ft. (18.3 m.) and even higher in some places. The Northern Flicker is often seen on the ground (in both city and country), feeding voraciously on the local ant population.

A long, rapid repetition of "KEE-KEE-KEE-KEE-KEE-KEE-KEE..." – also **loud and ringing**. A. C. Bent describes it as "WICK-WICK-WICK-WICK-WICK...". It also has a squeaky two-note call, with emphasis on the first syllable: a jerky or snappy "*WEE*KA-*WEE*KA-*WEE*KA-*WEE*KA-*WEE*KA...". Call note a loud, sharp "KEE-YER" or "KLEER".

EASTERN KINGBIRD

(see above)

GREAT-CRESTED FLYCATCHER

Nests in tree cavities in deciduous and mixed woodlands and in old orchards, anywhere from 10-70 ft. (3-21.3 m.) above the ground. It prefers areas near clearings or woodland borders.

A very loud single "WHEEP", or a loud burry "FRREEEP" (each note **rising** and on a fairly high pitch). This single note is sometimes repeated a few times in succession.

BLUE JAY

Forests, mixed woodlands (especially oak and pine), suburban areas, parks and city gardens. The nest is usually built quite high in a tree, about 10-30 ft. (3-9.1 m.), and it also has a preference for conifers, where they are available.

A **harsh**, piercing, repeated and 'steely' "JAAY–JAAY–JAAY...", or a down-slurred, screeching "JEEAH–JEEAH–JEEAH...", both **very loud**. Also two quick bursts "WHEEDLE-WHEEDLE", repeated after a generous pause, as well as a three-note "WHEEL-DE-LEE" song, with its sharp, "**creaking wheelbarrow**" quality.

AMERICAN CROW

(see above)

ONE NOTE REPEATED (continued)

BLACK-CAPPED CHICKADEE

Deciduous and mixed forests and in more open areas with scattered trees and bushes. The nest is built in tree cavities 4-10 ft. (1.2-3 m.) off the ground.

A **cheerful, bright** and quickly repeated "DEE-DEE-DEE-DEE-DEE-DEE-DEE...", often introduced by a squeaky and higher-pitched "CHICKA" or "SICKA". (see 2- and 3-note versions below)

TUFTED TITMOUSE

Deciduous woodlands, orchards, suburban areas and feeders. The nest is built in a tree cavity at variable heights, anywhere from 2-87 ft. (0.6-26.5 m.) off the ground.

A loud, clear and **whistled** "PEEER-PEEER-PEEER" repeated fairly quickly, with each note rising slightly toward the end. Its common two-note song sounds like "WHEEDLE-WHEEDLE-WHEEDLE", with the same qualities as the single-note song.

WHITE-BREASTED NUTHATCH

Deciduous and mixed woodlands and orchards. The nest is built in a natural cavity or old woodpecker hole from very low to 50 ft. (15.2 m.) off the ground.

A rapid series of nasal, low-pitched notes, "WA-WA-WA-WA-WA-WA-WA-WA..." or "KANK-KANK-KANK-KANK-KANK-KANK..." (a bit rough and burry).

BLUE-GRAY GNATCATCHER

Varied habitat ranging from scrub to wooded swamps to thick woodland, but quite often near water. Its dainty, hummingbird-like nest is built on a fairly small branch (often at a vertical fork), from a few feet (1 m.) above the ground, to very high – 70-80 ft. (21.3-24.4 m.).

A **thin**, rapid series of both **squeaky** and raspy notes, which is quite faint and **easily overlooked**. The call referred to here, is a high-pitched, rough and repeated "SEE-SEE-SEE-SEE...", with varying pauses in between.

CEDAR WAXWING

(see above)

AMERICAN REDSTART

Open deciduous and mixed woodlands, young second growth woods and in the thick growth of smaller trees or bushes on the edge of a larger forest, as well as in roadside trees, gardens and parks. It also likes willow thickets along streams or ponds. The nest is usually no more than 10 ft. (3 m.) off the ground in a sapling, tree, shrub or vine tangle.

A **high-pitched** and **variable** song, consisting of weak, yet emphatic, single notes (sometimes two-note phrases, similar to the Black and White Warbler's song). It is sometimes a repeated "TSEET-TSEET-TSEET-TSEET-TSEET.". More often though, it is delivered with the last note higher or lower. "TSEET-TSEET-TSEET-TSEET-*TSEEE*" (last note higher) or "TSEET-TSEET-TSEET-TSEE-O" (last note lower).

ONE NOTE REPEATED (continued)

II Repeated notes

NORTHERN CARDINAL

Woodland edges and in the brush and tangles of open woodlands, gardens and streamside thickets. It is often seen flitting in and out of tangles and thickets where its nest is built (if not in a small nearby tree), usually about 3-10 ft. (0.9-3 m.) off the ground. The Cardinal also likes to sing from high perches, such as the top of a high tree or a roof-top antenna, from which it will definitely attract your attention with its very loud and persistent singing.

A **very loud**, rich and drawn-out "TWEEER-TWEEER-TWEEER-TWEEER...", or a quicker "WHOIT-WHOIT-WHOIT-WHOIT...", or a sharp "CHET-CHET-CHET-CHET..." like a chatter (all repeated up to 7-8 times or more). Two-note songs include "*BI*RDY-*BI*RDY-*BI*RDY-*BI*RDY..." (accented on the first syllable) or "TU-*WEET* TU-*WEET* TU-*WEET* TU-*WEET*..." (accented on the last syllable).

TWO NOTES REPEATED

II Repeated notes

NORTHERN BOBWHITE

Farmlands, fields, open brushy areas and wood margins, where it often sings from a post or some other favourite perch. The nest is built on the ground.

A clearly whistled, medium-pitched "BOB – *WHITE*", the second note starting on the same pitch, but **rising sharply higher in exclamation**. It sometimes gives a three-note "BOB – BOB – *WHITE*". Each song may be repeated, and when it is, there is a generous pause in between each delivery.

NORTHERN FLICKER

(see above)

EASTERN KINGBIRD

(see above)

EASTERN PHOEBE

Open woodlands and around farm buildings and bridges. The nest is often built under a bridge or in a farm building, on a protected beam.

An **emphatic**, repeated, two-note song that sounds like "*FEE*-BEE" or "*FEE*-BREE", with the second note most often lower than the first and also raspy or burry.

EASTERN WOOD-PEWEE

Deciduous and mixed woodlands, especially bordering fields and clearings, as well as in orchards and shade trees. It is usually found higher up in the tree, where the nest is built on a small horizontal branch, about 20 ft. (6.1 m.) off the ground. It can vary, however, anywhere from 8-45 ft. (2.4-13.7 m.) high.

A **slow, drawn-out** "PEEE-*WEEE*", with an upward inflection on the second note. It is repeated after a generous pause, and it also "works in" a drawn-out "PEEE-YURR" every so often, with a downward inflection on the second syllable. (See three-note version below)

TWO NOTES REPEATED (continued)

LEAST FLYCATCHER

Open woodlands, wood margins, orchards, parks and shade trees. The nest is built in a tree 5-20 ft. (1.5-6.1 m.) up.

Two sharp, dry notes, repeated quickly, over and over. A snappy, emphatic "CHE-*BEK* CHE-*BEK* CHE-*BEK* CHE-*BEK*...", strongly accented on the second syllable.

BLUE JAY

(see above)

BLACK-CAPPED CHICKADEE

Deciduous and mixed forests, and in more open areas, with scattered trees and bushes.

A clear, sweet, whistled "*FEEE*-BEE" (the first note higher and longer), repeated after a brief pause. It also has a three-note song "*FEEE*-BEE-BEE", which quickly repeats the second note. This version is also repeated after a brief pause.

TUFTED TITMOUSE

(see above)

CAROLINA WREN

In moist woodland areas characterized by thick brush and tangles, and along streams and swamps with sufficient cover. The nest is usually less than 10 ft. (3 m.) off the ground in some kind of cavity, natural or man-made: woodpecker hole, tree stump or crotch, in stone walls, and around buildings and bridges.

A **very loud**, **rich** and sweet song. "TWEEDLE-TWEEDLE-TWEEDLE", or a three-note "*TWEE*DLE-DEE *TWEE*DLE-DEE *TWEE*DLE-DEE", both sung quickly.

BLUE-WINGED WARBLER

Found in overgrown, brushy meadows, open woodlands and forest edges, swamps and the edges of small streams, where the nest is built on, or just above the ground.

A two-note buzzy or raspy trill, with the second note lower and rougher than the first. A slow, **almost insect-like** "ZEEE-ZREEE".

NORTHERN CARDINAL

(see above)

TWO NOTES REPEATED (continued)

II Repeated notes

RUFOUS-SIDED TOWHEE

Open areas with thick undergrowth or shrubbery and along woodland edges and roadsides, where the nest is built on, or sometimes just over the ground.

The characteristic song is a three-note "DRINK-YOUR-*TEA-EE-EE-EE-EE*", with the last note prolonged, higher and trilled. The two-note version, referred to here, sounds like "DRINK-*TEA-EE-EE-EE-EE*", again with the last note prolonged, higher and trilled. It is quite musical and delivered at a slow, measured pace.

THREE NOTES REPEATED

II Repeated notes

NORTHERN BOBWHITE

(see above)

MOURNING DOVE

Open woods, orchards, fields with trees or shrubs and suburban gardens. The nest is built in a tree (with a preference for evergreens) 10–25 ft. (3-7.6 m.) up, or in shrubs, or even sometimes on the ground.

At a distance it sounds like a **slow**, sad "OOO–OOO–OOO", which is repeated after a short pause. Closer up you can hear the full four-note song, "OH-*WOOO* (rising) OOO–OOO–OOO", with the same qualities as above.

EASTERN WOOD-PEWEE

Deciduous and mixed woodlands, especially bordering fields and clearings, as well as in orchards and shade trees. It is usually found higher up in the tree, where the nest is built on a small horizontal branch, about 20 ft. (6.1 m.) off the ground. It can vary, however, anywhere from 8-45 ft. (2.4-13.7 m.) high.

The two-note song, a **slow, drawn-out** "PEEE-*WEEE*", with an upward inflection on the second note, usually sounds like a three-note "PEEE-A-*WEEEE*" (second note lower and the last with an upward inflection). As with the two-note version, it is repeated after a generous pause and it also "works in" a drawn-out "PEEE-YURR" every so often, with a downward inflection on the second syllable.

*OLIVE-SIDED FLYCATCHER

In conifer or mixed woodlands (deciduous and mixed on migration), where it likes the forest edges and clearings and more open areas. It is often seen on a dead branch at the top of a tree, taking flight after insects and returning to the same branch. The nest is usually built in a conifer, anywhere from about 7-50 ft. (2.1-15.2 m.) off the ground.

It sounds like a whistled "QUICK-*THREE*-BEERS" – a quick intro note, the second note highest, and the third drawn out and sliding slightly downward. It is repeated often.

THREE NOTES REPEATED (continued) — II Repeated notes

BLUE JAY
(see above)

BLACK-CAPPED CHICKADEE
(see above)

CAROLINA WREN
(see above)

BROWN-HEADED COWBIRD
(see above)

RUFOUS-SIDED TOWHEE
(see above)

SEVERAL VARYING NOTES — III Short songs

EASTERN BLUEBIRD

Open woodlands, orchards and any open country with a few trees or posts (for perching and nesting) and areas of open grass and fields. The nest is built in a natural cavity or, frequently, in one of the many birdhouses that are being provided nowadays.

A short, sweet, gentle and variable warble, sometimes introduced by a couple of "CHICK" notes. CHICK–PEEER-CHUR-WEE...PEEER-CHUR-WEE". The first note slurs downward, and the second note slides down slightly into the third (both on a similar pitch and lower than the first note). The call is a sweet "CHUR-WEE". There is also a longer version of this same song.

AMERICAN ROBIN

Woodlands, parks, gardens and lawns. The nest is usually about 5-25 ft. (1.5-7.6 m.) up in a tree or shrub, but it is also found on porches or ledges of buildings, on a post, or even sometimes on the ground. In cities and built-up areas, the Robin is probably most closely associated with the lawns and parks which provide it with its daily supply of earthworms. However, it does eat other insects, as well as fruits and berries when they become available.

A loud, **rolling**, "cheerful" song, consisting of a series of short, sweet phrases, rising and falling "CHEER*ILY*-CHEERY-CHEER*ILY*-CHEER" or "TWEEDLE-*DEET*-DEEO-TWEEDLE-*DEET*-DEE" (last note a bit hoarse) – often repeated many times. The final note of the "CHEERI*LY*" phrase (and the "*DEET*" note) is accented and higher. There is also usually a brief pause between deliveries. However it can be delivered as one long carolling song.

AMERICAN GOLDFINCH

Weedy fields, open woodlands, farmlands and roadsides, where the nest is usually built in a tree or shrub, about 3-10 ft. (0.9-3 m.) above the ground. The Goldfinch is fond of thistles and weeds, as a source of food, as well as for nesting materials.

This song can be a long song (usually in the spring) or a fairly short song (usually in the summer, after the start of nesting), but in either case it is a **canary-like** series of clear, sweet notes, combined with trills (less in summer) and characteristic **drawn-out squeaky notes** ("SWEEE", rising). The diagnostic flight song is a clear and whippy "PER-*CHICK*-O-REE", emphasized on the second note, and given on the uprise of its undulating flight. This is also worked into the regular song.

INDIGO BUNTING

Orchards, wood edges, clearings and brushy areas. The nest is built in a bush, small tree, or among the tangles and thickets, about 2-15 ft. (0.6-4.6 m.) off the ground.

This song consists of high-pitched "**pairs**" of notes, sharp and rhythmic, often with each pair at a lower pitch down the scale. It is delivered fairly quickly, but not rushed.

***WHITE-CROWNED SPARROW**

In winter it likes open woodlands, roadsides, wood margins and brush. It breeds in the far northern, open, stunted woodlands and scrub, where it builds its nest usually on the ground, or sometimes just over it, in a shrub or tree.

There are 2–3 clear, sweet, introductory notes (sounding like a White-throated Sparrow), followed by raspy (or husky) notes moving **down the scale**, and ending in a low trill. "ZWEE-ZA-ZA-ZOO-ZEE-ZOO". The first note is a little longer than the other introductory note(s). The last note is a low trill (sometimes a buzzy note), and the overall song is given at a moderate speed.

SONG SPARROW

Likes moist or swampy areas in woodland edges, streamside thickets, shrubby meadows and cattail swamps. However, it is also found in drier locations such as along country roads and fences. The nest is built on, or fairly close to the ground, among the brush or tangles.

Consists of two to three repeated sweet notes, followed by a short buzzy "*ZREE*", a lower liquid trill, and ending with a lower buzzy note (sometimes 2-3 notes). "SWEET-SWEET-SWEET-*ZREE*-SUGAR-IT" (last note may be repeated).

MOURNING DOVE

Open woods, orchards, fields with trees or shrubs and suburban gardens. The nest is built in a tree (with a preference for evergreens) 10-25 ft. (3-7.6 m.) up, or in shrubs, or even on the ground.

At a distance it sounds like a **slow**, sad "OOO–OOO–OOO", which is repeated after a generous pause. Closer up you can hear the full four-note song – "OH-*WOOO* (rising) OOO–OOO–OOO" (with the same qualities as above).

CERULEAN WARBLER

Upper levels of tall deciduous trees in forests and in open woodlands with little ground cover, and often near water. The nest is built quite high up, 20-50 ft. (6.0-15.2 m.), and sometimes even higher.

Several **rapid**, **buzzy** notes on one pitch, and then a **final buzzy note which is higher-pitched**. "ZREE-ZREE-ZREE-ZREE-*ZREEEE*"

BLACK-CAPPED CHICKADEE

Deciduous and mixed forests, in more open areas, with scattered trees and bushes. The nest is built in tree cavities 4-10 ft. (1.2-3 m.) off the ground.

A very snappy two-note introduction "CHICKA", followed immediately by a rapid series of "DEE-DEE-DEE-DEE-DEE..." notes, all with a squeaky, yet **cheerful and bright** quality The introduction is higher-pitched than the repeated notes.

CHESTNUT-SIDED WARBLER

Second growth deciduous forest or forest edges. Also overgrown, shrubby fields or pastures, or cut-over areas in the tangles and undergrowth. The nest is built very close to the ground in a shrub or sapling – about 1-4 ft. (0.3-1.2 m.).

A fast series of introductory notes (3-5) on the same pitch, almost like a trill, and then a "**snappy**" **ending**. It sounds like "SWEET-SWEET-SWEET-SWEET-TO-*BEAT*-CHA", with the second last note accented and highest, and then the last dropping.

AMERICAN REDSTART

Open deciduous and mixed woodlands, young second growth woods and thick growth of smaller trees and bushes on the edge of a larger forest, as well as in roadside trees, gardens and parks. It also likes willow thickets along streams or ponds. The nest is usually no more than 10 ft. (3 m.) off the ground in a sapling, tree, shrub or vine tangle.

A **high-pitched** and **variable** song, consisting of weak, yet emphatic, single notes (sometimes two-note phrases, similar to the Black and White Warbler's song). It is sometimes a repeated "TSEET-TSEET-TSEET-TSEET-TSEET". More often though, it is delivered with the last note higher or lower. "TSEET-TSEET-TSEET-TSEET-*TSEEE*" (last note higher) or "TSEET-TSEET-TSEET-TSEE-O" (last note lower).

CONTAINING A DISTINCT REPEATED NOTE OR PHRASE (cont'd) III Short songs

YELLOW WARBLER

Likes areas with scrub or brush or small trees, especially where they border marshes, swamps or other waterways. Also fond of brushy fences, hedgerows and roadside thickets, as well as apple orchards. The nest usually ranges from 2-12 ft. (0.6-3.7 m.) above the ground and is built in a small tree, shrub or tangle.

Several clear, **sweet** notes. A **rapid** "TWEET-TWEET-*TWEET*-TWEEDLE-DEEDLE-*DEET*" or "TWEET-TWEET-*TWEET*-TWEEDLE-DE-*DEET*", both with the last note rising.

GOLDEN-WINGED WARBLER

It likes areas overgrown with weeds and thickets (pastures, meadows or forest edges), usually with stands of larger trees or forest quite close by and providing shade for the nest. The nest is built on or close to the ground, quite often hidden at the base of a clump of grass, goldenrod or shrub.

A raspy, buzzing song of four notes, the first note long, and the last three shorter, and on a lower pitch. A lazy "*ZEEE*-ZREE-ZREE-ZREE".

MOURNING WARBLER

It builds its nest on or close to the ground in the thickets and tangles of moist northern woodlands or in the thick undergrowth along the edge of swamps. However, it is also found in dry, brushy areas and in roadside shrubbery.

A **loud**, **musica**l and short song which has considerable variation. Some examples are: "CHEE-CHEE-CHEE CHURR-*E*-AH" or "CHEE-CHEE-CHEE CHURR-AH" or, as R.T. Peterson describes it, "CHIRRY, CHIRRY, CHORRY, CHORRY (CHORRY lower)".

WHITE-THROATED SPARROW

A more northerly breeding sparrow found in open woodlands, woodland edges and clearings in the undergrowth, brush and thickets. The nest is usually built on the ground, but sometimes it is built just over the ground, in the undergrowth, or in a small tree.

One or two clear, whistled, high-pitched note(s), followed by three **3-note phrases**. "OH-*SWEET* CANADA-CANADA-CANADA" (second note higher). Usually sung fairly slowly, it has a **rhythmic** quality like the "WITCHITY-WITCHITY-WITCHITY" of the Common Yellowthroat. Often a three-note phrase will separate the two introductory notes.

MANY VARYING NOTES

IV Long songs

YELLOW-BILLED CUCKOO

Among the thickets of open woods, overgrown fields, streamside groves and in orchards. It is more common in the southern part of its range. The nest is built in a tree or shrub, usually 4-10 ft. (1.2-3 m.) off the ground.

A rapid, chattering "KEK-KEK-KEK-KEK-KEK", turning into "KYOLP-KYOLP-KYOLP", and ending with a few "KUT-A-KOWP"s. The delivery also **slows down** toward the end.

HOUSE WREN

Farmlands, gardens and open woods with brush, shrubs and tangles, where the nest is built in a natural cavity or crevice, or in a bird house.

A rapid burst of **squeaky**, **rising notes**, that ends in a slightly **lower sweet trill**. It begins as a distinctly rushed, squeaky sound and proceeds to a short, but rich trill, on a lower pitch.

BLUE-GRAY GNATCATCHER

(see above)

BROWN THRASHER

The nest is usually built on, or close to the ground in the thickets or tangles of woodland edges, or in low thick shrubby growth in open areas.

Characterized by each note or phrase being **repeated,** or sung in couplets. Its long series of notes and phrases ranges from harsh to sweet whistles, and is sung very deliberately. Each couplet is separated by a brief, but noticeable pause.

GRAY CATBIRD

Found in tangles or thickets, often along woodland edges, marshes or waterways, where the nest is usually built up to 6 ft. (1.8 m.) off the ground.

A **loud** jumbled **mixture** of squeaky, nasal, and sweet notes, interrupted every so often by a distinctive, **cat-like "mew" call**, which is different and much slower than the other notes.

NORTHERN MOCKINGBIRD

Open woodland edges, scattered trees and bushes in open areas, and around buildings in cities and towns, where the nest is built in a small tree or in shrubbery, usually fairly close to the ground – about 3-10 ft. (0.9-3 m.).

A **very loud** series of various notes and phrases, with each one **repeated several times** (6 or more) in its very long delivery. This very distinctive repetition is the key to identification.

EASTERN BLUEBIRD

(see above)

MANY VARYING NOTES (continued)

AMERICAN ROBIN

Woodlands, parks, gardens and lawns. The nest is usually 5-25 ft. (1.5-7.6 m.) up in a tree or shrub, but is also found on porches or ledges of buildings, on a post, or even sometimes on the ground. In cities and built-up areas the Robin is probably most closely associated with the lawns and parks which provide it with its daily supply of earthworms. However, it does eat other insects, as well as fruits and berries, when they become available.

A loud, **rolling**, "cheerful" song consisting of a series of short, sweet phrases, rising and falling "CHEER*ILY*-CHEERY-CHEER*ILY*-CHEER" or "TWEEDLE-DEET-DEEO TWEEDLE-DEET-DEE" (last note a bit hoarse). It usually has a brief pause between each delivery, but its early morning song is quicker and this pause is not noticeable. As a result, it sounds like **one long carolling song**. In this song the final note of the "CHEERILY" phrase (and the "DEET" note) is accented and higher.

WARBLING VIREO

(see above)

*TENNESSEE WARBLER

Open edges of northern coniferous and deciduous forests, often in a moist area with second growth, small trees and brush, where the nest is built on the ground.

A loud, staccato, 3-part song, more sharp and **dry** than musical. It starts slowly, and **gets faster**, as well as **louder**, ending in a trill. It is a persistent singer.

YELLOW-BREASTED CHAT

Dense tangles, thickets and brush on woodland edges, in overgrown pastures, and also along streams or swamps in similar heavy growth. The nest is built about 2-6 ft. (0.6-1.8 m.) above the ground.

A long series of notes, **slowly presented** (some single notes, some repeated several times) with **distinct pauses** between each phrase. The notes include:

- whistles - clear, and sometimes burry "WHOIT" notes.
- harsh "caw"s and raspy Blue Jay-like cries ("JEAHH").
- "kek"s or "crick"s

EUROPEAN STARLING

In cities and in the country, in parks, fields and farms, where there are orchards and scattered woods. It nests in any cavity (trees, buildings, bird houses) 10-25 ft. (3-7.6 m.) above the ground.

A series of chips, raspy and squeaky notes, and sharp twitterings, combined every so often with the characteristic drawn-out and down-slurred "*WHEEEE-ERR*".

MANY VARYING NOTES (continued)

IV Long songs

NORTHERN ORIOLE

Scattered trees, orchards, shade trees, parks and suburban trees. The nest is usually built quite high – about 20-30 ft. (6.1-9.1 m.) – but ranges anywhere from 6-60 ft. (1.8-18.3m.) above the ground.

A loud series of clear, **rich whistles** (some prolonged), with **harsh chicks** and burred notes thrown in, as well as rapid changes in pitch. One-note and two-note phrases are common, and many birds have a distinct, **whippy rhythm** in their song. Repeated notes and a harsh chatter may also be heard.

NORTHERN CARDINAL

Open woodlands, gardens and streamside thickets. It is often seen flitting in and out of tangles and thickets where its nest is built (if not in a small nearby tree), usually about 3-10 ft. (0.9-3 m.) off the ground. The Cardinal also likes to sing from high perches, such as the top of a high tree or a roof top antenna, from which it will definitely attract your attention with its very loud and persistent singing.

Its **very loud**, rich, one-note and two-note songs are often combined to form a long song with varying notes. One example is the following: "TWEEER–TWEEER–TWEEER" (each note slurred downward), followed immediately by a quick "WHOIT-WHOIT-WHOIT..." (each note rising). Each note or pair of notes within these combinations can be repeated 7-8 times or more.

HOUSE FINCH

(see above)

AMERICAN GOLDFINCH

Weedy fields, open woodlands, farmlands and roadsides, where the nest is usually built in a tree or a shrub 3-10 ft. (0.9-3 m.) above the ground.

A long **canary-like** series of clear, sweet notes, combined with trills and characteristic **drawn-out squeaky notes** ("SWEEE", rising). The diagnostic flight song is a clear and whippy "PER-*CHICK*-O-REE", or "CHEE-*CHI*-CHI-CHEE", emphasized on the second note, and given on the uprise of its undulating flight. It is also worked into the regular song.

ROSE-BREASTED GROSBEAK

Second growth woods, scrub and bushes by streams and clearings. The nest is usually built in a shrub or small tree, about 10-15 ft. (3-4.6 m.) off the ground.

A long series of short, **Robin-like whistles**, that are sweeter and higher-pitched than a Robin, and have a hint of **tremolo** that the Robin lacks. It also has shorter pauses, and therefore sounds more like a continuous delivery. Its call, a "high-pitched, short and squeaky 'KINK' " (A.A. Saunders), can be mixed in with the regular song.

MANY VARYING NOTES (continued)

IV Long songs

FIELD SPARROW

Woodland edges, overgrown pastures and brushy areas, meadows and clearings. Early nests are built near the ground and later nests are built a few feet (1 m.) higher.

A few slow, sweet, introductory notes, **accelerating** and flowing smoothly into a very rich, sweet, high-pitched song, and then ending in a **beautiful trill**. The song starts slowly , and then speeds up progressively into a rich trill. It can rise slowly as it speeds up, but it can also stay on the same pitch, or even drop.

CONSISTING OF SHORT VARIABLE PHRASES

IV Long songs

RED-EYED VIREO

Favours deciduous woods with thick undergrowth of saplings, about 6-10 ft. (1.8-3 m.) high, where it builds its nest at about eye level. It is also found in open woodlands, and near clearings and wood margins.

Short, sweet, **emphatic**, **Robin-like phrases** (2-3 notes), with brief pauses in between, repeated over and over. Although most phrases end with an upward inflection, there is enough variation (up and down at the end of each phrase) that it gives the impression of questions and answers.

YELLOW-THROATED VIREO

Although formerly associated with deciduous and mixed forests, it is now primarily a bird of open woodlands, forest edges, orchards and shade trees. The nest is typically built fairly high – over 20 ft. (6.1 m.) up in a tree.

Its song is similar to the Red-eyed Vireo's, but it is **slower**, lower-pitched, and has a rough or **hoarse** quality. One common combination of notes sounds like a burry, whistled "EE-LAY..........OH-LAY", (with the "EE-LAY" higher than the "OH-LAY"), repeated many times.

Chestnut-sided Warbler

Overviews by Habitat

MARSHES AND SWAMPS — Quick overview

SINGLE-NOTE SONG	I Very short songs
Sharp, nasal "PEENT" (with a buzzy or raspy quality), from forest floor	American Woodcock
Loud, sharp "SKEOW" or "KEOW"	Green-backed Heron
Loud, guttural "WORK" or "QUAWK"	Black-crowned Night Heron

THREE-NOTE SONG	I Very short songs
"oh-OOOOO-ooo", a long, mournful, wailing call, like a howling wolf	Common Loon
Squeaky, gurgling "COY-LA-*REE*" (rising), with the last note a raspy trill	Red-winged Blackbird

CHATTER OR TRILL	II Repeated notes
Dry rattle or rattling chatter, often given in flight	Belted Kingfisher
Squeaky, **jerky chatter**	Marsh Wren
Dry, fairly weak, slow trill "ZWEET-ZWEET-ZWEET..." with a husky quality	*Palm Warbler
Sweet, slow trill, like a musical, rich Chipping Sparrow	Swamp Sparrow

ONE NOTE REPEATED	II Repeated notes
Sharp, rather high-pitched "DEE-DEE-DEE-DEE-DEE..." (speed varies from fast to slow)	Killdeer
Sharp, nasal "PEENT" (with a buzzy or raspy quality), repeated after a generous pause	American Woodcock
Repeated "KRER-KRER-KRER", with a rolling of the "R" giving it a trilled quality (each note drops slightly at the end)	Red-bellied Woodpecker
Weak, high-pitched and rough "SEE-SEE-SEE-SEE..." (varying pauses between notes)	Blue-gray Gnatcatcher
Loud, rich, emphatic "TWEET-TWEET-TWEET-TWEET-TWEET"	Prothonotary Warbler
Sweet, slow, deliberate "SWEET-SWEET-SWEET-SWEET-SWEET" with a ringing or reedy quality	Swamp Sparrow

TWO NOTES REPEATED	II Repeated notes
Rising "KER-*WEE*" or "KA-*WEE*" repeated often	Sora
Nasal, resonant, bugling "KA-HONK KA-HONK KA-HONK"	Canada Goose
Sharp, fairly high-pitched "KILL-*DEE* KILL-*DEE* KILL-*DEE* KILL-*DEE*..."	Killdeer
Loud, rich "TWEEDLE-TWEEDLE-TWEEDLE"	Carolina Wren
Slow, almost insect-like "ZEEE-ZREEE" (second note rougher and lower)	Blue-winged Warbler
Very loud, rich "CHUR-*EE* CHUR-*EE* CHUR-*EE* CHUR-*EE* CHUR-*EE*"	Kentucky Warbler
Very loud, emphatic "*BEECHER-BEECHER-BEECHER-BEECHER-BEECHER*" (hesitant start and speeding up)	*Connecticut Warbler

THREE NOTES REPEATED	II Repeated notes
Deep, slow, pumping "OON-*KA*-LOONK" repeated with its hollow sound and rhythmic quality	American Bittern
Sharp, fairly high-pitched "*DEEE*-DEE-DEE...*DEEE*-DEE-DEE..." repeated many times	Killdeer

THREE NOTES REPEATED (continued)	II Repeated notes
Loud, rich "*TWEE*DLE-DEE *TWEE*DLE-DEE *TWEE*DLE-DEE"	Carolina Wren
Very loud, emphatic "CHICH-U-*EE* CHICH-U-*EE* CHICH-U-*EE* CHICH-U-*EE*" (hesitant start and speeding up)	*Connecticut Warbler
Loud, clear, rhythmic "*WIT*CHITY-*WIT*CHITY-*WIT*CHITY-*WITCH*"	Common Yellowthroat
Squeaky, gurgling "COY-LA-*REE*" (rising; last note a raspy trill), repeated after generous pause	Red-winged Blackbird

SEVERAL VARYING NOTES	III Short songs
Quick "YOODLE-OODLE-OO", a series of repeated, tremolo laughing calls	*Common Loon
Quick, rolling "*SEE*-SI-SI-*SEE*-SI-SI", sounding like "*Don't* Play A-*round* With Me" (weak and high-pitched)	Brown Creeper
Loud, liquid, hollow, flute-like song with a distinctive "*EO-LAY*" sound, ending in a trill	Wood Thrush
Sharp "CHICK" intro note, and short, sweet, **rapid warble** (moves quickly up and down in pitch)	Canada Warbler
Forced series of harsh clucks and a squeaky last note "CHACK–CHACK–KEEK-A-LEEK"	Common Grackle
"SWEET-SWEET-SWEET-*ZREE*-SUGAR-IT-IT-IT" – 3 sweet intro notes, a trill and buzzy ending	Song Sparrow
Loud, emphatic, sweet notes that speed up slightly and drop in pitch at the end "CHIP-CHIP-WHEET-WHEET-WHEET-TOO-TOO-TOO"	Northern Waterthrush
Slow, sweet intro notes or slurs (2-4), then quicker and dropping to a twitter "SEEE-SEEE-SEEE-SIREE-TWITTER-RIBBIT" or "SEEWEE-SEEWEE-SEEWEE-SIREE-TWITTER-RIBBIT"	Louisiana Waterthrush

CONTAINING A DISTINCT REPEATED NOTE OR PHRASE	III Short songs
Several tremulous "HOOTS" (commonly 8), sounding like "WHO-COOKS-FOR-*YOU*?...WHO-COOKS-FOR-*YOU*-ALL?"	Barred Owl
Sweet rapid "TWEET-TWEET-*TWEET* TWEEDLE-DEEDLE-*DEET*"	Yellow Warbler
Rapid chatter of stacatto notes speeding up and dropping "CHEE-CHEE-CHEE-CHEE CHE-CHE-CHE"	*Wilson's Warbler
Loud, rich "WITTA-WITTA-WI-*TE*-O" or "TA-WIT TA-WIT TA-WI-*TE*-O"	Hooded Warbler
Loud, high-pitched notes (single or double), and a lower, short trill "SWEET-SWEET-SWEET-TRRRR" or "SEEWEE-SEEWEE-SEEWEE-TRRRR"	Nashville Warbler
Variable – a loud, musical and short "CHEE-CHEE-CHEE-CHURR-*E*-AH", with a husky quality	Mourning Warbler

MANY VARYING NOTES	IV Long songs
Clear notes in a **descending whinny** and slowing down at the end	Sora
Very faint series of squeaky and raspy notes	Blue-gray Gnatcatcher
Loud mixture of squeaky, nasal and sweet notes and a slower **cat-like "MEW" call**	Gray Catbird
Long presentation of single or repeated notes with distinct pauses between each note or phrase	Yellow-breasted Chat

SINGLE-NOTE SONG	I Very short songs
Sharp, nasal "PEENT" (with a buzzy or raspy quality), from forest floor	American Woodcock
Loud, sharp "SKEOW" or "KEOW"	Green-backed Heron
Loud, guttural "WORK" or "QUAWK"	Black-crowned Night Heron
Weak, complaining or whining cry, like the "MEW" call of the Catbird. A down-slurred "EE-ERRR"	Yellow-bellied Sapsucker

CHATTER OR TRILL	II Repeated notes
Dry rattle or rattling chatter, often given in flight	Belted Kingfisher
Rapid twittering which stutters and changes speed (raspy and sharp), "ZEE-ZEE-ZEE-ZEEE-TEE-ZEE-TEE-ZEE"	Eastern Kingbird
Rapid, **dry, buzzy trill**, more rapid and weaker than the Chipping Sparrow	Worm-eating Warbler
Sweet, slow trill, like a musical, rich Chipping Sparrow	Swamp Sparrow

ONE NOTE REPEATED	II Repeated notes
Sharp, nasal "PEENT" (with a buzzy or raspy quality), repeated after a generous pause	American Woodcock
Series of nasal, ringing "COO-COO-COO" phrases (3-4 notes each)	Black-billed Cuckoo
Repeated "KRER-KRER-KRER", with a rolling of the "R", giving it a trilled quality (each note drops slightly at the end)	Red-bellied Woodpecker
Weak, complaining or whining cry, like the "MEW" call of the Catbird. Down-slurred "EE-ERRR" repeated slowly	Yellow-bellied Sapsucker
Slowly repeated, raspy, sharp notes, "ZEET–ZEET–ZEET–ZEET..."	Eastern Kingbird
Weak, high-pitched and rough "SEE-SEE-SEE-SEE..." (varying pauses between notes)	Blue-gray Gnatcatcher
High-pitched, emphatic "TSEET-TSEET-TSEET-TSEET-TSEET", delivered at moderate speed	American Redstart
Sweet, slow, deliberate "SWEET-SWEET-SWEET-SWEET-SWEET", with a ringing or reedy quality	Swamp Sparrow
Very loud, rich "TWEEER-TWEEER-TWEEER..." or "WHOIT-WHOIT-WHOIT-WHOIT..."	Northern Cardinal

TWO NOTES REPEATED	II Repeated notes
Slurred two-note "KIT-*ZEE*" (almost like one rising note), repeated fairly quickly	Eastern Kingbird
Emphatic "*FEE*-BEE" or "*FEE*-BREE" (second note lower and burry)	Eastern Phoebe
Very loud, rich "TWEEDLE-TWEEDLE-TWEEDLE" (delivered quickly)	Carolina Wren
Slow, almost insect-like "ZEEE-ZREEE" (seond note rougher and lower)	Blue-winged Warbler
Very loud, rich "CHUR-*EE* CHUR-*EE* CHUR-*EE* CHUR-*EE*"	Kentucky Warbler
Very loud, rich "*BIR*DY-*BIR*DY-BIRDY-*BIR*DY..." or "TU-*WEET* TU-*WEET* TU-*WEET*..."	Northern Cardinal

THREE NOTES REPEATED	II Repeated notes
Very loud, rich, whistled "*TWEE*DLE-DEE *TWEE*DLE-DEE *TWEE*DLE-DEE"	Carolina Wren

SEVERAL VARYING NOTES	III Short songs
Ascending, rapid spiral of hollow, flute-like notes	★Swainson's Thrush
Loud, liquid song, with hollow, flute-like notes and a distinctive "*EO-LAY*" sound, ending in a trill	Wood Thrush
Snappy song with a "CHICK" or "CHICK-SEE" intro, one version sounding like "CHICK-SEE-PUT-THE-GA*ZE*BO- UP"	White-eyed Vireo
Sharp "CHICK" intro note, and a short, sweet, **rapid warble** (moves quickly up and down in pitch)	Canada Warbler
Emphatic, sweet notes that speed up and drop in pitch at the end "CHIP-CHIP-WHEET-WHEET-WHEET-TOO-TOO-TOO"	Northern Waterthrush
Slow, sweet intro notes or slurs (2-4), then quicker and dropping to a twitter "SEEE-SEEE-SEEE-SIREE-TWITTER-RIBBIT" or "SEEWEE-SEEWEE-SEEWEE-SIREE-TWITTER-RIBBIT"	Louisiana Waterthrush
"SWEET-SWEET-SWEET-*ZREE*-SUGAR-IT-IT-IT" – 3 sweet intro notes, a trill and a lower buzzy ending	Song Sparrow

CONTAINING A DISTINCT REPEATED NOTE OR PHRASE	III Short songs
Several, rapid, buzzy notes on one pitch and a **final buzzy note which is higher**	Cerulean Warbler
High-pitched, emphatic "TSEET-TSEET-TSEET-TSEE-O (ending lower, or "*TSEEE*" ending higher)	American Redstart
Sweet, rapid "TWEET-TWEET-*TWEET* TWEEDLE-DEEDLE-*DEET*"	Yellow Warbler
Rapid chatter of stacatto notes speeding up and dropping "CHEE-CHEE-CHEE-CHEE CHE-CHE-CHE"	★Wilson's Warbler
Loud, rich "WITTA-WITTA-WI-*TE*-O" or "TA-WIT TA-WIT TA-WI-*TE*-O" ("TE" higher and "O" lower)	Hooded Warbler

MANY VARYING NOTES	IV Long songs
Rapid, chattering "KEK-KEK-KEK-KEK..." into "KYOLP-KYOLP-KYOLP" and slowing with a few "KUT-A-KOWP"s	Yellow-billed Cuckoo
Very faint series of squeaky and raspy notes	Blue-gray Gnatcatcher
Loud mixture of squeaky, nasal and sweet notes and a slower **cat-like "MEW" call**	Gray Catbird
Long presentation of single or repeated notes with distinct pauses between each note or phrase	Yellow-breasted Chat
Loud, highly variable series of notes (like Purple Finch), rich and sweet (like Robin), some repeated notes and a two-note burry ending	Orchard Oriole
Variable – a very loud, rich "TWEEER-TWEEER-TWEEER-WHOIT-WHOIT-WHOIT-WHOIT" (one and two note phrases)	Northern Cardinal
Series of short, **Robin-like whistles** (sweeter, higher-pitched, and shorter pauses), with a wavering, **tremolo quality**	Rose-breasted Grosbeak

SINGLE-NOTE SONG	I Very short songs
Sharp, nasal "PEENT" (with a buzzy or raspy quality), from the forest floor	American Woodcock
Loud, raspy scream, slurring downward "KEEAHHRR"	Red-tailed Hawk
High-pitched, shrill whistle, drawn-out, and weaker toward the end "KWEE-E-E-E-E" or "CHE-WEE-E-E"	Broad-winged Hawk
Harsh, **raspy scream or hissing**, with a cat-like quality (repeated after an interval)	Barn Owl
Weak, complaining or whining cry, like the "MEW" call of the Catbird. A down-slurred "EE-ERRR" (can be repeated slowly)	Yellow-bellied Sapsucker
Very loud single "WHEEP" or burry "FREEEP", each rising (can be repeated a few times in succession)	Great-crested Flycatcher
Loud, raspy, nasal "CAW" (may be repeated several times in succession)	American Crow

CHATTER OR TRILL	II Repeated notes
Soft, **muffled trill**, delivered with a wavering or tremulous quality	Screech Owl
Rapid, **dry, buzzy trill**, more rapid and weaker than the Chipping Sparrow	Worm-eating Warbler
Pleasant, **ringing trill**, with a slightly metallic quality (speed and pitch can vary)	Dark-eyed Junco

ONE NOTE REPEATED	II Repeated notes
Sharp, nasal "PEENT" (with a buzzy or raspy quality), from the forest floor	American Woodcock
Series of repeated screams, each slurring downward "KEEAHH-KEEAHH-KEEAHH"	Red-shouldered Hawk
Muffled thumping sound, speeding up to a rapid flurry "THUMP–THUMP–THUMP-THUMP-THUMP...PRRRR'	Ruffed Grouse
Loud "KEE-KEE-KEE-KEE-KEE...", similar to the Flicker's song, but louder (also slight changes in speed and pitch)	Pileated Woodpecker
Repeated "KRER-KRER-KRER", each note dropping slightly and with a rolling of the "R", giving it a trilled quality	Red-bellied Woodpecker
Weak, complaining or whining cry, like the "MEW" call of the Catbird. A down-slurred "EE-ERRR" repeated slowly	Yellow-bellied Sapsucker
Very loud "WHEEP" or burry "FRREEEP", each rising and repeated a few times in succession	Great-crested Flycatcher
Harsh, piercing and 'steely' "JAAY–JAAY–JAAY..." or a down-slurred, screeching "JEEAH–JEEAH–JEEAH...", both very loud	Blue Jay
Loud, raspy, nasal "CAW" repeated several times in succession	American Crow
Cheerful, bright and quickly repeated "DEE-DEE-DEE-DEE..."	Black-capped Chickadee
Loud, clearly whistled "PEEER-PEEER-PEEER" (each note rising) repeated fairly quickly	Tufted Titmouse
Rapid, nasal, low-pitched "WA-WA-WA-WA-WA..." or "KANK-KANK-KANK-KANK..." (a bit rough and burry)	White-breasted Nuthatch
Weak, high-pitched and rough "SEE-SEE-SEE-SEE..." (varying pauses between notes)	Blue-gray Gnatcatcher
High-pitched, emphatic "TSEET-TSEET-TSEET-TSEET-TSEET", delivered at moderate speed	American Redstart

TWO NOTES REPEATED — **II Repeated notes**

Series of repeated screams, each slurring downward "KEEAHH-KEEAHH-KEEAHH..." (the slur sometimes sounds like 2 notes repeated)	Red-shouldered Hawk
Two (or three) quick bursts "WHEEDLE-WHEEDLE-(WHEEDLE)", repeated after a generous pause – quite pleasant and musical but still has a sharp quality to it	Blue Jay
Clear, sweet whistled "*FEEE*-BEE", first note higher and longer, repeated after a brief pause	Black-capped Chickadee
Loud, clearly whistled "WHEEDLE-WHEEDLE-WHEEDLE" repeated fairly quickly	Tufted Titmouse
Slow, drawn-out "PEEE-*WEEE*" (second note slurred upward) repeated slowly	Eastern Wood-Pewee
Thin, high-pitched "*WEE*-SEE *WEE*-SEE *WEE*-SEE...", first note higher and emphasized (repeated rapidly)	Black and White Warbler
Very loud, rich "CHUR-*EE* CHUR-*EE* CHUR-*EE* CHUR-*EE*" emphasized on the second syllable	Kentucky Warbler
Very loud, emphatic "*BEECH*ER-*BEECH*ER-*BEECH*ER-*BEECH*ER-*BEECH*ER" (hesitant start then speeding up)	*Connecticut Warbler
Loud, clear "*TEACH*ER-*TEACH*ER-*TEACH*ER-*TEACH*ER..." repeated quickly and getting louder	Ovenbird

THREE NOTES REPEATED — **II Repeated notes**

At night, a rhythmic, snappy "*WHIP*-POOR-*WILL*" repeated over and over	Whip-poor-will
Slow, drawn-out "PEEE-A-*WEEE*" (last note slurred upward) repeated slowly	Eastern Wood-Pewee
Musical, rolling "WHEEL-DE-LEE" with a sharp "creaking wheelbarrow" quality, repeated after a short pause	Blue Jay
Clear, sweet whistled "*FEEE*-BEE-BEE" , first note higher and longer, repeated after a brief pause	Black-capped Chickadee
Very loud, emphatic "CHICH-U-*EE* CHICH-U-*EE* CHICH-U-*EE* CHICH-U-*EE*" (hesitant start then speeding up)	*Connecticut Warbler

SEVERAL VARYING NOTES — **III Short songs**

Quick, rolling "*SEE*-SI-SI-*SEE*-SI-SI" ("*Don't* Play A-*round* With Me"), weak and high-pitched	Brown Creeper
Loud, liquid, hollow and flute-like song with a distinctive "*EO-LAY*" sound, ending in a trill	Wood Thrush
Descending series of hollow, flute-like notes "VA-VEER-VEER-VEER-VEER"	Veery
Series of buzzy notes (3-5) rising up the scale "ZEEP-ZEEP-ZEEP-ZEEP-*ZEEE*" at a moderate speed	Black-throated Blue Warbler
Sharp "CHICK" intro note, and short, sweet, **rapid warble** (moves quickly up and down in pitch)	Canada Warbler
Short, sweet, Robin-like phrases "TWEER-TWEER-TUWEET-TUWEET-TWEER", delivered with a hoarse quality	Scarlet Tanager

CONTAINING A DISTINCT REPEATED NOTE OR PHRASE — III Short songs

Several low-pitched "HOOTS" (3-8), often with second and third notes quicker "WHOO–HOO-HOO–WHOO–WHOO"	Great-horned Owl
Several tremulous "HOOTS" (commonly 8), sounding like "WHO-COOKS-FOR-*YOU*?...WHO-COOKS-FOR-*YOU*-ALL?"	Barred Owl
Snappy, higher-pitched "CHICKA" intro followed by a rapid "DEE-DEE-DEE-DEE-DEE..." (squeaky yet bright and cheerful)	Black-capped Chickadee
Series of buzzy notes (3-5), with the last note higher "ZEEP-ZEEP-ZEEP-ZEEP-ZEEE" at a moderate speed	Black-throated Blue Warbler
Several, **rapid**, buzzy notes, with the last note higher "ZREE-ZREE-ZREE-ZREE-*ZREEE*"	Cerulean Warbler
Short, weak, very high-pitched "SWEET-SWEET-SWEET-*TRRRR*", last note a higher-pitched, slow, chirping trill. Also a quick "SEET-SEET-SEET-SEET-SEET-SEEDLEE-*SEET*", last note rising extremely high	Blackburnian Warbler
High-pitched, emphatic "TSEET-TSEET-TSEET-TSEE-O (ending lower, or "*TSEEE*" ending higher)	American Redstart
Loud, rich "WITTA-WITTA-WI-*TE*-O" or "TA-WIT TA-WIT TA-WI-*TE*-O" ("*TE*" higher, "O" dropping)	Hooded Warbler
Loud, high-pitched notes (single or double), and a lower short trill "SWEET-SWEET-SWEET-TRRRR" or "SEEWEE-SEEWEE-SEEWEE-TRRRR"	Nashville Warbler

MANY VARYING NOTES — IV Long songs

Soft, **muffled trill**, delivered with a wavering or tremulous quality	Screech Owl
Very faint series of squeaky and raspy notes, delivered rapidly and easily overlooked	Blue-gray Gnatcatcher
Loud staccato song, sharp and dry, and given **in three parts**. It starts slowly, speeds up and ends in a trill	*Tennessee Warbler
Short **Robin-like whistles** (with a **tremolo quality**), but sweeter, higher-pitched and more carolling than the Robin	Rose-breasted Grosbeak

CONSISTING OF SHORT VARIABLE PHRASES) — IV Long songs

Short, sweet, emphatic, **Robin-like phrases** (2-3 notes each) with brief pauses between each	Red-eyed Vireo
Short phrases, slower and lower than the Red-eyed Vireo's (rough or hoarse quality and longer pauses). A burry, whistled "EE-LAY...OH-LAY" with the "EE-LAY" higher than the "OH-LAY"	Yellow-throated Vireo
Short, sweet, **Robin-like phrases**, but **slower, sweeter and simpler** than the Red-eyed Vireo's song	Solitary Vireo

SINGLE-NOTE SONG | I Very short songs

Loud, raspy scream, slurring downward "KEEAHHRR"	Red-tailed Hawk
Loud, raspy, nasal "CAW" which may be repeated several times in succession	American Crow
Deep, nasal "GRONK" or other croaking calls, lower in pitch than the Crow's	Common Raven

CHATTER OR TRILL | II Repeated notes

Sweet, slow, trill "SWEE-WHEE-WHEE-WHEE-WHEE..."	Yellow-rumped Warbler
High, soft, **musical chirping** or trill, sweeter and fuller than the Chipping Sparrow's trill, and usually slower	Pine Warbler
Pleasant, **ringing trill**, with a slightly metallic quality (pitch and speed can vary)	Dark-eyed Junco

ONE NOTE REPEATED | II Repeated notes

Loud "KEE-KEE-KEE-KEE-KEE...", similar to the Flicker's song, but louder (also slight changes in speed and pitch)	Pileated Woodpecker
Repeated "KRER-KRER-KRER", with a rolling of the "R", giving it a trilled quality (each note drops slightly at the end)	Red-bellied Woodpecker
Loud, raspy, nasal "CAW" repeated several times in succession	American Crow
Deep, nasal "GRONK" or other croaking call (lower in pitch than the Crow's), repeated several times in succession	Common Raven
Series of nasal, twangy notes, more nasal and higher than the White-breasted Nuthatch "KNG-KNG-KNG-KNG..." (like a nasal "KING")	Red-breasted Nuthatch
Weak, very high-pitched series of notes (commonly 4-6) "SEE-SEE-SEE-SEE"	★Cape May Warbler
Sweet, rapid series of notes "SWEE-WHEE-WHEE-WHEE-WHEE..."	Yellow-rumped Warbler
Series of weak, high-pitched, tinny notes, louder in the middle "TSEE-TSEE-TSEE-*TSEE-TSEE-TSEE*-TSEE-TSEE-TSEE"	★Blackpoll Warbler

TWO NOTES REPEATED | II Repeated notes

Rapid "TEESI-TEESI-TEESI-TEESI" which is weak, short and high-pitched	★Bay-breasted Warbler

THREE NOTES REPEATED | II Repeated notes

Whistled "QUICK-*THREE*-BEERS" (second note highest, the third drawn out and dropping slightly), repeated often	★Olive-sided Flycatcher

SEVERAL VARYING NOTES | III Short songs

Quick, rolling "*SEE*-SI-SI-*SEE*-Si-SI" ("*Don't* Play A-*round* With Me"), weak and high-pitched	Brown Creeper
Very high-pitched series of "TSEE" notes (each rather long) ascending, then abruptly **dropping into a soft chatter**	Golden-crowned Kinglet
Ascending, rapid spiral of hollow flute-like notes, rolling up the scale	★Swainson's Thrush
Introductory, flute-like note, followed by several, clear, rising and falling, reedy notes "HEY-BREVITY-BREE" (repeated on different pitches)	Hermit Thrush
Rapid, buzzy trill, rising and snapping at the end "DSEEEEEEEEE-UH"	Northern Parula Warbler

SEVERAL VARYING NOTES (continued)
III Short songs

Buzzy "ZOO-*ZEE*-ZOO-ZOO-*ZEE*" ("TREES-*TREES*-MURMURING-*TREES*", third and fourth notes clearer and quicker)	Black-throated Green Warbler
Series of buzzy notes (3-5) **rising up the scale** "ZEEP-ZEEP-ZEEP-ZEEP-*ZEEE*" at a moderate speed	Black-throated Blue Warbler
Loud, rapid and **highly variable series of notes** (sweeter and clearer than the House Finch, with a softer trill ending)	Purple Finch

CONTAINING A DISTINCT REPEATED NOTE OR PHRASE
III Short songs

Several buzzy notes on the same pitch with the last buzzy note higher and usually rising. "TSWEE-TSWEE-TSWEE-TSWEEEE"	Northern Parula Warbler
Quick "ZEE-ZEE-ZEE-ZEE-ZEE-ZOO-ZEE", with the "ZOO" lower (clearer than its slower, buzzy song above)	Black-throated Green Warbler
Series of buzzy notes (3-5), with the last note higher "ZEEP-ZEEP-ZEEP-ZEEP-*ZEEE*" at a moderate speed	Black-throated Blue Warbler
Short, weak, rapid and variable. A whistled "SEEYA-SEEYA-SEEYA-*SOON*", last note higher, or "SEEYA-SEEYA-*SEAT*-YA"	Magnolia Warbler
Sweet, slow, trill (or slower, rapid series of notes), with the ending higher or lower	Yellow-rumped Warbler
Short, weak, very high-pitched "SWEET-SWEET-SWEET-*TRRRR*", last note a higher-pitched, slow, chirping trill. Also a quick "SEET-SEET-SEET-SEET-SEET-SEEDLEE-*SEET*", last note rising extremely high	Blackburnian Warbler

MANY VARYING NOTES
IV Long songs

High-pitched, sweet, three-note phrases ("TWIDDLE-*DEE* TWIDDLE-*DEE* TWIDDLE-*DEE*"), introduced by several, high-pitched, squeaky notes and a musical chatter (also a two-note version "HEDGY-HEDGY-HEDGY", emphasizing the first syllable)	Ruby-crowned Kinglet
Loud staccato song, sharp and dry, and given **in three parts**. It starts slowly, speeds up and ends in a trill	★Tennessee Warbler
Loud, rapid and **highly variable series of notes** (sweeter and clearer than the House Finch, with a softer trilled ending)	Purple Finch

CONSISTING OF SHORT VARIABLE PHRASES)
IV Long songs

Short, sweet, **Robin-like phrases**, but slower, sweeter and simpler than the Red-eyed Vireo's song	Solitary Vireo

SINGLE-NOTE SONG	I Very short songs
Loud, raspy scream, slurring downward "KEEAHHRR"	Red-tailed Hawk
Loud, raspy, nasal "CAW" (may be repeated several times in succession)	American Crow

TWO-NOTE SONG	I Very short songs
Very loud, harsh croaking "KROOOK-OOK"	Ring-necked Pheasant
Clearly whistled, medium-pitched "BOB – *WHITE*", the second note rising higher in exclamation	Northern Bobwhite

THREE-NOTE SONG	I Very short songs
Clearly whistled, medium-pitched "BOB – BOB – *WHITE*", the last note rising sharply higher in exclamation	Northern Bobwhite
Squeaky, gurgling "COY-LA-*REE*" (rising), with the last note a raspy trill	Red-winged Blackbird
Two very short, bubbly, gurgling sounds, followed by a thin, high-pitched, short whistle "GLUG-LA-*SEEE*"	Brown-headed Cowbird

ONE NOTE REPEATED	II Repeated notes
Sharp, quite high-pitched "DEE-DEE-DEE-DEE-DEE..." repeated many times (speed varies)	Killdeer
Sharp, nasal "BEEK – BEEK – BEEK..." (often in the evening sky)	Common Nighthawk
Long, rapid "KEE-KEE-KEE-KEE-KEE..." or "WICK-WICK-WICK..." (loud and ringing)	Northern Flicker
Loud raspy, nasal "CAW" repeated several times in succession	American Crow

TWO NOTES REPEATED	II Repeated notes
Nasal, resonant bugling "KA-HONK KA-HONK KA-HONK"	Canada Goose
Sharp, fairly high-pitched, repeated "KILL-*DEE* KILL-*DEE* KILL-*DEE*..." with the second syllable higher and emphasized	Killdeer
Clearly whistled, medium-pitched "BOB – *WHITE*", (rising sharply higher in exclamation), repeated after a generous pause	Northern Bobwhite
Jerky or snappy "*WEE*KA-*WEE*KA-*WEE*KA-*WEE*KA...", with a squeaky quality	Northern Flicker

THREE NOTES REPEATED	II Repeated notes
Sharp, high-pitched, repeated "*DEEE*-DEE-DEE...*DEEE*-DEE-DEE... *DEEE*-DEE-DEE..." repeated many times	Killdeer
Clearly whistled, medium-pitched "BOB – BOB – *WHITE*", (last note rising sharply higher), repeated after a generous pause	Northern Bobwhite
Squeaky, gurgling "COY-LA-*REE*" (rising; last note a raspy trill), repeated after a generous pause	Red-winged Blackbird
Two short, gurgling sounds, then a thin, high-pitched, short whistle "GLUG-LA-*SEEE*", repeated after a generous pause	Brown-headed Cowbird

SEVERAL VARYING NOTES — III Short songs

Sweet, gentle, variable warble (sometimes intro "CHICK" notes) "CHICK–PEEER-CHUR-WEE...PEEER-CHUR-WEE"	Eastern Bluebird
Rolling, "cheerful" series of short, sweet phrases, rising and falling "CHEERI*LY*-CHEERY-CHEERI*LY*-CHEER"	American Robin
Hesitating series of harsh clucks, ending with a high-pitched, squeaky note "CHACK–CHACK–KEEK-A-LEEK"	Common Grackle
Leisurely 4-5 note sweet, **slurred whistle** (first 3 notes slurring down; last 2 notes starting high again, also slurring down)	Eastern Meadowlark
Canary-like series of clear sweet notes (and trills) and drawn-out, squeaky notes (also its "PER-*CHICK*-O-REE" flight song)	American Goldfinch
"SWEET-SWEET-SWEET-*ZREE*-SUGAR-IT-IT-IT" – 3 sweet intro notes, a trill and a lower buzzy ending	Song Sparrow

MANY VARYING NOTES — IV Long songs

A couple of high-pitched, chirping notes slowly, then quickly into a rushed series of disjointed, **tinkling notes** (weak and unmusical)	Horned Lark
Sweet, gentle, variable warble (sometimes intro "CHICK" notes) "CHICK–PEEER-CHUR-WEE...PEEER-CHUR-WEE"	Eastern Bluebird
Rolling, "cheerful" series of short, sweet phrases, rising and falling "CHEERI*LY*-CHEERY-CHEERI*LY*-CHEER"	American Robin
Exuberant, bubbling, overflow of short notes that tend to trip over each other as the song speeds up	Bobolink
Series of chips, raspy and squeaky notes, and sharp twitterings, as well as its characteristic, down-slurred "*WHEEEE-ERR*"	European Starling
Canary-like series of clear, sweet notes (and trills) and drawn-out squeaky notes (also its "PER-CHICK-O-REE" flight song)	American Goldfinch
A few slow intro notes **accelerating** into a rich, high-pitched song and beautiful, **rich trill** at the end	Field Sparrow
Often three short intro notes followed by **two longer buzzy notes** (second lower) "TSIP-TSIP-TSIP-TSEEEE-TSAAAAY"	Savannah Sparrow

SINGLE-NOTE SONG	I Very short songs
Loud, raspy scream, slurring downward "KEEAHHRR"	Red-tailed Hawk
Sharp, nasal "PEENT" (with a buzzy or raspy quality), from the forest floor	American Woodcock
Harsh, **raspy scream or hissing**, with a cat-like quality (repeated after an interval)	Barn Owl
Very loud single "WHEEP" or burry "FREEEP", each rising (can be repeated several times in succession)	Great-crested Flycatcher
Loud, raspy, nasal "CAW" (may be repeated several times in succession)	American Crow

TWO-NOTE SONG	I Very short songs
Very loud, harsh croaking "KROOOK-OOK"	Ring-necked Pheasant
Clearly whistled, medium-pitched "BOB – *WHITE*", the second note rising sharply higher in exclamation	Northern Bobwhite

THREE-NOTE SONG	I Very short songs
Clearly whistled, medium-pitched "BOB – BOB – *WHITE*", the last note rising higher in exclamation	Northern Bobwhite
Slow, sad "OOO–OOO–OOO", heard from a distance (slurred intro note heard closer up); a generous pause when repeated	Mourning Dove
Two very short, bubbly, gurgling sounds, followed by a thin, high-pitched, short whistle "GLUG-LA-*SEEE*"	Brown-headed Cowbird

CHATTER OR TRILL	II Repeated notes
Soft, **muffled trill**, delivered with a wavering or tremulous quality	Screech Owl
High-pitched, rapidly repeated and **noisy twittering** (often seen in the sky over towns and cities)	Chimney Swift
Rapid twittering (with a raspy, sharp quality), which stutters and changes speed "ZEE-ZEE-ZEE-ZEEE-TEE-ZEE-TEE-ZEE"	Eastern Kingbird
High-pitched, thin trill or trilled note (chirpy or buzzy rather than sweet or musical) "SREEE – SREEE – SREEE"	Cedar Waxwing
Soft, high-pitched, **musical chirping or trill** (sweeter, fuller and usually slower than the Chipping Sparrow's trill)	Pine Warbler
Dull unmusical twitter or trill, consisting of **rapidly repeated sharp chips**	Chipping Sparrow

ONE NOTE REPEATED	II Repeated notes
Sharp, nasal "PEENT" (with a buzzy or raspy quality), from the forest floor, which is repeated after a generous pause	American Woodcock
Series of repeated screams, each slurring downward "KEEAHH-KEEAHH-KEEAHH"	Red-shouldered Hawk
Slow, sad "OOO–OOO–OOO", heard from a distance (slurred intro note heard closer up); a generous pause when repeated	Mourning Dove
Series of fairly nasal, ringing "COO-COO-COO" phrases (3-4 notes each)	Black-billed Cuckoo
Fairly high-pitched, but throaty or harsh "QUEER–QUEER–QUEER", with each note rising slightly in exclamation	Red-headed Woodpecker
Repeated "KRER-KRER-KRER", each note dropping slightly and with a rolling of the "R", giving it a trilled quality	Red-bellied Woodpecker

ONE NOTE REPEATED (continued)	**II Repeated notes**
Sharp, nasal "BEEK – BEEK – BEEK..." repeated with a short pause in between (sometimes sounds like "BEE-ICK")	Common Nighthawk
Long, rapid "KEE-KEE-KEE-KEE-KEE..." or "WICK-WICK-WICK..." which is loud and ringing	Northern Flicker
Fairly slow "ZEET–ZEET–ZEET..." with a raspy, sharp quality	Eastern Kingbird
Very loud "WHEEP" or a burry "FRREEEP", each rising and repeated a few times in succession	Great-crested Flycatcher
Harsh, piercing and 'steely' "JAAY–JAAY–JAAY..." or a down-slurred, screeching "JEEAH–JEEAH–JEEAH...", both very loud	Blue Jay
Loud, raspy, nasal "CAW" repeated several times in succession	American Crow
Cheerful, bright and quickly repeated "DEE-DEE-DEE-DEE-DEE..."	Black-capped Chickadee
Loud, clearly whistled "PEEER-PEEER-PEEER" (each note rising) repeated fairly quickly	Tufted Titmouse
Rapid, nasal, low-pitched "WA-WA-WA-WA..." or "KANK-KANK-KANK-KANK..." (a bit rough and burry)	White-breasted Nuthatch
Weak, high-pitched and rough "SEE-SEE-SEE-SEE..." (varying pauses between notes)	Blue-gray Gnatcatcher
High-pitched, thin trill or trilled note, slowly repeated with a chirpy or buzzy quality (not musical) "SREEE – SREEE – SREEE..."	Cedar Waxwing
High-pitched, emphatic "TSEET-TSEET-TSEET-TSEET-TSEET...", delivered at moderate speed	American Redstart
Very loud, rich "TWEEER-TWEEER-TWEEER..." or "WHOIT-WHOIT-WHOIT-WHOIT..."	Northern Cardinal

TWO NOTES REPEATED	**II Repeated notes**
Series of repeated screams, each slurring downward "KEEAHH-KEEAHH-KEEAHH"	Red-shouldered Hawk
Clearly whistled, medium-pitched "BOB – *WHITE* (rising sharply higher in exclamation), repeated after a generous pause	Northern Bobwhite
Jerky or snappy "*WEE*KA-*WEE*KA-*WEE*KA-*WEE*KA...", with a squeaky quality	Northern Flicker
Slurred, two-note "KIT-ZEE" (second syllable emphasized and sounding like one sharp rising note), repeated fairly quickly	Eastern Kingbird
Emphatic "*FEE*-BEE" or "*FEE*-BREE" (second note lower and burry)	Eastern Phoebe
Drawn-out "PEEE-*WEEE*" (second note slurred upward) repeated slowly	Eastern Wood-Pewee
Two sharp, dry notes, repeated quickly over and over; a snappy, emphatic "CHE-*BEK* CHE-*BEK* CHE-*BEK*..."	Least Flycatcher
Two (sometimes three) quick bursts "WHEEDLE-WHEEDLE" with a pleasant, musical, yet sharp quality, repeated with generous pauses	Blue Jay
Clear, sweet, whistled "*FEEE*-BEE", first note higher and longer, repeated after a brief pause	Black-capped Chickadee
Loud, clearly whistled "WHEEDLE-WHEEDLE-WHEEDLE" repeated fairly quickly	Tufted Titmouse

TWO NOTES REPEATED (continued)	II Repeated notes
Very loud, rich "TWEEDLE-TWEEDLE-TWEEDLE" (delivered quickly)	Carolina Wren
Slow, almost insect-like "ZEEE-ZREEE" (second note rougher and lower)	Blue-winged Warbler
Very loud, rich "*BIRDY*-*BIRDY*-*BIRDY*..." or "TU-*WEET* TU-*WEET* TU-*WEET*..."	Northern Cardinal
Short "DRINK-*TEA-EE-EE-EE-EE*" with the last note prolonged, higher and trilled; quite musical and delivered fairly slowly	Rufous-sided Towhee

THREE NOTES REPEATED	II Repeated notes
Clearly whistled, medium-pitched "BOB – BOB – *WHITE*" (last note rising sharply higher), repeated after a generous pause	Northern Bobwhite
Slow, sad "OOO–OOO–OOO", heard from a distance (slurred intro note heard closer up); a generous pause when repeated	Mourning Dove
Drawn-out "PEEE-A-WEEE" (last note slurred upward) repeated slowly	Eastern Wood-Pewee
Whistled "QUICK-*THREE*-BEERS" (second note highest, the third drawn out and dropping slightly) repeated often	*Olive-sided Flycatcher
Musical, rolling "WHEEL-DE-LEE" with a sharp, "creaking wheelbarrow" quality, repeated after a short pause	Blue Jay
Clear, sweet, whistled "*FEEE*-BEE-BEE", first note higher and longer, repeated after a brief pause	Black-capped Chickadee
Very loud, rich, whistled "*TWEE*DLE-DEE *TWEE*DLE-DEE *TWEE*DLE-DEE"	Carolina Wren
Two short, gurgling sounds, then a thin, high-pitched, short whistle "GLUG-LA-*SEEE*", repeated after a generous pause	Brown-headed Cowbird
"DRINK-YOUR-*TEA-EE-EE-EE-EE*" with the last note prolonged, higher and trilled;quite musical and delivered fairly slowly	Rufous-sided Towhee

SEVERAL VARYING NOTES	III Short songs
Quick, rolling "*SEE*-SI-SI-*SEE*-SI-SI" (*Don't* Play A-*round* With Me"), weak and high-pitched	Brown Creeper
Sweet, gentle, variable warble (sometimes intro "CHICK" notes) "CHICK–PEEER-CHUR-WEE...PEEER-CHUR-WEE"	Eastern Bluebird
Rolling, "cheerful" series of short, sweet phrases, rising and falling "CHEERILY-CHEERY-CHEERILY-CHEER"	American Robin
Snappy song with a "CHICK' or "CHICK-SEE" intro, one version sounding like CHICK-SEE-PUT-THE-GAZEBO-UP"	White-eyed Vireo
Warbling song that **rambles up and down**, with a slightly burry quality and **ends on an upswing** (common and repeated often)	Warbling Vireo
Series of thin, raspy, or buzzy notes (6–10) climbing up the scale "ZEE-ZEE-ZEE-ZEE-ZEE-ZEE..." (rising and getting faster)	Prairie Warbler
Hesitating series of harsh clucks, ending with a high-pitched, squeaky note "CHACK–CHACK–KEEK-A-LEEK"	Common Grackle
Rich one- and two-note phrases, some harsh notes mixed in, with quick changes in pitch and a **whippy or snappy rhythm**	Northern Oriole

SEVERAL VARYING NOTES (continued)	III Short songs
Short, sweet, Robin-like phrases "TWEER-TWEER-TUWEET-TUWEET-TWEER", delivered with a hoarse quality	Scarlet Tanager
Short, sweet, Robin-like phrases, like the song of the Scarlet Tanager, but **not as burry** (call notes like "CHICKY-TUCKY-TUCK")	Summer Tanager
Bubbly, loud and **highly variable series of notes** sung quickly and ending in a burry or harsh "CHURRR' (longer and dropping)	House Finch
Loud, rapid and highly variable series of notes (**sweeter and clearer than the House Finch**, with a softer trill ending)	Purple Finch
Canary-like series of clear, sweet notes (and trills) and drawn-out squeaky notes (also its "PER-CHICK-O-REE" flight song)	American Goldfinch
High-pitched **pairs of notes**, sharp and rhythmic, often with each pair at a lower pitch **down the scale**	Indigo Bunting
Two or three clear, sweet intro notes, followed by husky notes moving down the scale "ZWEE-ZA-ZA-ZOO-ZEE-ZOO"	*White-crowned Sparrow
"SWEET-SWEET-SWEET-*ZREE*-SUGAR-IT-IT-IT" – 3 sweet intro notes, a trill and a buzzy ending	Song Sparrow

CONTAINING A DISTINCT REPEATED NOTE OR PHRASE	III Short songs
Several low-pitched "HOOTS" (3-8), often with second and third notes quicker "WHOO–HOO-HOO–WHOO–WHOO"	Great-horned Owl
Slow, sad four-note song "OH-WOOO (rising) OOO–OOO–OOO", which is repeated after a generous pause	Mourning Dove
Several **rapid**, buzzy notes, with the last note higher "ZREE-ZREE-ZREE-ZREE-*ZREEE*"	Cerulean Warbler
Snappy higher-pitched intro "CHICKA", followed immediately by a rapid series of "DEE-DEE-DEE..." notes, all with a squeaky yet cheerful quality	Black-capped Chickadee
Quick series of notes (3-5) on the same pitch, with a snappy ending "SWEET-SWEET-SWEET-SWEET-TO-*BEAT*-CHA"	Chestnut-sided Warbler
High-pitched, emphatic "TSEET-TSEET-TSEET-TSEE-O" (ending lower, or "*TSEEE*" ending higher)	American Redstart
Sweet, rapid "TWEET-TWEET-*TWEET* TWEEDLE-DEEDLE-*DEET*" ("SWEET-SWEET-*SWEET* SWEETER-THAN-*SWEET*")	Yellow Warbler
Raspy, buzzing song of four notes, the first note longer and on a higher pitch. A lazy "*ZEEE*-ZREE-ZREE-ZREE"	Golden-winged Warbler
Loud, musical and short song, with a husky quality (highly variable) "CHEE-CHEE-CHEE CHURR-*E*-AH"	Mourning Warbler
One or two clear note(s) and then three 3-note phrases "OH-*SWEET*-CANADA-CANADA-CANADA" (slowly)	White-throated Sparrow

MANY VARYING NOTES	IV Long songs
Series of notes, sounding like a soft, **muffled whinny**, descending in pitch and with a tremulous quality	Screech Owl
Rapid, chattering "KEK-KEK-KEK-KEK..." into "KYOLP-KYOLP-KYOLP" and slowing with a few "KUT-A-KOWP"s	Yellow-billed Cuckoo

MANY VARYING NOTES (continued)	IV Long songs
Rapid burst of squeaky, rising notes, that **ends in a slightly lower, sweet trill**	House Wren
Very faint series of squeaky and raspy notes, delivered rapidly and easily overlooked	Blue-gray Gnatcatcher
Long series of notes, ranging from harsh to sweet whistles, **sung in couplets** (deliberately and separated by brief pauses)	Brown Thrasher
Loud mixture of squeaky, nasal and sweet notes and a slower, **cat-like "MEW" call** (no repetition)	Gray Catbird
Very loud collection of different notes and calls, with **each one repeated many times** in succession (6 or more)	Northern Mockingbird
Sweet, gentle, variable warble (sometimes intro "CHICK" notes) "CHICK–PEEER-CHUR-WEE...PEEER-CHUR-WEE"	Eastern Bluebird
Rolling, "cheerful" series of short, sweet phrases, rising and falling "CHEERI*LY*-CHEERY-CHEERI*LY*-CHEER"	American Robin
Warbling song that **rambles up and down**, with a slightly burry quality and **ends on an upswing** (common and repeated often)	Warbling Vireo
Loud, staccato song, sharp and dry, and given **in three parts**. It starts slowly, speeds up and ends in a trill	*Tennessee Warbler
Long presentation of single or repeated notes, with distinct pauses between each note or phrase	Yellow-breasted Chat
Series of chips, raspy and squeaky notes, and sharp twitterings, as well as its characteristic, down-slurred "*WHEEEE-ERR*"	European Starling
Loud, **highly variable series of notes** (like Purple Finch), rich and sweet (like Robin), some repeated notes and a **two-note burry ending**	Orchard Oriole
Rich, one- and two-note phrases, some harsh notes mixed in, with quick changes in pitch and a **whippy or snappy rhythm**	Northern Oriole
Variable – very loud, rich "TWEEER-TWEEER-TWEEER-WHOIT-WHOIT-WHOIT-WHOIT" (one- and two-note phrases)	Northern Cardinal
Bubbly, loud and **highly variable series of notes**, sung quickly and ending in a **burry or harsh "CHURRR"** (longer and dropping)	House Finch
Loud, rapid and **highly variable series of notes** (sweeter and clearer than the House Finch, with a **softer trilled ending**)	Purple Finch
Canary-like series of clear, sweet notes (and trills) and drawn-out squeaky notes (also its "PER-CHICK-O-REE" flight song)	American Goldfinch
Series of short, **Robin-like whistles** (sweeter, higher-pitched, and shorter pauses), with a wavering, **tremolo quality**	Rose-breasted Grosbeak
A few slow intro notes **accelerating** into a rich, high-pitched song and beautiful, **rich trill** at the end	Field Sparrow

CONSISTING OF SHORT VARIABLE PHRASES	IV Long songs
Short, sweet, emphatic, **Robin-like phrases** (2-3 notes each) with brief pauses between each	Red-eyed Vireo
Short phrases, slower and lower than the Red-eyed Vireo's (rough or hoarse quality and longer pauses). A burry, whistled "EE-LAY...OH-LAY" with the "EE-LAY" higher than the "OH-LAY"	Yellow-throated Vireo

Part 3

Going for a Walk

Introduction

In this section I have tried to create "in story form" an outline of what birds you might or should see (again in the breeding season) in each habitat, as you work your way through that habitat. The emphasis, in each case, is on *where to look* and *what to listen for* during your walk. Throughout this section I have used capitals to draw attention to the songs as well as to noteworthy descriptions and characteristics. My intention here is to make these significant sections stand out while casually reading, but more importantly to make quick reference and identification easier, while skimming or searching right in the field. These songs and descriptions are the keys to quick, effective identification.

As was pointed out in the introduction to this book, although most of the birds listed are quite common and widespread in the East, some of the birds are more locally common than others and some of the "northern breeders" may be seen only during migration in many areas. Each time a "northern breeder" is mentioned I have drawn attention to the fact in order to distinguish them as a special case. As a final check in order to establish exactly what birds to expect in your particular area, I mention again the information on ranges included in Part I for each bird, as well as refer the reader to the excellent range maps in the more popular bird guides.

I Marshes and Swamps

You are walking in the relatively open area around a pond which has marshy borders, with a scattering of small trees, scrub and bushes, or along a swampy or forested wetland area. Both of these wetland habitats provide an abundance of food as well as an interesting variety of potential nesting sites. As a result, they attract a similarly interesting variety of birds.

As you walk around the marsh, you will probably hear the "SQUEAKY, JERKY CHATTER" of the Marsh Wren among the cattails and reeds. You might also hear the "SWEET, SLOW TRILL" (sometimes single repeated sweet notes) of the Swamp Sparrow. The rhythmic "*WIT*CHITY-*WIT*CHITY-*WIT*CHITY" of the Common Yellowthroat is sure to catch your attention, as it skulks low in the reeds, or flits about in the surrounding bushes. One of the most common sounds in any marsh is the strident "COY-LA-*REE*" (rising up the scale, with the last note a harsh, raspy trill) of the Red-winged Blackbird. Overhead, a "DRY, RATTLING CHATTER" announces the presence of the Belted Kingfisher, as it flies rapidly to a new look-out or favourite perch, over the water.

Other birds often seen in the brush, scrub and small trees around the marsh include the Common Grackle, with its series of harsh clucks, rising and then ending in a high-pitched, squeaky note ("CHACK–CHACK–KEEK-A-LEEK"), the Song Sparrow (2-3 repeated, sweet notes, followed by a short buzzy "ZREE", a lower liquid trill, and ending with a lower, buzzy note – sometimes 2-3 notes, ("SWEET-SWEET-SWEET-*ZREE*-SUGAR-IT"), and the Yellow Warbler, with its rapid "TWEET-TWEET-*TWEET*-TWEEDLE-DEEDLE-*DEET*" (or "SWEET- SWEET-*SWEET*-SWEETER-THAN-*SWEET*" with the last note rising), which it repeats as it flits quickly from branch to branch among the smaller trees. The Gray Catbird's favourite haunt is the brush and tangles, and its distinctive "CAT-LIKE 'MEW' CALL" (a downward-slurred, raspy and squeaky note) is a common sound in this habitat, either given alone or as part of its full song, which is a "LOUD JUMBLE OF SQUEAKY, NASAL AND HIGH-PITCHED NOTES."

On the ground you may see a Killdeer, if the ground is fairly gravelly or sandy. Its loud "DEE-DEE-DEE..." or "KILL-*DEE* KILL-*DEE* KILL-*DEE*..." make it difficult to miss. You may also see Canada Geese ("KA-HONK KA-HONK KA-HONK"), if the shoreline vegetation is to their liking for nesting, or a Palm Warbler (with its dry, slow, slightly buzzy trill, "ZWEET-ZWEET-ZWEET-ZWEET-ZWEET-ZWEET") during migration, or even an American Woodcock (a single nasal "PEENT"), if there is a second growth wooded area near the marsh. If your marsh is on the edge of a deep northern lake a Common Loon could be another bonus sighting, or you may hear its wolf-like wailing call ("oh-OOOOO-ooo") or tremolo laughing calls (a quick "YOODLE-OODLE-OO") in the distance.

A swamp is nothing more than a forested wetland, which is flooded at least part of the year. This type of habitat can yield some other interesting, though, in many cases, less common species than those I have just mentioned. The beautiful golden-yellow Prothonotary Warbler (a sweet, emphatic and loud "TWEET-TWEET-TWEET-TWEET-TWEET-TWEET"), which nests in a tree cavity just above the water, is found here, and among the ground vegetation you might see the Kentucky Warbler (a very loud, emphatic and rich "CHUR-*EE* CHUR-*EE* CHUR-*EE* CHUR-*EE* CHUR-*EE*", emphasized on the second syllable), the Connecticut Warbler (a very loud, rich chirping song, which starts out slowly and speeds up "*BEE*CHER-*BEE*CHER-*BEE*CHER-*BEE*CHER-*BEECH*", or a three note version that sounds like "CHICH-U-*EE* CHICH-U-*EE* CHICH-U-*EE* CHICH-U-*EE*"), or the Palm Warbler (as mentioned above, a dry, slow, slightly buzzy trill "ZWEET-ZWEET-ZWEET-ZWEET-ZWEET-ZWEET'). These last two warblers are northern breeders, but can be seen and heard on migration, in a variety of habitats.

Other birds which are fond of the tangles and thickets around the swamp include the Yellow Warbler (a rapid "TWEET-TWEET-*TWEET*-TWEEDLE-DEEDLE-*DEET*"), the Nashville Warbler (a loud "SWEET-SWEET-SWEET-SWEET-TRRRR" or "SEEWEE-SEEWEE-SEEWEE-TRRRR", both with the final trill lower), the Wilson's Warbler, another northern breeder, with its series of staccato notes, dropping in pitch, and speeding up at the end ("CHEE-CHEE-CHEE-CHEE CHE-CHE-CHE"), the Canada Warbler, with its "SHORT, SWEET, VERY RAPID AND FIDGETY (up and down in pitch) WARBLE", introduced by a sharp "CHIP" or "CHICK" note, and the Carolina Wren (a loud, rich "TWEEDLE-TWEEDLE-TWEEDLE" or "*TWEE*DLE-DEE *TWEE*DLE-DEE *TWEE*DLE-DEE"). You might also be lucky enough to see the Hooded Warbler ("WITTA-WITTA-WI-*TE*-O", the "*TE*" higher and emphasized), the Mourning Warbler (a sweet, chirpy and loud song, first higher, and then lower "CHEE-CHEE-CHEE-CHURR-*E*-AH, CHEE-CHEE-CHEE-CHURR-AH"), the Blue-winged Warbler (a raspy, buzzy and slow "ZEEE-ZREEE", second note lower), or the Yellow-breasted Chat, with "ITS LONG, SLOW DELIVERY" of clear and burry whistles, harsh "caw"s and raspy Blue Jay-like calls, as well as some "kek"s or "crick"s thrown in for good measure. It has LONG PAUSES between each note or series of notes, and this makes it very distinct. You may also see the Blue-gray Gnatcatcher, but you will have to listen carefully for its song, a "THIN, RAPID SERIES OF BOTH SQUEAKY AND RASPY NOTES", which is quite faint and easily overlooked even in the breeding season. Its call is a high-pitched, rough and repeated "SEE-SEE-SEE-SEE-...". As your walk nears its end, you may hear, in nearby moist woodlands, the hollow, flute-like and yodelling phrases of the Wood Thrush, echoing in the distance ("*EO-LAY*" or "*EO-EO-LAY*").

II Streamside Groves and Thickets

This habitat includes those areas along streams where there are small stands of trees, as well as those areas where tangles, vines and small shrubs are present, and provide the necessary cover and protection desired by some species.

As you walk along the bank of such a stream, you will come across many of those birds which are commonly found in and around marshes and swamps. The "DRY RATTLE" of the Belted Kingfisher may attract your attention, or the repeated, single sweet notes of the Swamp Sparrow may be heard "SWEET-SWEET-SWEET-SWEET-SWEET-SWEET" (sometimes a sweet, slow trill). This is one of the favourite haunts of the Song Sparrow, which gives its "SWEET-SWEET-SWEET-*ZREE*-SUGAR-IT" (or a similar version) quite regularly, from among the shrubs and trees. It is also a favourite of the Gray Çatbird ("LOUD JUMBLE OF SQUEAKY, NASAL AND SWEET NOTES" and its "CAT-LIKE 'MEW' CALL"), which is usually seen low among the tangles. Less shy and retiring than the Catbird is the Yellow Warbler, which flits about among the stands of willow and alder, as it sings its quick, sweet "TWEET-TWEET-*TWEET*-TWEEDLE-DEEDLE-*DEET*" (or "SWEET-SWEET-*SWEET*-SWEETER-THAN-*SWEET*" with the last note rising). You are almost sure to hear the Carolina Wren before you see it, with its loud, rich "TWEEDLE-TWEEDLE-TWEEDLE" or "*TWEE*DLE-DEE *TWEE*DLE-DEE *TWEE*DLE-DEE". At dawn or dusk, especially in spring, you may even hear that characteristic, raspy, nasal "PEENT" of the American Woodcock, coming from ground level, among the scrubby edges or alder stands.

Continuing your walk, you are likely to encounter the buzzy, sputtering, sharp trill or twittering of the Eastern Kingbird (a series of "ZEE-ZEE-ZEE" notes). It could also be singing its slower, repeated "ZEET–ZEET–

ZEET..." notes, or its slurred "KIT-*ZEE*" (emphasized and rising sharply on the "*ZEE*", and sounding like one slurred note), which can be repeated fairly quickly. It is a fairly common song around streams and ponds, since it likes nesting in the small trees and shrubs along streams, often nesting right over the water. The characteristic "CHIP" call of the Northern Cardinal is another common sound among the streamside thickets, as the male and female slip quickly in and out of sight, going about their business. The very loud, sweet, one-note and two-note phrases of the Cardinal (which make up its song) may be delivered from a more elevated perch, such as the top of a nearby tree, and their sheer volume and richness make them almost unmistakeable. A loud "TWEEER-TWEEER-TWEEER..WHOIT-WHOIT-WHOIT-WHOIT...", or a two-note "*BIRDY-BIRDY-BIRDY*...", are common examples of its very impressive song.

Other birds to watch for, especially among the thickets, are the White-eyed Vireo (a quick, snappy song, introduced by a sharp "CHICK" note "CHICK-PUT-THE-GA*ZE*BO-UP"), the Yellow-breasted Chat (a LONG, SLOW DELIVERY of various whistles, harsh notes and "kek"s with LONG PAUSES after each note or series of notes), the Hooded Warbler (WITTA-WITTA-WI-*TE*-O", the "*TE*" higher and emphasized), and the Kentucky Warbler (a loud, rich "CHUR-*EE* CHUR-*EE* CHUR-*EE* CHUR-*EE* CHUR-*EE*", second syllable emphasized).

Coming from the thickets you may also hear the distinctive songs of these birds: the Blue-winged Warbler sings a raspy, buzzy and slow "ZEEE-ZREEE" (second note lower), with an almost insect-like quality, the Canada Warbler sings a "SHORT, SWEET, VERY RAPID AND FIDGETY (up and down in pitch) WARBLE" introduced by a sharp "CHIP" or "CHICK" note, and the Wilson's Warbler (a northern breeder) sings a series of staccato notes dropping in pitch and speeding up at the end ("CHEE-CHEE-CHEE-CHEE CHE-CHE-CHE").

Although the Black-billed Cuckoo prefers more wooded areas than the Yellow-billed Cuckoo, both species can be found in streamside shrubs and thickets. The Black-billed Cuckoo sings a rapid series of nasal and ringing "COO-COO-COO" notes (3-4 to a series), while the Yellow-billed Cuckoo delivers a rapid chattering "KEK-KEK-KEK-KEK-KEK", turning into "KYOLP-KYOLP-KYOLP" and ending with a few "KUT-A-KOWP"s, as it slows down toward the end. Another distinctive song, the "RAPID, DRY, BUZZY TRILL" of the Worm-eating Warbler, may be heard if your stream passes by a hilly area of deciduous forest, with shrubs and leaf-covered ground – its preferred nesting habitat.

Higher up in the trees bordering the stream, you are likely to see an American Redstart (a series of high-pitched, weak, yet emphatic, single notes [sometimes two-note phrases, similar to the Black and White Warbler]: "TSEET-TSEET-TSEET-TSEET-TSEET", with the last note often higher or lower). You may also see the Blue-gray Gnatcatcher, but you will have to listen carefully for its song, a "THIN, RAPID SERIES OF BOTH SQUEAKY AND RASPY NOTES", which is quite faint and easily overlooked even at the height of the breeding season. Its call is a high-pitched, rough and repeated "SEE-SEE-SEE-SEE...". Much easier to see and hear is the beautiful Rose-breasted Grosbeak, as it sings among the bushes and small trees. It sings a long series of short, "ROBIN-LIKE WHISTLES" (although "SWEETER AND HIGHER-PITCHED" than the Robin and with a hint of tremolo that the Robin lacks), that has a fairly jerky, up and down quality to it.

Still higher up in the trees, you may be lucky enough to see a Cerulean Warbler (several rapid, buzzy notes and a final, higher-pitched, buzzy note: "ZREE-ZREE-ZREE-ZREE-*ZREEE*"). Another bird to be on the lookout for is the Eastern Phoebe, which is not so much attracted to the groves or the thickets along the stream, as it is to the strategic placement of a bridge. This bird particularly likes to build its nest on a protected beam, under a bridge or often in a farm building. Its presence will be announced by its emphatic "*FEE*-BEE" or "*FEE*-BREE", with the first note higher and emphasized, and the second note often more raspy or burred.

Finally, if the area you are walking in has smaller fir and spruce trees on the border of a more mature coniferous forest, you may hear the "ASCENDING SERIES OF HOLLOW, FLUTE-LIKE NOTES" of the Swainson's Thrush rolling up the scale. If the area is mixed conifer and deciduous, you are more likely to hear the hollow, flute-like and yodelling phrases of the Wood Thrush, which prefers deciduous trees for nesting ("*EO-LAY*" or "*EO-EO-LAY*").

III Deciduous Forests

This habitat attracts birds which like the deep woods, as well as the edges and open areas of such woods.

As you set out for a walk among the hardwoods, you may have your attention diverted to the sky overhead, for this too is the home of the Red-tailed Hawk, and its loud, raspy, downward-slurred scream, "KEEAHHRR", is its way of proclaiming the fact. Nearby fields provide a steady supply of food. Continuing on, you are bound to hear the harsh, 'steely' "JAAY–JAAY–

JAAY..." or down-slurred "JEEAH–JEEAH–JEEAH..." of the Blue Jay. It may also be giving its repeated two-note or three-note phrases, which are less easily recognized by the casual birder. The two-note version sounds like "WHEEDLE-WHEEDLE", two quick bursts, which are quite pleasant and musical, and are repeated after a generous pause. The three-note version has its characteristic "creaking wheelbarrow" sound: a musical, rolling "WHEEL-DE-LEE", which is repeated after a brief pause.

The American Crow will be obvious by its size, as it flaps its huge wings just above the tree-tops, and utters its loud, raspy, nasal "CAW" (not as deep or resonant as the Common Raven's harsh or croaking notes, which are not associated with the deciduous forest). Another common song of the hardwoods, likely to be heard during your walk, is that of the White-breasted Nuthatch. It is a rapid, nasal and low-pitched "WA-WA-WA-WA-WA-WA...", or more burry "KANK-KANK-KANK-KANK...", delivered as it moves along from one tree trunk to the next, in search of insects.

In the more open areas or borders of the forest is where you'll find the Great-crested Flycatcher and the Eastern Wood-Pewee. Listen for the loud, single "WHEEP" or more burry "FRREEEP" (each rising) of the Great-crested Flycatcher, which may be repeated several times in succession. The Eastern Wood-Pewee sings its slow, drawn-out "PEEE-*WEEE*" or "PEEE-A-*WEEE*" (both with the last note rising), with a down-slurred "PEEE-YURR" thrown in every so often. In the more open areas of the forest, you will also hear the quickly repeated, cheerful "DEE-DEE-DEE..." notes (introduced by a higher-pitched squeaky "SICKA" or "CHICKA") of the Black-capped Chickadee. It may also be giving its clear, sweet, whistled "*FEEE*-BEE" song (first note higher and longer), which is repeated after a brief pause.

You will have to listen carefully for the "THIN, RAPID SERIES OF BOTH RASPY AND SQUEAKY NOTES" that belong to the Blue-gray Gnatcatcher. Its high-pitched and rough "SEE-SEE-SEE..." notes may also be heard coming from the trees overhead. The Tufted Titmouse, if there are any about, will be much easier to pick out, with its loud, clear, whistled "PEEER-PEEER-PEEER", delivered fairly quickly, or its whistled, two-note "WHEEDLE-WHEEDLE-WHEEDLE".

The four birds that follow are birds whose songs are often confused with the song of the American Robin and its sweet "CHEERI*LY*-CHEERY" phrases. Whereas the song of the Robin consists of 4-6 short, carolling phrases, followed by a pause, some of the vireos repeat their short phrases, over and over, with the same pause between each individual phrase. The word "carolling" would not apply. The Red-eyed Vireo is a very common bird of the deciduous forests. It gives "SHORT, SWEET, EMPHATIC, ROBIN-LIKE PHRASES", each separated by a brief pause and repeated over and over again. It sometimes gives the impression of questions and answers, as the ending, usually rising, sometimes drops in reply. Less common, the Solitary Vireo's song is "*SLOWER*, HIGHER AND *SWEETER* THAN THE RED-EYED VIREO'S", as well as having each phrase simpler and more to the point.

Listen for the hoarse or burry version of the Robin's song, delivered by the Scarlet Tanager, with its "TWEER-TWEER-TUWEET-TUWEET-TWEER", which moves up and down in pitch as it proceeds. The Rose-breasted Grosbeak, which prefers second growth woods by streams and clearings, has a "MUCH SWEETER AND HIGHER-PITCHED SONG THAN THE ROBIN", with less noticeable pauses between the phrases. It also has a hint of tremolo, which the Robin lacks, that makes it sound like a more "professional" singer. The Yellow-throated Vireo, which has been compared to the American Robin and the Red-eyed Vireo, has, to me, a much more distinct song. It sings a much slower song, with a rough or hoarse quality. One version sounds like a burry "EE-LAY..........OH-LAY" ("EE-LAY" higher), with a long pause between the two phrases. It repeats this with a similar long pause between deliveries.

The Cerulean Warbler likes the heights in deciduous forests and will be heard singing its rapid, buzzy "ZREE-ZREE-ZREE-ZREE-*ZREEE*" (first notes on the same pitch and the final note higher). The Blackburnian Warbler also likes the heights, but it is found in deciduous forests, only in the southern portion of its range. Its song is a short, weak and very high-pitched "SWEET-SWEET-SWEET-TRRRR" (last note an even higher-pitched trill). In contrast, you will find the American Redstart in young, second growth woods and among the thick growth of smaller trees on the edge of the forest. Listen for its weak, yet emphatic, individual notes, or two-note phrases ("TSEET-TSEET-TSEET-TSEET-TSEET" or "TSEETA-TSEETA-TSEETA-TSEETA-TSEETA"). The ending is often higher or lower, and can be alternated.

As you walk through the woods, there are many songs which will draw your attention downward, to the leaf-covered floor of the forest, or to the thickets and tangles that dominate the understory in places. One of the most characteristic songs of these lower reaches is the loud, clear "*TEACH*ER-*TEACH*ER-*TEACH*ER..." of the Ovenbird. It is accented on the first syllable and gets louder as it progresses. From the moist areas of the forest floor, you will also hear the descending, series of flute-like, hollow notes, belonging to the Veery: "VA-VEER-VEER-VEER-VEER", down the scale. From this same, moist habitat, you may hear another thrush. The Wood Thrush sings a loud, liquid song, with each phrase ending in a trill. Listen for the hollow, flute-like, thrush sound, and its distinctive "*EO-LAY*" sound (or "*EO-EO-LAY*") that gives it a "yodelling" quality.

Some of the warblers you might come across in the thickets and tangles of these moist, deciduous woodlands include the Hooded Warbler (a very loud, rich and clear "WITTA-WITTA-WI-*TE*-O", with the "*TE*" louder and higher, and the "O" lower), the Kentucky Warbler (a very loud, emphatic and rich "CHUR-*EE* CHUR-*EE* CHUR-*EE* CHUR-*EE* CHUR-*EE*", emphasized on the second syllable), the Connecticut Warbler (a northern breeder), with its very loud, clear "*BEE*CHER-*BEE*CHER-*BEE*CHER-*BEE*CHER-*BEECH*", which speeds up noticeably as it proceeds (as does its "CHICH-U-*EE*" three-note version), or you may hear the Canada Warbler singing its "SHORT, QUICK, SWEET AND FIDGETY (quickly up and down in pitch) WARBLE", which is introduced by a sharp "CHICK" or "CHIP".

If you are in an area of the forest which has a leaf-covered, shrubby hill-side, preferably with a stream nearby, you are in the ideal habitat for a Worm-eating Warbler. You will recognize it by its "RAPID, DRY, BUZZY TRILL". Another ground-nester partial to this ravine or hillside location is the Black and White Warbler, which is most often seen creeping along tree limbs, like a nuthatch, looking for insects. It sings a rapid, high and thin "*WEE*SEE-*WEE*SEE-*WEE*SEE...", with the first note higher and emphasized.

Throughout the forest, anywhere there is thick undergrowth, you might also hear the Ruffed Grouse, as it slowly thumps its wings and then speeds this action up into a rapid flurry. This "RAPID, MUFFLED THUMPING" is a common sound of spring in the deciduous forest.

Two ground-nesting warblers that prefer the forest edge and second growth woodlands, where there are brush and thickets, are the Nashville Warbler (loud, sweet notes, followed by a trill, on a lower pitch: "SWEET-SWEET-SWEET-SWEET-TRRR"), and the Tennessee Warbler ("SHORT, STACCATO NOTES GETTING FASTER AND LOUDER AND ENDING IN A TRILL"), a northern breeder which is noted for its persistent singing. The Black-throated Blue Warbler likes similar conditions, but is usually found in a mixed conifer-hardwood forest, where the nest is commonly constructed in a conifer sapling, but also in saplings of hardwoods, and in laurel and rhododendron thickets. Listen for its buzzy "ZEEP-ZEEP-ZEEP-ZEEP-*ZEEE*", with the last note noticeably higher.

If you are late on the trail, toward evening, or even on into dark, you may hear the raspy, nasal "PEENT" of the American Woodcock, or the snappy "*WHIP*-POOR-*WILL*" (of the bird by the same name, emphasized on the first and last notes), repeated over and over again, with almost no pause in between. In the south the Whip-poor-will's song is replaced by the equally snappy four notes repeated of the Chuck-will's-widow. All of these songs are delivered from the forest floor, and are delivered at a time when just about every other bird has already called it a day.

IV Evergreen Forests

The conifer forests, with their lush, cool, dense greenery have a special attraction for another large group of birds, many of them warblers. In general, this habitat includes those birds (dealt with in this book) which inhabit the conifer forests, as well as the edges and open areas of these forests.

Going for a walk in an evergreen forest is usually a refreshing experience (if we can overlook the insects), with its cool breezes, pleasant aromas and quiet solitude. Some of the birds encountered in and around the evergreen forest have rather distinctive songs. The Common Raven likes the tops of large conifers to nest in, when rocky ledges are not available, and its deep nasal "GRONK" is hard to mistake (or its other harsh notes, which are lower in pitch than the American Crow). Its close relative, the American Crow, will nest in either deciduous or coniferous forests, but it has a preference for conifers and usually nests high in the tree. Its harsh "CAW" is higher-pitched than the call of the Raven, but like the Raven it may be repeated several times in succession.

The Red-breasted Nuthatch, which builds its nest in tree cavities in conifers, has a very distinctive series of twangy, nasal notes ("KNG–KNG–KNG–KNG...", like a nasal "KING", sung at a moderate pace), which it delivers as it quickly picks its way, moving from one tree to the next. Still another inhabitant of the conifer forests with a very distinctive song is the Olive-sided Flycatcher (a northern breeder). It sings its famous "QUICK-*THREE*-BEERS" (emphasized and rising on the second note) at a moderate speed, and it is likely to be seen, setting out after insects from a dead branch at the top of a tree, and returning to the same spot, time after time. It tends to like the more open areas of the forest – the edges and clearings.

As you continue through the greenery, you are very likely to cross the path of a Ruby-crowned Kinglet. You will know it by its beautiful song, which consists of "HIGH-PITCHED, SWEET, 2- or 3-NOTE PHRASES (HEDGY-HEDGY-HEDGY or TWIDDLE-*DEE* TWIDDLE-*DEE*

TWIDDLE-*DEE*), INTRODUCED BY SEVERAL HIGH-PITCHED NOTES AND A MUSICAL CHATTER". Its nest may be found fairly close to the ground, but it may also be found in a tree as high as 100 ft. (30 m.) above the ground. The Yellow-rumped Warbler also has a great range in its nesting height, although it is usually found nesting only a short distance overhead. Its song is a sweet, slow, trill, "WHEE-WHEE-WHEE-WHEE-WHEE..." or a slightly sharper, sibilant "SWEE-WHEE-WHEE-WHEE..." (ending can also rise or drop).

Two other birds which have a similar wide range in nesting heights among the conifers include the Black-throated Green Warbler (with its slow, buzzy "ZOO-*ZEE*-ZOO-ZOO-*ZEE*", or its faster "ZEE-ZEE-ZEE-ZEE-ZEE-ZOO-ZEE"), and the Northern Parula Warbler (a loud, buzzy trill, rising and then snapping at the end, "DSEEEEEEEEE-UH", or several buzzy notes on the same pitch with the last buzzy note higher and usually rising, "TSWEE-TSWEE-TSWEE-*TSWEEEE*"). The Blackburnian Warbler is a bird that likes the heights and is found in the tops of fir and spruce trees. Its bright orange-yellow colour may attract your attention, but its short, weak, very high-pitched song might not ("SWEET-SWEET-SWEET-*TRRRR*", ending with a higher-pitched, slow, chirping trill). If the area you are in is dominated by pines, you will probably hear the "SOFT, HIGH-PITCHED, MUSICAL CHIRPING OR TRILL" of the Pine Warbler. It is sweeter, fuller and usually slower than the Chipping Sparrow's trill.

Both the Yellow-rumped Warbler (mentioned above) and the Magnolia Warbler can be found nesting at fairly lofty heights, but, like the Olive-sided Flycatcher, they are also birds of the more open areas and edges of conifer forests, as well as stands of smaller evergreens. When you find yourself in this type of habitat, listen for the sweet slow trill of the Yellow-rumped, "WHEE-WHEE-WHEE-WHEE-WHEE..." or a slightly sharper, sibilant "SWEE-WHEE-WHEE-WHEE..." (ending can also rise or drop) or the fairly weak, rapid, two-note phrases of the Magnolia Warbler ("WEETO-WEETO-WEETEE-*EET*", last note rising, or "SEEYA-SEEYA-*SEAT*-YA").

Three other warblers (all northern breeders) to listen for in the low conifer forests and forest edges are the Tennessee Warbler ("SHORT, STACCATO NOTES GETTING FASTER AND LOUDER AND ENDING IN A TRILL"), the Cape May Warbler (commonly 4-6 notes but as many as 11-12, which are high-pitched, weak and all on the same pitch: "SEE-SEE-SEE-SEE"), and the Blackpoll Warbler, (a series of weak, yet emphatic, single "TSEE" notes, that "GET STRONGER TOWARD THE MIDDLE AND THEN WEAKER AGAIN TOWARD THE END"). Look for the Tennessee Warbler and the Blackpoll Warbler on or fairly close to the ground. However you'll have to look up to see the Cape May, which likes to build its nest high in a spruce or fir, along the forest edge. Finally, in the smaller firs and spruce trees, along the border of mature coniferous forests, preferably in damp areas, and near streams, is where you will find the Swainson's Thrush (also a northern breeder). Its song is an "ASCENDING RAPID SPIRAL OF HOLLOW, FLUTE-LIKE NOTES", rolling up the scale.

In areas where the coniferous forest begins to blend with deciduous forest in a mixed forest habitat, several new birds introduce themselves. Although the Swainson's Thrush (mentioned above) could be found in this mixed woodland habitat, it would more likely be the Hermit Thrush that you would find here. Its song consists of a long, distinct, introductory, flute-like note, followed by several clear, rising and falling, reedy notes, in a slow, yodelling cadence ("HEY-BREVITY-BREE", last note higher, or "HEY-BREVITY-BREVITY", on the same pitch).

You will probably hear the Solitary Vireo singing its "SHORT, SWEET, ROBIN-LIKE NOTES, SIMPLY AND SLOWLY, WITH DISTINCT PAUSES BETWEEN EACH PHRASE". Two warblers are attracted to this mixed woodland habitat. You'll have to listen carefully for the short, weak, rapid and high-pitched "TEESI-TEESI-TEESI" (R.T. Peterson) of the Bay-breasted Warbler (another northern breeder). The song of the Black-throated Blue Warbler is more distinctive. Listen for 3-5 evenly spaced, husky or buzzy notes, on a fairly high pitch, with the last note noticeably higher and slurring upward ("ZEEP-ZEEP-ZEEP-ZEEP-*ZEEE*").

V Grasslands, Fields and Meadows

The habitat being explored here is a typically open area that has vegetation, but has not yet turned over to trees and shrubbery. Under the heading grasslands, which usually gives the impression of tall, lush prairie grasses, blowing in the wind, I have also included open, manicured lawns such as those found in gardens, parks and golf courses in a more urban type of setting.

As you walk through a field in open or farm country (with grass and a scattering of short growth and weeds), you are very likely to see a bird, which is quite common, but is probably more closely associated with the air above, than with the fields that it hunts in. That is the Red-tailed Hawk. It is easily recognized by its loud, raspy, downward-slurred scream, "KEEAHHRR", which is given as it soars in the sky overhead. Another similar case is the Common Nighthawk, since it is most often seen "winging it" after insects in the waning light of the evening sky, and not so often in the open country, where it nests. Its sharp, nasal "BEEK – BEEK – BEEK..." sounds a bit like the American Woodcock (but the Woodcock's version would only be heard on the ground).

As noticeable in the air as on the ground, simply because of its size, is the American Crow. Its loud, raspy, nasal "CAW", which can be repeated several times in succession, will definitely attract your attention, if it has escaped it to this point. As the Crow quietens down, you might hear the sweet warble of the Eastern Bluebird. All it needs is a post or tree (for perching and nesting) in the open fields and it is happy. You will hear its short, sweet, gentle and variable warble, sometimes introduced by a couple of "CHICK" notes. "CHICK–PEEER-CHUR-WEE...PEEER-CHUR-WEE"

Continuing your walk through this grassy field, you hear a loud, harsh, croaking "KROOOK-OOK". This is the Ring-necked Pheasant, and it is usually very secretive and well hidden in the grass, as it forages on the ground. Also, especially if your field borders a pond or lake, you may come upon some nesting Canada Geese, obvious by their size and appearance, and also by their 2-note "breaking" "KA-HONK KA-HONK KA-HONK". In this same field, you may see the Northern Bobwhite on a post or other favourite perch, as it delivers its clearly whistled "BOB – *WHITE*" (with the second note rising higher in exclamation). Open fields and meadows are also the home of the Eastern Meadowlark. Its heavy-winged flight is as distinctive as its leisurely, down-slurred 4- or 5-note song (a clear, sweet, whistled "SEE-YOU-SOON" slurring downward, then starting high again "NOT-NOW", also slurring downward).

As you proceed, you may hear the strident "COY-LA-*REE*" (last note emphasized, rising and trilled) of the Red-winged Blackbird, for it is just as much at home here as in a cattail marsh, or other wet area. One of the most beautiful songs you are likely to hear on this outing is that of the Field Sparrow. "IT STARTS SLOWLY AND SPEEDS UP, ENDING IN A BEAUTIFUL, RICH TRILL". Where the field has a little thicker covering of weeds and thistles, you are sure to find the American Goldfinch, feeding on the thistles. It will probably be singing its "CANARY-LIKE SONG", which combines "DRAWN-OUT SQUEAKY NOTES AND TRILLS" with its diagnostic, whippy "PER-*CHICK*-O-REE" (emphasized on the second note). This phrase is also commonly delivered on the uprise of its undulating flight. In this same type of growth, along a roadway or fence is where you should find the Song Sparrow. Its song consists of two to three repeated sweet notes, followed by a short, buzzy "ZREE", a lower liquid trill, and ending with a lower buzzy note (sometimes two to three notes). "SWEET-SWEET-SWEET-*ZREE*-SUGAR-IT-IT-IT".

As was mentioned at the beginning, some birds find the close-cut and well maintained grasslands of parks, lawns and golf courses to their liking. The following birds are found in the farm country and open grasslands that you were just walking in, but they also have a special association with this more urban type of habitat. First among this group is the American Robin, a familiar sight on just about any newly cut or newly watered lawn. Its persistent singing is most noticeable in the early morning or evening, with its "CHEERI*LY*-CHEERY" phrases filling the air in both country and city. The Northern Flicker devours countless ants, as it scours parks and lawns, and its loud, rapid, repeated "KEE-KEE-KEE-KEE-KEE-KEE...", or "*WEE*KA-*WEE*KA-*WEE*KA-*WEE*KA..." are common sounds of the grasslands, fields and open woodlands that it frequents.

European Starlings ("RASPY, SQUEAKY NOTES AND SHARP TWITTERINGS, AND ITS CHARACTERISTIC, DOWN-SLURRED 'WHEEEE-ERR'"), Brown-headed Cowbirds (2 very short, bubbly, gurgling sounds, followed by a thin, high-pitched, short whistle "GLUG-LA-*SEEE*") and Common Grackles (short, forced, harsh clucks, ending in a high-pitched, squeaky note, "CHACK–CHACK–KEEK-A-LEEK") are often seen in flocks, feeding on lawns and in fields. Killdeer often frequent similar grassy areas, and their sharp, piercing cries (a repeated "DEE-DEE-DEE..." or 3-note "*DEEE*-DEE-DEE...*DEEE*-DEE-DEE..." are common sounds in these areas. They are hard to miss, as they are easily disturbed and protest loudly.

VI Open Woodlands and Brushy Areas

This habitat grouping includes areas that have tree covering, but in a rather open, or scattered fashion (orchards, parks or second growth areas with small trees and bushes for example). It also includes brushy areas that adjoin woodlands, or brushy areas that are found along roadsides, fencerows or in clearings. I have tried to limit the birds in this category to those which are identified with such open woodlands and such open areas. I include here those birds who inhabit the brushy borders of forests but who are also at home nesting in other more open brushy areas away from the forest. Those birds whose primary association is with the forest itself (and its brushy or open areas) have been dealt with in previous categories. Some overlap in the habitat categories is inevitable though. There are those birds, for instance, who are just as much at home in the deep woods as they are in the more open woodlands or orchards. In fact the very reason I chose to join the two habitat types dealt with here, is that so many of the birds of the brushy areas are also associated with open woodlands and wood margins. Because this habitat grouping includes orchards, parks and the transition zones between forests and fields, it offers a rich diversity of conditions and surroundings, and an amazing variety of birds.

Open woodland areas are probably the most accessible of all the habitats listed here. You could be walking in a local park or cemetery, or along a country road, or simply sitting in your camp-site, or on the verandah of your favourite country retreat, and you could hear many of the birds listed for this habitat.

One common song of the open woodlands (often confused by many people for an owl) is the soft "OOO–OOO–OOO" of the Mourning Dove, as it sits on a wire or a branch. The Eastern Kingbird may be singing its raspy, twittering, high-pitched notes (a series of "ZEE-ZEE-ZEE notes which sputter and change speed), as it flits about after insects, often in smaller trees. It could also be singing its slower, repeated "ZEET–ZEET–ZEET..." notes or its slurred "KIT-*ZEE*" (emphasized and rising sharply on the "*ZEE*", and sounding like one slurred note). Another common song you are very likely to hear is the loud and rapidly repeated "KEE-KEE-KEE-KEE-KEE-KEE-KEE..." of the Northern Flicker, or its squeaky, two-note "*WEE*KA-*WEE*KA-*WEE*KA-*WEE*KA...".

Every bit as common as the Flicker's strident song is the dainty, cheerful "CHICKA-DEE-DEE-DEE" of the Black-capped Chickadee. It may also be giving its characteristic two-note "*FEEE*-BEE" (first note higher and longer), or a three-note version which quickly repeats the last note. The bird which is named for its "FEE-BEE" song, the Eastern Phoebe, gives a much more emphatic delivery. Its repeated "*FEE*-BEE", or "*FEE*-BREE" song usually has the second note lower and also raspy or burry. It has a special preference for areas around farm buildings and bridges (for nesting). You may just as easily hear the slow drawl of the Eastern Wood-Pewee, "PEEE-*WEEE*" (or "PEEE-A-*WEEE*"), with an upward inflection on the last note, and a downward-slurred "PEEE-YURR", which is thrown in every once in a while for variety. This series of phrases is usually repeated many times, with a generous pause between each delivery. In the upper levels of tall deciduous trees is where you will find the Cerulean Warbler, especially where ground cover is sparse. It sings a rapid, buzzy "ZREE-ZREE-ZREE-ZREE-*ZREEE*" (first notes on the same pitch and the final note higher).

As you move about, the loud, rising "WHEEP" or "FRREEEP" (single or repeated a few times) of the Great-crested Flycatcher is sure to catch your attention. Another loud entertainer of the open woodlands is the Blue Jay, with its harsh, 'steely' "JAAY–JAAY–JAAY...", or its down-slurred "JEEAH–JEEAH–JEEAH...". It may also be giving its two- or three-note phrases, which are not as easily recognized by the casual birder. The two-note version sounds like "WHEEDLE-WHEEDLE", two quick bursts, which are quite pleasant and musical, and are repeated after a generous pause. The three-note version has its characteristic "creaking wheelbarrow" sound: a sharp, yet musical, rolling "WHEEL-DE-LEE", which is repeated after a brief pause. Not as high up in the trees, a rapid, low-pitched "WA-WA-WA-WA-WA-WA-WA..." or burry "KANK-KANK-KANK-KANK-KANK-KANK..." tells us that the White-breasted Nuthatch is nearby.

It is also quite likely that you will hear the song of the Least Flycatcher during your walk. Its snappy and emphatic two-note song is repeated over and over: "CHE-*BEK* CHE-*BEK* CHE-*BEK*..." (strongly accented on the second syllable). Among the trees or scrub you may also come across the Blue-gray Gnatcatcher whose distinctive song is quite faint and easily overlooked ("A THIN, RAPID SERIES OF BOTH SQUEAKY AND RASPY NOTES"). Its call is a high-pitched, rough and repeated "SEE-SEE-SEE-SEE...".

The Warbling Vireo's song is definitely one of the more common and persistent songs of the open woodlands, and it is fairly easy to identify with practice. "IT WARBLES QUICKLY UP AND DOWN" as it progresses (with a slightly 'burry' quality), and then "ENDS ON AN UPSWING". Listen for this diagnostic last note, which always finishes the song on an upswing. During the spring migration you could very easily come upon the Olive-sided Flycatcher in the open areas of deciduous and mixed woodlands. You will recognize its very distinctive, whistled "QUICK-*THREE*-BEERS" (second note highest and the last note drawn out and sliding slightly downward). After migration it is found on its breeding grounds in the open areas of northern coniferous and mixed woodlands.

The American Robin's song consists of a series of sweet, "cheerful", two- and three-note phrases ("CHEERI*LY*-CHEERY-CHEERI*LY*-CHEER"), which is then repeated, after a noticeable pause. From spring into early summer, it serenades us in the very early morning (often before sunrise) and in the evening. The pause between deliveries is not as noticeable during its early morning concerts and as a result it sometimes sounds more like one continuous carolling song. Many of the vireo songs have a similar sound to that of the Robin, in that they have short sweet phrases. However the phrases are usually more abrupt and with longer pauses between each. The word "carolling" would not apply.

For instance, a very common song of the open woodlands is that of the Red-eyed Vireo. You will hear "SHORT, SWEET, EMPHATIC, ROBIN-LIKE PHRASES, WITH SHORT PAUSES IN BETWEEN" that are delivered over and over again. It sometimes gives the impression of questions and answers, as the ending, usually rising, sometimes drops in reply. Although the Yellow-throated Vireo's song has similarities to that of the Red-eyed Vireo, you will notice that its short phrases are much slower, lower-pitched and have a rough or hoarse quality. One common combination sounds like a burry "EE-LAY.......... OH-LAY" ("EE-LAY" higher), with a long pause between the two phrases. It is repeated with a similar long pause between deliveries.

During your walk in the open woodlands you may also come across two other birds whose songs have been compared to that of the American Robin. If you hear a Robin singing with a distinct hoarse or burry quality, chances are you're listening to a Scarlet Tanager. It sings "TWEER-TWEER-TUWEET-TUWEET-TWEER", and the song moves up and down in pitch as it proceeds. The Rose-breasted Grosbeak, which prefers second growth woods and bushes by streams and clearings, "HAS A MUCH SWEETER AND HIGHER-PITCHED SONG THAN THE ROBIN," with less noticeable pauses between the phrases. It also has a hint of tremolo, which the Robin lacks, that makes it sound like a more "professional" singer.

Both the Carolina Wren and the Northern Cardinal have very loud and beautiful songs. The Carolina Wren, which tends to sing from a lower perch, sings a loud, rich and sweet "TWEEDLE-TWEEDLE-TWEEDLE", or a three-note "*TWEE*DLE-DEE *TWEE*DLE-DEE *TWEE*DLE-DEE" (both sung quickly). The Cardinal, which likes to sing from a more elevated perch, also sings a very loud, rich song, but it tends to repeat its one- and two-note phrases many times, as well as combine them. Some common examples include a drawn-out "TWEEER-TWEEER-TWEEER-TWEEER...", or a quicker "WHOIT-WHOIT-WHOIT-WHOIT...", or a "CHET-CHET-CHET-CHET...", like a chatter, any of which could be combined with its two-note songs that sound like "*BIRDY-BIRDY-BIRDY-BIRDY...*" (emphasized on the first syllable), or "TU-*WEET* TU-*WEET* TU-*WEET* TU-

WEET..." (accented on the last syllable). In the same area, you may hear the Tufted Titmouse whose song also has similarities to that of the Carolina Wren. However, its loud, whistled "PEEER-PEEER-PEEER", or its two-note "WHEEDLE-WHEEDLE-WHEEDLE" (both of which are sung fairly quickly) are more clear and whistled than the full, rich song of the Carolina Wren.

As you proceed on your walk, your attention may be drawn to one of four birds in the sky overhead. You may hear the loud, raspy, downward-slurred scream of the Red-tailed Hawk ("KEEAHHRR"), or the "HIGH-PITCHED, NOISY 'TWITTERING' " of several Chimney Swifts, or, especially in the evening sky, several Common Nighthawks, uttering their sharp, nasal "BEEK – BEEK – BEEK..." sounds, as they fly about, erratically, after insects. Finally, you may see the American Crow, as it flaps its huge wings just above the tree-tops, and utters its loud, raspy, nasal "CAW" (once, or several times in succession).

Back on the ground again, and suddenly there's a flurry of activity. You find yourself on the edge of an old apple orchard. Up in the tree in front of you is a blue bird that is singing "HIGH-PITCHED PAIRS OF NOTES", with each pair at a lower pitch down the scale. This is the Indigo Bunting. Then, in the tree next to it, you hear the sweet, rapid "TWEET-TWEET-*TWEET*-TWEEDLE-DEEDLE-*DEET*" (or "SWEET-SWEET-*SWEET*-SWEETER-THAN-*SWEET*" with the last note rising) of the Yellow Warbler, and see it flitting from branch to branch. Not far from there you see some movement in a large shrub with red berries on it. A pair of Cedar Waxwings gives its distinctive high-pitched, buzzy trilled notes (or longer single clear note): "SREEEE – SREEEE – SREEEE...",as they feed on the berries. Then a Northern Oriole pipes in with its "LOUD SONG, WHICH IS A SERIES OF CLEAR, RICH WHISTLES" (some prolonged), with harsh clicks and burry notes thrown in, as well as "RAPID CHANGES IN PITCH". The rapid changes in pitch give its song a rather whippy rhythm.

Over by the field, emerging from a hole in one of the apple trees, an Eastern Bluebird sings its short, sweet, gentle warble, which it introduces with a "CHICK" note: "CHICK–PEEER-CHUR-WEE...PEEER-CHUR-WEE". As you walk over to inspect, the flash of an American Goldfinch catches your eye, and as it feeds on a thistle in the neighbouring field, you can hear it singing. Its "CANARY-LIKE SONG" consists of clear, sweet notes, combined with trills and obvious "DRAWN-OUT, SQUEAKY NOTES". It also works in, what is usually referred to as its "diagnostic" flight song – a clear and whippy "PER-*CHICK*-O-REE", emphasized on the second note. As it flies off, you hear this phrase, delivered on the uprise of its undulating flight.

In this same field, but coming from the clearing, over by the edge of the adjoining forest, is the beautiful, rich trill of the Field Sparrow. It starts with a few slow, sweet, introductory notes and then "ACCELERATES INTO THAT VERY RICH, SWEET, HIGH-PITCHED SONG AND BEAUTIFUL TRILL". Finally, you notice the very distinctive sharp twitter or trill of the Chipping Sparrow. Its "RAPIDLY REPEATED, SHARP CHIPS" are being sung from the top of a small shrub. (The very similar, but softer and sweeter trill of the Pine Warbler would be heard in areas of open pine woods, but it can be found in mixed or deciduous growth during migration.) Although, this has been a fictional re-creation of what might be seen and heard on a walk through an apple orchard, it is, in reality, quite possible, on a good day, to see all of these birds, and probably a good many more. A good ear can make identification much simpler, and can make your outing that much more enjoyable.

Some of the more common birds that you are likely to find in the thickets and tangles of the open woodlands include the Brown Thrasher, the Mockingbird, the Gray Catbird and the White-eyed Vireo. The Brown Thrasher commonly REPEATS EACH NOTE OR PHRASE, SINGING IN COUPLETS. Its song has both harsh and sweet whistles, sung deliberately, with a noticeable pause between each couplet. The Mockingbird has a "LONG SERIES OF VERY LOUD NOTES AND PHRASES, WITH EACH ONE *REPEATED MANY TIMES*".

The Gray Catbird, on the other hand, has "*NO REPETITION* IN ITS LOUD, JUMBLED MIXTURE OF SQUEAKY, NASAL AND SWEET NOTES", but it does have a very distinctive "CAT-LIKE 'MEW' CALL", which is different and much slower than its other notes. Listen for this call which is sometimes repeated several times on its own, with generous pauses in between. The White-eyed Vireo will catch your attention with its snappy, short song, which begins with a "CHICK" or "CHICK-SEE", and then is followed immediately (in one common version) by what sounds like "PUT-THE-GA*ZE*BO-UP", strongly accented and rising on the "*ZE*" and then dropping. Another version leaves the last note off ("CHICK-BUILD-THE-GA*ZE*BO"). It also utters a rapid "CHICK-*THREE*-BEERS" (the "*THREE*" rising and emphasized).

Another bird often found among the tangles and in the brushy areas of open woodlands and wood margins is the Song Sparrow, whose song consists of two to three repeated sweet notes, followed by a short, buzzy

"ZREE", a lower liquid trill, and ending with a lower buzzy note (sometimes two to three notes), "SWEET-SWEET-SWEET-*ZREE*-SUGAR-IT-IT-IT". It is quite common and likes moist areas or streamside thickets, but is also found along roadsides and in drier areas. Still other birds to be found here include the Rufous-sided Towhee, with its distinct, three-note "DRINK-YOUR-*TEA-EE-EE-EE-EE* (last note prolonged, higher and trilled), the American Redstart (high-pitched, weak, yet emphatic, individual notes, or sometimes two-note phrases, similar to the Black and White Warbler's song: "TSEET-TSEET-TSEET-TSEET-TSEET" or "TSEETA-TSEETA-TSEETA-TSEETA-TSEETA" (last note often higher or lower).

You may also hear the Chestnut-sided Warbler, which gives its three to five quick, introductory notes (almost like a trill), and then a snappy ending: "SWEET-SWEET-SWEET-SWEET-TO-*BEAT*-CHA" (the "*BEAT*" accented and highest, and the last note dropping), the Prairie Warbler, with its series of thin, buzzy notes (6-10), climbing up the scale: "ZEE-ZEE-ZEE-ZEE-ZEE..." (rising and getting faster), the Blue-winged Warbler, giving its slow, almost insect-like "ZEEE-ZREEE" (second note lower and rougher) and the Mourning Warbler, which has a loud, musical and short song with considerable variation and a burry or husky delivery: "CHEE-CHEE-CHEE CHURR-*E*-AH" or "CHEE-CHEE-CHEE CHO-CHO-CHO". Here too you will find the Tennessee Warbler ("SHORT STACCATO NOTES GETTING FASTER AND LOUDER AND ENDING IN A TRILL"), although it will be seen mainly in migration in many areas, since it is, once again, one of those northern breeders.

In the brushy areas of open woodlands, two other sparrows should be expected. First you should hear the White-throated Sparrow, singing its very distinctive and rhythmic "OH-SWEET CANADA-CANADA-CANADA" (high and sweet, and with a similar rhythm to the "WITCHITY-WITCHITY-WITCHITY" of the Common Yellowthroat, but with a slower delivery). The White-crowned Sparrow would be heard mainly in migration, since it breeds in the far northern, stunted woodlands. Its song starts like the White-throated Sparrow's, but follows through with husky or raspy, notes moving down the scale, and ending in a low trill: "ZWEE-ZA-ZA-ZOO-ZEE-ZOO". Both cuckoos are also fond of the thickets in and around open woodland areas. The Black-billed Cuckoo prefers more wooded areas than the Yellow-billed Cuckoo. You will recognize it by its repeated series of "COO-COO-COO" notes (given 3-4 to a series). The notes have a fairly nasal and ringing quality, unlike the soft "COO"s of the Mourning Dove. The Yellow-billed Cuckoo has a very distinctive song, progressing from a rapid chattering "KEK-KEK-KEK-KEK-KEK" to a series of "KYOLP-KYOLP-KYOLP-KYOLP" notes, and then ending with a few "KUT-A-KOWP"s, as the delivery slows down toward the end.

The Northern Bobwhite and the Ring-necked Pheasant are two birds, found among the brushy areas of open woodlands, that have almost unmistakeable songs. The Bobwhite gives a clearly whistled, medium-pitched "BOB – *WHITE*" (the second note rising sharply in exclamation), or a three note "BOB – BOB – *WHITE*". The Ring-necked Pheasant is usually well hidden in the grass or tangles and gives a very loud, harsh, croaking "KROOOK-OOK", which sounds like the "rooster call" horn on an old car, and is emphasized sometimes on the first syllable and sometimes on the second.

Less common among the tangles of open woodlands is the Yellow-breasted Chat. Its strange mixture of calls has always been a treat for me, simply because it is so different and distinct. "IT IS A LONG SERIES OF NOTES, SLOWLY PRESENTED (some single notes, some repeated several times), WITH VERY DEFINITE PAUSES BETWEEN EACH PHRASE". There are clear and burry whistles, harsh "caw"s and Blue Jay-like cries, as well as "kek"s and "cricks"s.

We've been overlooking some of the less spectacular (plain) birds thus far on our walk, but they are too common to avoid. The European Starling is seen and heard anywhere in open woodland areas where there are cavities to nest in. While it mimics many other birds, its characteristic song consists of "CHIPS, RASPY AND SQUEAKY NOTES, AND SHARP TWITTERINGS", combined every so often with its diagnostic "DRAWN-OUT AND DOWN-SLURRED 'WHEEEE-ERR". Another bird that can't be avoided, especially by those birds whose nests it parasitizes, is the Brown-headed Cowbird. It scours the woods and thickets, waiting for that opportune moment to slip one of its eggs into the nest of an unsuspecting finch, warbler, flycatcher, vireo or other suitable victim. Its song, fittingly, is not likely to draw much attention. It is a quick little song, consisting of two very short, bubbly, gurgling sounds, followed by a thin, high-pitched, short whistle: "GLUG- LA-*SEEE*".

The male House Finch, when the sun catches it just right, is a spectacular bird, but quite often its brilliant red is hidden, and it becomes just another dull "sparrow" to a lot of people. However, its lively song is ever-present and it is spreading as this little bird continues to expand its range to the north, west, and south. It is sung very quickly and consists of "A BUBBLY, LOUD, HIGH-PITCHED AND MUSICAL SERIES OF NOTES, VARIABLE

AND IRREGULAR" with sharp changes in pitch. It often "ENDS IN A BURRY OR HARSH 'CHURRR'" (or a more biting "VEEER" or "JEEER"), which is longer than the other notes and slides downward. It is found in open woodlands, but it is very much at home in cities and suburbs, and also very close to human habitation. Then there's the Common Grackle, far from plain in many people's eyes, with its shiny, irridescent, purplish feathers and golden eyes. It tends to congregate and nest in colonies and you will recognize it with its harsh "CHACK"s and high-pitched, squeaky note ("CHACK–CHACK–KEEK-A-LEEK"). You will notice it in fairly open areas, often damp, where it nests in shrubs, in single trees or in groves (preferably conifers).

Finally, as you head back, after a full day of birding in the open woodland and its adjoining areas, and assuming you still have some energy and interest left, don't forget to listen for the sharp, nasal "PEENT" (with that raspy or buzzy quality) of the American Woodcock. It is delivered while on the ground, and it is heard most frequently at dawn and dusk during the breeding period in spring. You may also be lucky enough to see its flight displays which are accompanied by a light twittering or trill as the bird climbs, and then a series of chirps or warbles as the bird descends to the ground again.

Horned Lark

Part 4

Other Common Bird Songs

I WATERBIRDS

1. GREEN-BACKED HERON

(I SINGLE NOTE SONG)

SONG – A **loud, sharp** "SKEOW" or "KEOW" (1 syllable) that seems to finish before it starts. It also utters low, clucking notes.

HABITAT – Lakes, ponds, marshes or streams with some woodland or shrubs, nesting singly or in colonies. It also will nest in woods and orchards away from water.

RANGE – *Summer* – S. Ontario and south throughout the e. U.S. Also casual into the eastern Canadian provinces. *Winter* – Atlantic coast (Carolinas south), Gulf coast and Florida southward.

2. BLACK-CROWNED NIGHT HERON

(I SINGLE NOTE SONG)

SONG – A **loud, guttural** "WORK" or "QUAWK". A similar sound can be obtained by forcing the word "work" quickly, in a loud whisper, with just a slight throaty quality. It is very distinctive in its wet or marshy setting.

HABITAT – Salt or fresh water areas, with trees, marshes, bushes or thickets. It generally roosts in trees during the day and is seen feeding commonly at dawn and dusk. It is not strictly nocturnal.

RANGE – *Summer* – Atlantic and Gulf coast states, as well as along the St. Lawrence R., around the lower Great Lakes and down the Mississippi R. *Winter* – Atlantic (Cape Cod south) and Gulf coasts, Florida, and up the Mississippi R. to Illinois and Indiana.

3. AMERICAN BITTERN

(II THREE NOTES REPEATED)

SONG – A deep, **slow, pumping** "OON-*KA*-LOONK", emphasized on the second syllable. It is repeated several times and can be heard over a long distance. It has been described as sounding like an old-fashioned wooden pump, because of its deep guttural and **hollow** sound and its **rhythmic**, almost mechanical, cadence, as the phrase is repeated over and over.

HABITAT – Marshes, bogs and wet meadows in fresh or salt water, where it prefers dense vegetation – cattails, bulrushes and grasses.

RANGE – *Summer* – From n. Ontario, s. Quebec and Newfoundland, south to n. Arkansas, s. Pennsylvania and down the Atlantic coast to N. Carolina. *Winter* – Atlantic coast (Cape Cod south), Florida and the Gulf coast.

4. SORA

(IV MANY VARYING NOTES and II TWO NOTES REPEATED)

SONG – A **descending "whinny"** of clear, sweet notes (12-15), which starts very quickly and then **slows down** and levels off in pitch toward the end. Other calls include its springtime, plaintive "love song", a rising "KER-*WEE*", or "KA-*WEE*", repeated often, a sharp "PEEK", or a sharp "QUEEP-EEP-IP-IP-IP-IP", with the first two notes slower and the rest quicker.

HABITAT – Freshwater marshes, borders of sloughs, bogs and wet grassy meadows. In fall and winter, commonly found in salt marshes and rice fields.

RANGE – *Summer* – Northern one third of the U.S. (c. Missouri to Washington D.C. north), up to n. Ontario, c. Quebec and Newfoundland. *Winter* – Florida, the Gulf coast and up the Atlantic coast.

II HAWKS

5. RED-SHOULDERED HAWK

(II ONE or TWO NOTES REPEATED)

SONG – A series of loud, repeated screams, each one **slurring downward**. "*KEE*AHH-*KEE*AHH-*KEE*AHH...". These short screams sound like single, down-slurred notes, but there is also a definite two tone or two syllable emphasis to the delivery at times. The repetition gives it a rhythmic quality.

HABITAT – Moist woodlands, wooded river bottoms, farm country and open pine woods and palmettos in Florida.

RANGE – *Summer* – Throughout e. Canada and the U.S. *Winter* – S. Ontario and the s. Great Lakes states southward.

6. BROAD-WINGED HAWK

(I ONE NOTE SONG)

SONG – A high-pitched, **shrill whistle**, which is **drawn out** and gets weaker toward the end. "KWEE-E-E-E-E" or "CHE-WEE-E-E". The first part of this whistle is almost like a quick stutter sometimes, giving it a two-syllabled effect.

HABITAT – Forests, usually deciduous, and often near ponds or streams.

RANGE – *Summer* – From n. Florida, throughout the U.S., to c. Ontario, s. Quebec and New Brunswick. *Winter* – S. Florida and southward

III OWLS

7. SCREECH OWL

(II A TRILL and IV MANY VARYING NOTES)

SONG – A series of short notes that sound like a soft, **muffled whinny**. The series of notes descend in pitch and have a sad or melancholy tone. It also gives a similar sounding **trill**, which stays on one pitch. Both of these are delivered with a wavering or **tremulous quality**.

HABITAT – Woodlands, orchards, parks and urban shade trees, where the nest is built in a natural cavity, woodpecker hole or birdhouse.

RANGE – *Summer* – S. Ontario and all the e. U.S. except n. Maine and n. Minnesota, Michigan and Wisconsin. *Winter* – Same.

8. GREAT-HORNED OWL

(III CONTAINING A DISTINCT REPEATED NOTE)

SONG – 3-8 loud, **low-pitched hoots**, often with the second and third notes ("hoots") given quickly. "WHOO – HOO-HOO – WHOO – WHOO".

HABITAT – From heavy forest to open country, often where Red-tailed Hawks are found. It often nests in an old hawk's nest or the nest of another large bird, as well as in natural tree cavities and on rocky ledges.

RANGE – *Summer* – N. Ontario and Quebec to Newfoundland and throughout the e. U.S. *Winter* – Same.

9. BARRED OWL

(III CONTAINING A DISTINCT REPEATED NOTE)

SONG – A series of **tremulous hoots** (higher-pitched than the Great-horned Owl), which are loud and emphatic. It consists of 2 series of 4-5 notes, **rhythmic** and strongly emphasized that sound like "WHO-COOKS-FOR-*YOU*?... WHO-COOKS-FOR-*YOU*-ALL?" (last note dropping in pitch and volume).

HABITAT – Dense forests and swampy woodlands, often where Red-shouldered Hawks nest. It nests in a tree cavity or in an old bird's nest.

RANGE – *Summer* – N. Ontario and c. Quebec to Nova Scotia and throughout the e. U.S. *Winter* – Same.

10. BARN OWL

(I SINGLE NOTE SONG)

SONG – A harsh, **raspy scream** or hissing, with a cat-like quality, which is repeated after an interval.

HABITAT – Woodlands, buildings (farm and town), trees, cliffs and burrows.

RANGE – *Summer* – S. Ontario and all of the e. U.S. (with the exception of the Appalachians and the N.E., and n. Michigan, Wisconsin and Minnesota). *Winter* – Same.

IV WOODPECKERS

11. RED-HEADED WOODPECKER

(II SINGLE NOTE REPEATED)

SONG – A fairly high-pitched, but **throaty** or harsh "QUEER – QUEER – QUEER" with **each note rising** slightly in exclamation, and repeated fairly slowly.

HABITAT – Open woodlands and more open stands of trees, including or chards, golf courses, shade trees and scattered trees in open fields, as well as in agricultural areas where there are dead trees for nesting.

RANGE – *Summer* – S. Ontario and all of the e. U.S., except the N.E. and the tip of Florida. *Winter* – E. U.S., except the most northerly Great Lakes states.

12. PILEATED WOODPECKER

(II SINGLE NOTE REPEATED)

SONG – A loud "KEE-KEE-KEE-KEE...", much like the Northern Flicker's song but louder, as well as more variable, with **slight changes in speed and pitch** as it proceeds.

HABITAT – Mature conifer or deciduous forests, or in mixed woodlands. It is less common than the Flicker.

RANGE – *Summer* – N. Ontario and s. Quebec to Nova Scotia and throughout the e. U.S. *Winter* – Same.

13. RED-BELLIED WOODPECKER

(II SINGLE NOTE REPEATED)

SONG – A repeated "KRER – KRER – KRER" or "CHURR – CHURR – CHURR", with a rolling of the "R" giving it a **trilled quality**. **Each note also drops slightly** at the end. Speed of delivery varies

HABITAT – Any woodlands including groves, stands of scattered trees and shade trees in towns, quite often beside streams, creeks and swamps.

RANGE – *Summer* – S.w. Ontario and throughout the e. U.S. except the N.E. and portions of the most northerly Great Lakes states. *Winter* – Same.

14. YELLOW-BELLIED SAPSUCKER

(I SINGLE NOTE SONG AND II SINGLE NOTE REPEATED)

SONG – A weak, complaining or **whining cry**, which sounds like the "MEW" call of the Catbird. A **downward-slurred** "EE-ERRR", which is repeated slowly.

HABITAT – Woodlands, often near streams or lakes.

RANGE – *Summer* – N. Ontario and c. Quebec to Newfoundland, south into the n.e. states and Allegheny mountains, as well as the most northerly Great Lakes states. *Winter* – Atlantic coast (New York to Florida) and the southern half of the U.S.

V MISCELLANEOUS

15. HORNED LARK

(IV MANY VARYING NOTES)

SONG – The song **starts slowly**, being introduced by a couple of high-pitched chirping notes but it picks up quickly into its characteristic **rushed series of disjointed tinkling notes.** In flight, song is repeated over and over, high in the air. The overall quality is **weak and unmusical**. The call is a sharp "TI-SICK", a shrill "TSEEE" or "TSEE-DE-REE".

HABITAT – Grasslands, prairies, golf courses, open fields, barren or bare ground and tundra.

RANGE – *Summer* – Throughout all of eastern Canada and the U.S., except the s.e. region and Gulf states. *Winter* – Most of the e. U.S., except the n. Great Lakes states, south Atlantic and Gulf coast areas and Florida.

16. BROWN CREEPER

(III SEVERAL VARYING NOTES)

SONG – The song is short, **weak** and **very high-pitched** and is heard mainly on the breeding grounds. A quick, rolling "*SEE*-SI-SI-*SEE*-SI-SI" with the first and fourth notes higher and emphasized. ("*Don't* Play

A-*round* With Me"). The call note which may be mixed in with the song is heard more often during migration, as the bird forages up the trunk of a tree. It consists of one high-pitched, short and **wavering** "SEEEE", similar to the call note of the Golden-crowned Kinglet.

HABITAT – Mixed and coniferous woodlands and scattered trees in swamps, where it builds its nest behind the loose bark of a tree.

RANGE – *Summer* – N. Ontrio and c. Quebec to Newfoundland, south to the n.e. states and Appalachians and the northern Great Lakes states. *Winter* – Same, but also throughout the e. U.S. to c. Florida.

17. GOLDEN-CROWNED KINGLET

(III SEVERAL VARYING NOTES)

SONG – A **very high-pitched** series of "TSEE" notes (each rather long) **ascending** and then abruptly **dropping** into a soft chatter. Call notes are a series of very high-pitched, thin "TSEE" notes, similar to the call notes of the Brown Creeper.

HABITAT – Coniferous woodlands and any woodland area in winter.

RANGE – *Summer* – N. Ontario and s. Quebec to Newfoundland, the n.e. states and Appalachians, and portions of the northern Great Lakes states. *Winter* – S. Ontario to Newfoundland and all of the e. U.S. except the Florida peninsula.

18. NORTHERN WATERTHRUSH

(III SEVERAL VARYING NOTES)

SONG – Loud, **emphatic**, sweet notes that **speed up** slightly and **drop in pitch** at the end. The song usually consists of 8-10 rich, musical notes, which are sung at a fairly quick pace, although definitely not rushed. "CHIP-CHIP-WHEEET-WHEEET-WHEEET-TOO-TOO-TOO". The call note is a sharp "CHIP".

HABITAT – Swampy woodlands, wet thickets and the banks of streams or ponds.

RANGE – *Summer* – N. Ontario and Quebec to Newfoundland, the n.e. states down to W. Virginia, as well as the n. Great Lakes states. *Winter* – Tip of Florida to n. S America.

19. LOUISIANA WATERTHRUSH

(III SEVERAL VARYING NOTES)

SONG – This song starts with 2-4 loud, **slow**, high-pitched, sweet notes or slurs (each note usually slurred upward) followed by a series of **much quicker notes**, which are quite variable and **drop in pitch** and sound like a chatter or twitter. "SEEE-SEEE-SEEE-SIREE-TWITTER-RIBBIT" or "SEEWEE-SEEWEE-SEEWEE-SIREE-TWITTER-RIBBIT".

HABITAT – Swampy woodlands, ravines and the edges of creeks. It has a special preference for damp areas with running water nearby (mountain streams and brooks).

RANGE – *Summer* – Gulf states north into New England; also to w. New York and the tip of L. Michigan further west, as well as into s.w. Ontario. *Winter* – W. Indies, Mexico and S. America.

20. BOBOLINK

(IV MANY VARYING NOTES)

SONG – An **exuberant**, bubbling overflow of notes (ranging up and down with no two notes the same) that rises in pitch and **speeds up** as it progresses. This loud, clear series of short notes produces a rather disjointed song and the **notes tend to run into each other**, or trip over each other, as the song speeds up. It sometimes gives the impression of having too many notes to deliver in too short a time. Sung from a perch or in flight.

HABITAT – Open grasslands, hayfields and weedy, moist meadows.

RANGE – *Summer* – C. Ontario, s. Quebec to Nova Scotia and the e. U.S. north of W. Virginia. *Winter* – S. America.

21. ORCHARD ORIOLE

(IV MANY VARYING NOTES)

SONG – Its song has been compared to that of the Purple Finch, with its **loud, highly variable series of notes**, and also, in quality, to that of the Robin (rich and sweet). However, unlike these two, the Orchard Oriole has **some repeated single notes and pairs of notes** and the ending is sometimes "burry", like the Scarlet Tanager's rough notes, and noticeably **downslurred** ("WEE-YO").

HABITAT – Orchards, parks, woodland edges and streamside groves, as well as nearer human habitation in the shade trees of both town and country.

RANGE – *Summer* – S. Ontario and all of the e. U.S. with the exception of the N.E., portions of the northern Great Lakes states and s. Fla. *Winter* – Mexico to n. S. America.

22. SUMMER TANAGER

(III SEVERAL VARYING NOTES)

SONG – A series of short, **sweet, Robin-like phrases,** much **like the song of the Scarlet Tanager, but louder and not as harsh or burry**. Its characteristic call notes sound like a sharp, staccato "CHICKY-TUCKY-TUCK" or "CHICKETY-TUCKY-TUCK".

HABITAT – Open pine-oak woodlands, orchards, groves or shade trees.

RANGE – *Summer* – All but the northern third of the e. U.S. (c. Ohio south) and the s. tip of Florida. It is casual further north. *Winter* – Mexico to S. America.

23. DARK-EYED JUNCO

(II A TRILL)

SONG – A pleasant, **ringing trill**, with a slightly metallic quality. It is similar to the Chipping Sparrow's song but softer, sweeter and more "ringing". There can be a difference in pitch (or speed) from one rendition to another.

HABITAT – Forested regions (conifer and mixed) and, in winter, in open woods, weedy fields, thickets and roadsides and also common at feeders.

RANGE – *Summer* – N. Ontario and Quebec to Newfoundland, south to the northern Great Lakes states, the N.E. and down the Appalachians. *Winter* – S. Ontario and Quebec to Newfoundland and all of the e. U.S. except s. Florida.

24. PURPLE FINCH

(III SEVERAL or IV MANY VARYING NOTES)

SONG – Its song is **similar to the House Finch's** loud, rapid and highly variable series of notes but it is not as burry **(sweeter and clearer)** and it also lacks the harsh "CHURR" ending, having instead a **softer trill** sometimes.

HABITAT – More open woodlands (preferring conifer stands), parks and orchards.

RANGE – *Summer* – From c. Ontario, s. Quebec and Newfoundland, south through the n.e. states to the Virginias and continuing west around the Great Lakes. *Winter* – From s. Ontario to Nova Scotia and throughout the e. U.S., except s. Florida.

25. SAVANNAH SPARROW

(III SEVERAL VARYING NOTES)

SONG – Like the Song Sparrow, it often has **3 short, introductory notes**. In the case of the Savannah Sparrow, these notes are **followed by two longer, buzzy notes** (second one lower), which have been described as insect-like. "TSIP-TSIP-TSIP-TSEEEE-TSAAAAY" (last note lower).

HABITAT – Open areas of grassy vegetation from northern tundra and sedge bogs, to prairie grasslands and hayfields, to salt marshes, dunes and shore lines.

RANGE – *Summer* – Throughout e. Canada and the n. one third of the e. U.S. (into W. Virginia, Ohio, Indiana, Illinois and Missouri). *Winter* – Atlantic coast (Cape Cod south to Florida) and Gulf states north to Illinois and Missouri.

For Further Reading

Bent, Arthur Cleveland. *Life Histories of North American Birds.* 26 vols. New York: Dover Publications, 1961-1968. Originally published by the U.S. National Museum, 1919-1968.

Blachly, Lou and Jenks, Randolph. *Naming the Birds at a Glance.* New York: Alfred A. Knopf, Inc., 1989.

Bull, John and Farrand, John, Jr. *The Audubon Society Field Guide to North American Birds: Eastern Region.* New York: Alfred A. Knopf, Inc., 1977.

Collins, Henry Hill, Jr. and Boyajian, Ned R. *Familiar Garden Birds of America.* Boston: G.K. Hall & Co., 1985.

Connor, Jack. *The Complete Birder.* Boston: Houghton Mifflin Co., 1988.

Godfrey, W. Earl. *The Birds of Canada.* Ottawa: National Museums of Canada, 1986.

Grosvenor, Gilbert and Wetmore, Alexander. *The Book of Birds.* Washington D.C: National Geographic Society, 1939. Vols. I, II.

Harrison, Colin. *A Field Guide to the Nests, Eggs and Nestlings of North American Birds.* Toronto: Collins, 1978.

Harrison, Hal H. *American Birds in Color.* New York: Wm. H. Wise & Co. Inc., 1948.

Harrison, Hal H. *A Field Guide to Birds' Nests east of the Mississippi River.* Boston: Houghton Mifflin Co., 1975.

Harrison, Hal H. *Wood Warblers' World.* New York: Simon and Schuster, 1984.

Mackay, Barry, Kent. *Eighty More Land Birds to Know.* Toronto: Book Society of Canada Ltd, 1968.

Mackenzie, John P.S. *The Complete Outdoorsman's Guide to Birds of Eastern North America.* Boston: Houghton Mifflin Co., 1977.

Mathews, F. Schuyler. *A Field Book of Wild Birds and Their Music.* New York: G. P. Putnam & Sons, 1921.

McElroy, Thomas P., Jr. *The Habitat Guide to Birding.* New York: Alfred A. Knopf Inc., 1974.

Mckenny, Margaret. *Birds in the Garden and How to Attract Them.* New York: Grosset & Dunlap, 1939.

The National Geographic Society Field Guide to the Birds of North America. Washington D.C.: National Geographic Society, 1983.

Pasquier, Roger F. *Watching Birds: An Introduction to Ornithology.* Boston: Houghton Mifflin Co., 1977.

Pearson, T. Gilbert. *Birds of America.* New York: Garden City Publishing Co., 1936.

Peterson, Roger Tory. *A Field Guide to the Birds East of the Rockies.* 4th ed. Boston: Houghton Mifflin Co., 1980.

Peterson, Roger Tory. *The Bird Watcher's Anthology.* New York: Harcourt Brace and Co., 1957.

Peterson, Roger Tory. *Birds Over America.* New York: Dodd Mead & Company, 1948.

Peterson, Roger Tory and Fisher, James. *Wild America*. London: Collins, 1956.

Pettingill, Olin Sewall, Jr. *A Guide to Bird Finding East of the Mississippi*. 2nd ed. New York: Oxford University Press, 1977.

Piatt, Jean. *Adventures in Birding: Confessions of a Lister.* New York: Alfred A. Knopf, Inc., 1973.

Pough, Richard H. *Audubon Guides: All the Birds of Eastern and Central North America*. Garden City, New York: Doubleday & Company, Inc., 1953.

Proctor, Noble. *Song Birds: How to Attract Them and Identify Their Songs.* Toronto: B. Mitchell, 1988.

Robbins, Chandler S., Bruun, Bertel and Zim, Herbert S. *Birds of North America*. 2nd ed. New York: Golden Press, 1983.

Saunders, Aretas A. *A Guide to Bird Songs*. New York: Doubleday & Co. Inc., 1951.

Speirs, J. Murray. *Birds of Ontario.* Toronto: Natural Heritage/Natural History Inc., 1985. Vols. I, II.

Stokes, Donald W. and Stokes, Lillian Q. *A Guide to Bird Behaviour. A Guide to Bird Behaviour.* Vol.s I- 3. Toronto: Little, Brown and Company, 1979-1989.

Vardaman, James M. *Call Collect, Ask For Birdman.* New York: McGraw-Hill Book Company, 1980.

RECORDS AND TAPES

A Field Guide to Bird Songs. Cornell Laboratory of Ornithology. 2 records to accompany, page by page, R.T. Peterson's *A Field Guide to the Birds* 2nd ed.

Also a newer version of *A Field Guide to Bird Songs,* introduced in 1983, [records or tapes] to accompany Peterson's 4th ed. of *A Field Guide to the Birds.*

A Field Guide to Western Bird Songs. Cornell Laboratory of Ornithology. 3 records to accompany, page by page, R.T. Peterson's *A Field Guide to Western Birds.* 2nd ed.

The Federation of Ontario Naturalists has a series of records produced by Houghton Mifflin Co., Boston, under the following titles: *[1] Finches, [2] Thrushes, Wrens and Mockingbirds, [3] Warblers and [4] Songs of Spring.*

An excellent instructive set of tapes and booklet, called *Birding By Ear* by Richard K. Walton and Robert W. Lawson, was brought out in 1989 by Houghton Mifflin Co., Boston.

Two other tapes with text and explanation of bird song are *Song Birds: How to Attract Them and Identify Their Songs* [listed above under author, Noble Proctor], produced in 1988 and *Wild Sounds of the Northwoods* by Lang Elliot and Ted Mack, produced in 1990.

Index

NOTE: *Page numbers in italics refer to illustrations.*

ERNIE JARDINE has two children and lives in Toronto, where he has been a high school teacher for the last twenty-seven years. His interest in birding began as a youngster. He has maintained this interest throughout, and now describes it as more of a passion. This passion has taken him all over the world: many of the countries of Europe (including Iceland), the Caribbean and Central America, Hawaii and most parts of the U.S. and Canada. He has been doing photography almost as long as he has been birding, and his camera is always close at hand on these trips. For many years he has had a special interest in bird song and this book is the culmination of that interest.

PHOTO: KEITH NICHOLLS

DON CAVIN lives in Fenelon Falls, Ontario, with his photographer wife, Barbara. Don cannot remember a time that he wasn't drawing and painting, or observing birds. Since his childhood these interests have only increased in intensity. He is also a talented musician, who can switch from one instrument to another with ease. However, his prime focus remains birding and art. Although he has concentrated almost exclusively on landscape painting over the last dozen years, he was enthused that this project allowed him once again to blend his two favourite interests: birds and art. He has won many awards and his work is in private collections in North America and overseas.